COPAGANDA

WHY THE CONSTITUTION DOESN'T APPLY TO YOU

I.C. THRUIT

Amana Mission Publishing Ink
Alternative Press

To Incite Insight

Dedicated to the prisoners of war, and the heroic activists striving to free us all.

Copaganda™ : Why the Constitution Doesn't Apply to You

ISBN-13:978-0615511702
(Amana Mission Publishing Ink Alternative Press)

This is a work of political persuasion and media criticism. Every word contained herein is purely the opinion of the author, a summary of news or other media, or a quotation deriving from documented speech by another party. All people and events mentioned in this book are already the subject of media reporting and have been presented in other venues. Nothing in this volume should be construed as an endorsement of illegal behavior, or discouragement of it. Nor ought anything contained in any part of this work be regarded as legal advice; the author is not an attorney, and no attorney has endorsed any part of this writing. Legal theories are presented for the sake of argument; try them in court at your own risk. Good luck, however.

WARNING: *These thoughts are insubordinate and subversive.* The author and publisher intend to incite insight with this publication. We are not to be held liable for what our readers may do after being helped to see through it. If you are a member of law enforcement, or employed by the State in a court or prison setting, please go to www.leap.cc and join the organization there, if you have not already, before reading this book. Welcome aboard! Together we can end this awful perversion of Justice.

Table of Contents

Worth a Thousand Words:
About the Cover

The cover of *Copaganda* is a work of conceptual art, as well as a way of taking full advantage of the already-included four-color printing option. Nearly as much forethought and planning went into the design of the cover as the creation of the interior text. Certainly more talent and patience went into it. New software was painstakingly mastered; the limits of the five-year-old student model laptop was reached and all too frequently surpassed. Art makes computers hot and very bothered!

After all the alarming clicks of death followed by abruptly darkened screens, ten-minute lollygagging spinning rainbows heralding each critical save, and other technical devils fighting to keep this book from the world, we have a symbolic rendering which mirrors the themes discussed in the Articles.

The heart of the surreal image is the incongruous arrest of Lady Justice, represented as a partial self-portrait juxtaposed with the trappings of traditional courthouse statue versions. Clad in a torn tie-die summer dress, she has been blindsided as well as blindfolded, disarmed and looted of her savings.

Depriving her of everything she values, including free movement of her arm, Officer Sam is in the midst of heartlessly clicking the cuffs on another defenseless citizen. Clad in his traditional red, white, and blue, Sam has added a pair of shades and jackboots to the ensemble, sporting a utility belt for hanging weapons along with a Kevlar vest.

As she kneels in submission to the overwhelming force capturing her, she clutches her scale, the archetypal symbol of fairness and deliberation, but also, in the eyes of police, illegal drug paraphernalia, not to mention evidence of intent to distribute.

One pan of the scale holds a sheaf of calendar pages, steadily rising as unrecoverable months fall from her life. Precious time she took for granted, her ever-shrinking future, is disappearing before her blinded eyes. The other side is loaded with incriminating evidence spilling from the sleeve of Officer Sam. Every baggie that lands on the pile depresses her fate, causing yet more months to tumble irrevocably away.

The planting of contraband has multiple layers of significance. First, Sam is actually creating the problem he purports to solve, literally and figuratively. The furor and uproar is generated when he arrives on an otherwise placid scene. Clearly Lady Justice is no threat to anyone, despite her ornamental sword. Bringing her to jail will make no one else any safer.

Another level of implication suggests that Sam, being the source of the very drugs for which he intends to rob her of everything, is nothing but a blackmailer staging the frame. Taken in this context, the scene being depicted is less an arrest than a mugging.

Not only is Officer Sam filling the scales of justice with fraud, he is tampering with the balance, putting more weight on the drugs than their gravity justifies.

Crouching behind the jackboot of the bow-legged cop is a representative of broadcast Media, faithfully rolling tape while Justice meets disaster. Careful to point the camera away from Sam's nefarious planting of evidence, his job is to ensure that coverage is angled from the officer's point of view.

Like all Feds, Sam drives a black SUV. The door is emblazoned with the shield of the Thought Police, indicating that *Uncle Sam* and *Big Brother* bear more than a family resemblance. The rear door, the one which shuts on hapless arrestees as the world of confinement closes in, is inscribed with the fantastically frank and accurate motto, *"To Harass & Extort."*

He will tell you that there is nothing sinister about the way he stalks random strangers, groping them and picking their pockets, as if what any given person is carrying has suddenly become his urgent business.

"What am I supposed to do? She was standing there, right outside the courthouse, holding a sword and a scale. I knew right then, I was either dealing with a fencer or a drug dealer. When fencing drug dealers wait outside the courthouse to sell drugs and stab children, it is my job and duty to disarm them and fully interrupt their lives." Like a drunk uncle who won't let you finish a phrase or excuse yourself to the bathroom, not to mention the other things drunk uncles do, Sam is an unremitting nuisance who won't take no for an answer or get his hands out of your pants.

This Uncle is drunk on the power to pen the fate of his unwilling nephews and nieces, to compel them to appear on command, and hunt them with his vast posse if they dare to flee.

His hopes and dreams for you are to see you languish in a cell through the best years of your life. Sam is never afraid to hit you up for some bread, even after slamming the door shut in your face, always managing to imply that for some unknown reason you owe him something. He might send a check every once in while, paying back part what of he took without asking, but it will never equal what he has raided from the piggy banks of his large and unfortunate family.

We didn't ask for this jerk to meddle in our lives, but there he is, everywhere we go, stern and overbearing, full of strangely misinformed ideas about propriety and his role in the moral welfare of others. A cherished symbol of mindless loyalty, who got his big break urging us to war, Uncle Sam is an unconscionable bully with an insatiable appetite for control. He wants *you* to feed the prison-industrial beast with your body, mind and soul.

As Justice falls into the clutches of the sociopath, the reporter dutifully records the daily bust, beaming the cruelty into our living rooms so that we are desensitized to abuse by the long arm of the law, coming to accept it as part of the rough luck we are due for daring to be born in this country.

Behind them a bleak prison wall stands, topped by barbed wire, reminding those of us who are relatively free, that we are always just a few yards away from the absolute loss of freedom.

ARTICLE I:
Criminals Under Color of Authority

"Do not expect justice where might is right."—Plato

You are sleeping soundly in your own bed, minding your own business. At the moment, that business happens to be peacefully dreaming. It does not matter what you are dreaming about. Perhaps you are working out psychological issues in a strange symbolic milieu you barely comprehend, or living out a heroic destiny which fate has not been kind enough to bestow on your waking hours. Maybe it is a sordid orgy scene involving movie stars. The possibilities are limitless in the realm of unfounded freedom.

No matter what is going on, it's all in your head, and so it is your business, no one else's. You've locked your door, and by the rules of polite society, no one ought disturb you with so much as a phone call at this hour, except in the direst of emergencies.

At first, you think the loud thumping you hear is merely one of those odd unpredictable wrinkles dreamers are prone to encounter, an eruption of the unconscious. Then something breaks very nearby, and a riot of sounds dissolve the entire world. Scuttling jackboots approach. The dream has become nightmare, and you are fully awake.

Your bedroom door flies open with a kick. Bleary-eyed and confused, you are dragged to the floor in your nighttime garb or lack thereof. The masked men shout orders, shine flashlights and demand forcefully to know where they can find your treasures. They begin to ransack the house, heedless of the mayhem they are wreaking. Furniture is ripped apart, cabinets emptied, floorboards loosened in search of valuables. Walls are pummeled in hopes that secret safes are concealed within.

The home invasion rapidly escalates into a kidnapping, as all occupants of the house are bound and ushered into cars. Taken to another location, you are locked in a tiny cramped room, separated from your loved ones and forced to compete with strangers for a spot of stained concrete. A single clogged toilet, supposed to meet your collective sanitary needs, fills the scarce air with unbelievable stench.

After hours of silent waiting, you and the other captives are shackled together and brought before the godfather of the operation, who explains why you've been kidnapped and names your ransom price. As he states the outrageous figure, you realize that your nightmare is just beginning. You haven't that much in the whole world. You may never get out of this awful place.

The perpetrators of this sequence have committed a horrible and violent crime. Everyone in the gang ought to be charged and sentenced accordingly. Instead, they will be praised, and eventually promoted within their organization, and it is the victims who face loss of some, or even all, of their lives.

Donald Scott learned this in the hardest of all ways when his two-hundred-acre ranch in Ventura County, California, was invaded by armed criminals acting under the color of authority. Still disoriented from the previous night's drinking, Scott thought the men breaking into his house were aggressive process servers attempting to illegally deliver papers related to his divorce. He brought out a gun to meet the intruders, and was fatally shot, never to learn the sinister motive behind his untimely demise.

It turned out that the men breaking into his home were thirty-one members of various police agencies, including LA County Sheriffs, DEA, National Park Service, and even National Guard, all on the property to serve a search warrant for up to four thousand plants of marijuana. These widely divergent entities had converged on Scott's property to rescue the country from the obvious threat to National security posed by such a large field of green. Clearly this was an emergency of Federal proportions, a dangerous operation calling for maximum paramilitary force.

There was only one problem, other than the troublesome dead man— there was absolutely no marijuana growing on the property. There was not so much as a seed, or even a pipe. Although authorities employed canine units, helicopters, and a high-tech Jet Propulsion Laboratory device for detecting traces of cannabis, the massive raid yielded no fruit whatsoever. Donald Scott, survivors tearfully explained, did not grow marijuana, or even smoke it. He was an alcohol man.

The ranch had been viewed with covetous eyes by the Park Service, who had put it on the list of properties the agency would like to acquire. Scott's land, bordered on three sides by National Park, was worth an estimated five million dollars. And it was in the way.

As the investigation ensued, Michael Bradbury, the Ventura County DA, who had jurisdiction despite having been completely excluded from the raid operation, found compelling evidence of impropriety in the deadly affair. It began to look as if the probable cause for the warrant had been concocted, with the sole intention of seizing Scott's attractive land. The

Bradbury report stopped short of calling it a conspiracy, however.

Scott's widow wasn't so shy. "As I sat there on the patio, I realized, these sons of bitches are a *hit squad* for the US government!"

Under Federal forfeiture statutes, the agencies participating in the incursion could divvy up the booty amongst themselves. The murderous invasion was motivated, not by any urgency of public safety, but pure institutional greed. Supporting this assertion was the presence of two forfeiture agents on the scene, as well as the fact that pre-raid preparations had included officers examining Tax Assessor reports on the property. A particularly damning piece of evidence was a hand-written note on a parcel map referring to the value of adjacent land recently sold for $800,000. Bradbury could find no legitimate justification for an interest in this information, which was irrelevant to the cultivation investigation.

Then there is the faulty search warrant, containing conflicting pretexts for the raid, predicated on what were clearly false claims of between fifty and four thousand live plants under cultivation. The non-existent marijuana had been "positively identified" through visual inspection; it was allegedly hung from branches of trees. This unlikely method supposedly explained the lack of photographic corroboration.

"The Los Angeles Sheriff's Department was motivated, at least in part, by a desire to seize and forfeit the ranch for the government," concluded Bradbury's shocking report. Shocking, not merely because of the implication that Scott was murdered in a broad-daylight multimillion dollar heist, but in that a prosecutor would admit it.

If a group of private citizens were to undertake such a crime, and commit murder in the commission of it, no one involved would be allowed to escape prosecution. Most of those convicted of even peripheral involvement would receive many years or even life in prison.

Of course, it would be very difficult for any private citizen to do what the police do every day—rob individuals of their real estate at gunpoint. There simply is no means by which such a theft could be effected, without the force of the government itself.

The county and Federal authorities settled with the deceased's estate for five million dollars, without admitting fault. His grieving widow noted that this figure is quite a price to pay, considering authorities did not concede the wrongness of her husband's death. The government was more willing to part with a mountain of taxpayer coin than denounce and punish the public employees who had perpetrated this travesty.

Not only were none of the police prosecuted for the murder, none were even seriously disciplined. In fact, Deputy Gary Spencer, who led the operation and actually fired the killing shot, continued to defend his actions and smear his victim, who was doubtless rolling in his grave, five years later.

"Sometimes people get warned and we don't find anything," Spencer claimed. "I wouldn't call it botched, because that would say that it was a mistake to have gone there in the first place, and I don't believe that."

One wonders what Spencer would consider a mistake, if not the death by cop of a man who was in no discernible way breaking the law. Spencer is clearly not haunted by the ghost of the man he killed. In fact, he sued DA Bradbury for his damning report—and was ordered to pay $50,000 to cover court costs instead. That's what happens when you sue a lawyer.

Perhaps he *would* consider it a mistake that he is on audio recording, lying to a concerned neighbor who called just minutes after the slaying to find out what the gunshots were all about. Scott's answering machine was still recording when the call came in, unbeknownst to Deputy Spencer. The neighbor asked, "Hello, is this, uh, uh, Donald?"

Spencer, with unmitigated gall, answered, "No, no, it's a *friend* of his. Who's this?"

If this is how Spencer treats his friends, one truly fears for his enemies. When the neighbor asked if Donald was there, the cop who killed him lied again.

"Uh, he's busy, what's up?" Scott was busy being dead, but who's to quibble with the word of a sworn law enforcement agent?

Land grabs, false pretexts, and government-sponsored murder are nothing new in these United States; after all, this vast nation was settled through slaughter of natives for the ground beneath their feet.

Under the Constitution, citizens have the right to expect to be free of such treatment. That guarantee is enshrined in the Fifth Amendment, which clearly states that no person shall be "deprived of life, liberty, or property without due process of law."

The forfeiture legislation by which Scott's killers were hoping to profit is just one of the many unconstitutional measures attendant to prohibition. Because the idea of dictating personal habits is itself contrary to the values of a just society, many of the props supporting these tenuous practices are also at odds with the protections adopted at the foundation of the union. In the name of fighting substances which are held to cause dubious harm, much more definitive damage is inflicted on individuals and families who may or may not have broken these very foolish rules.

Kathryn Johnston was another innocent bystander slain in her home by shock troops. Johnston was a ninety-two-year-old grandmother, who had lived alone in her west Atlanta home for seventeen years. A victim of sloppy police work and outright conspiracy, her death spurred widespread outrage at the sheer excess of the government addiction to drug enforcement.

The neighborhood where Mrs. Johnston lived was poor and dangerous, and as an elderly woman living alone, she was afraid of criminals. Home security was a top priority for her, and in the past year she had scraped up the funds from relatives to install both burglar bars and extra locks.

To defend herself, she kept a rusty handgun at the ready, so when three uninvited guests burst through her door, the frightened woman grabbed her weapon and prepared to repel the invaders or die trying.

It is not completely unknown for individuals of advanced age to deal drugs; retirement can be lean, and the job involves very little heavy lifting. Nevertheless, all indications are that Mrs. Johnston was not one such, despite the attempts of her killers to paint her so.

When three members of Atlanta's Narcotics Task Force burst through her door on a no-knock raid, they saw a gun pointing back at them. Instead of backing away, as a reasonable person facing an unanticipatedly fair gunfight would do, the cops started firing randomly, as if they were starring in an action flick.

Thirty-nine shots were fired by the cops, an average of thirteen apiece, striking not only the terrified old lady on the couch with five bullets, including the shot which entered her heart and ended her life, but wounding each of the officers as well.

Her lone discharge missed the intended targets by several feet, suggesting that, even armed, Johnston was not a good enough shot to make a credible threat to armed police garbed in Kevlar vests and bearing riot shields. Either that, or she was kind enough to use her first round for a warning shot, a courtesy the jackboots did not return.

The cops were also gravely incompetent with their firearms, but they had certainly learned to pull the trigger. Each sustained an injury from friendly fire, which is remarkable in itself, since they wore flak jackets. They somehow managed not only to shoot each other, but to strike the only parts of their bodies left exposed.

The incompetence does not end there. Incredibly, one of the killer cops, Jason R. Smith, handcuffed the suspect as she took her last breaths, and proceeded to plant three bags of marijuana in the basement of the house, so as to frame his victim and cover his ass.

Smith orchestrated the put-up job like he'd been doing it all his life. Killing a drug suspect in cold blood is usually no big deal, since it is presumed that those who won't balk at getting high will have no scruples or cautions about taking a shot at the men trying to put them in a little box, but there tends to be a public outcry when the victim is utterly innocent as Johnston clearly was.

After being released from the hospital, Smith contacted his snitch and pressured him to falsely swear to having bought crack at Johnston's house. Helping cops get away with murdering an innocent grandmother was too much for confidential informant Alex White, and he instead turned State's evidence on his police handlers. He called the Feds and told his story to local television news. He said although the cops had instructed him to say he had been there to buy crack, he'd never visited the house in question.

If it weren't for White's courage, the truth might never have come out. Here were some filthy dirty cops, concocting evidence and suborning false testimony. All indications were that this cheating was a regular pattern, which had worked well for the relatively unsupervised narcotics squad at the expense of their innocent victims.

The details being released about this incident kept shifting from the very first reports; for example, it was frequently reported that officers had gone to the wrong house by mistake, or that the injuries inflicted on her attackers had been caused by her gunfire, rather than each other's. At first it was reported that an undercover officer had made a crack purchase at Johnston's home from someone named Sam, but that story dissolved as well under scrutiny.

The Atlanta Police Department slowly backed away from the raiders and their conflicting stories, as it became more and more obvious that there were layers of lies concealing webs of deceit. The entire narcotics unit was put on paid leave, and the investigation was turned over to Federal prosecutors.

Smith and his compatriots had evidently been getting away with these frame-and-bust operations for a while, garnering brownie points for bringing in arrests, without having to actually detect any drugs. This time, though, they had gone too far, and the outrage at the murder of Kathryn Johnston was too much to contain.

It developed at trial that the probable cause for the warrant the cops were there to serve was fraudulent, the statement of an unreliable informant which was attributed to Mr. White because of his superior credibility.

The three officers were convicted of violating her civil rights under the color of authority in Federal court, receiving sentences of five, six, and ten years for these machinations. Community leaders denounced these relatively light sentences from courts which routinely send drug defendants to prison for twice as long. Two of the three also pled to State manslaughter charges and were given concurrent sentences.

Nevertheless, in this rare case the police were held criminally liable for their death-dealing. The city of Atlanta opened a probe, promised reforms, and paid Johnston's family a multimillion-dollar settlement. Lamentably, these "reforms" included expanding the task force to thirty members and adding a requirement that their urine be regularly tested for drugs, instead of abolishing the unit entirely.

One question raised by this case is whether all this fuss would have gotten action if, instead of the evidence-planting and witness-tampering being exposed, Smith and the others had successfully painted Johnston as the dealer they claimed. Would her life really have been worth less, if she had actually been selling a few dime bags of pot or even the crack the officers originally claimed?

When cops suborn perjury, plant stashes, falsify warrants, and fabricate confessions, there is precious little their victims can do to redress the absolute destruction of their lives which results, even if they survive the experience. As a general rule, criminal defendants are not believed in court when their testimony contradicts the statements of one or more sworn officers. Being the subject of criminal prosecution, your word, truthful as it may be, doesn't mean much to a judge, no matter what outrageous falsehoods stream from the mouths of cops.

Narcotics officers have every motivation to lie. They have quotas to fill, superiors to impress, property to confiscate, grudges to settle, misconduct to conceal, aggression to vent, prejudices to indulge, privacy to unconstitutionally breach, and no one watching over them except a system that needs them to do its dirty work, and their comrades, who honor a code of silence.

That the government stirs sluggishly to punish the most egregious trampling of rights is often expedient. The crime of such officers is not the way in which they brought down the mighty hammer of the law on the innocent, but the failure to cover the cover-up. Embarrassing the Force is what sends the worst cops to live with their victims behind bars.

For agencies with a charter to violently enforce every trivial regulation on the general public, the police can be rather lax on those who betray the basic character of their job by falsifying evidence. One example of this is the appalling case of Officer Richard Chrisman, who for some reason was carrying around a dirty crack pipe, and conspired to use it in setting up a homeless woman in Phoenix, Arizona.

The entire episode, including the part where Chrisman passes the paraphernalia to his partner just before it was "found" in the woman's dress, was caught on what would become a widely disseminated video. The scene was kept under wraps, but emerged when Chrisman later fell under investigation for a deranged on-duty shooting of an unarmed suspect's head. The question is why he was allowed to stay on the job after he'd already been caught framing innocent suspects.

Chrisman's excuse, which he told the investigators with a straight enough face to keep his job, was that he did it because he wanted to get "a rise out of her" and that he "thought it would be funny." Yeah. Like a felony charge for something you know damn well was not yours is a real knee-slapper.

It's obvious from the footage that the officers are conniving to plant evidence of a felony in her clothing. Also clear is the agitation of the woman as she's being set up, causing officers to restrain her by the neck. Yet Chrisman wrote off this highly illegal abuse of authority as a gag, as if on-duty officers have nothing better to do with their taxpayer-funded hours than pretending to bust the homeless for laughs.

This was enough to convince internal affairs that what they had on their hands was an irrepressible prankster, who was just so misunderstood by humorless subjects who don't get the joke about going to jail for no reason at all. They suspended Chrisman for one whole day, put him on the list of problem officers, and then sent him back out with a gun and arrest powers to patrol the streets looking for "bad guys."

Five years later, when Chrisman went too far during a domestic disturbance call and was charged with murder in the slaying of Danny Rodriguez, the video spread far and wide, as part of the department finally cutting loose the rabid hound. This time he'd gone too far. Not only did he shoot Rodriguez like a mad dog, but he shot the dog as well. Chrisman had a history of being unreliable, the Media reported. Yup, sure is one bad apple ruining the bunch.

We're left to wonder, though, why his department would tolerate any sort of evidence tampering, even in jest. Doesn't such abuse violate the very premise of the job? And how come these top cops, of a breed who never accept any of *our* excuses along those lines, believed that planting a crack pipe was just Chrisman's zany sense of humor, rather than an obvious attempt to fabricate cause for arrest?

Jose Guerena was a veteran of two tours in Iraq. At the age of twenty-six, he was finally ready to enjoy civilian life with his wife, Vanessa, and their two young sons. Having taken on the responsibility of funding his family's move to a new house, he had just begun to sleep off a twelve-hour graveyard shift on May 5, 2011, when his life became a casualty of a different war on the domestic front.

Literally working in the mines, Asarco Mission Mine to be exact, in order to pay the bills, Guerena was a loyal, hardworking citizen, the kind of dutiful, well-meaning patriot whose gravest flaw is trusting the government. Nevertheless, he died in a hail of over seventy bullets, fired at him by soldiers on an even vaguer mission than the one he'd just returned from. Twenty-two pieces of high-powered lead found their mark ending the fight before it started.

Confronted with what he assumed was a violent gang of thugs engaged in robbery, Guerena armed himself with the AR-15 which he kept for just such an occasion, and sent his wife and son to hide in the closet. It was the last time they would see him alive. As he'd been trained, he steeled himself for a firefight with the hostile insurgents attempting to breach the perimeter. Stormtroopers swarmed his home and rained lead on the lone Marine. The safety of Guerena's weapon was still on when it was pried from his cold dead fingers.

Vanessa called 911, still unsure of who had shot her husband, but desperate to get help for him before he bled to death. The dispatchers delivered the customer service you might expect from a cheap cell phone company. She begged them to send an ambulance for over five minutes, while Jose lay dying. Precious minutes were consumed in confusion over whether the emergency assistance call was coming from the same house currently being raided, and what that meant to the Department. Paramedics were delayed over an hour outside the home by the anxious police, while any chance Guerena had of surviving the event disappeared.

The SWAT team which invaded his home in Tucson, Arizona, was there to serve a search warrant pertaining to some sort of drug conspiracy case, which also included three other homes in the neighborhood. They not only didn't find any drugs, they apparently weren't even *looking* for them. A long-term investigation focusing on some of his family members had shown none of the suspects handling, or even in proximity to, narcotics.

The armed force was called in, not to locate a stockpile of contraband, but rather to seek ledgers and paperwork which allegedly showed Guerena to be peripherally involved in this ring. Although the Sheriff's department emphasized that *one* of the four raids yielded some money and signs of dealing, nothing of the sort was recovered in the Guerenas' home. One out of four is a pretty crappy batting average when you're swinging at human lives.

We may never know whether the police actually found the incriminating evidence, as they claimed, or simply planted it to frame their departed defendant. Faced with a massive lawsuit, the Sheriff's department has every motivation to posthumously convict their victim.

Lieutenant Michael O'Connor said it well, with perhaps unintentional candor. "Sometimes home invasions *look* like a narcotic search warrant. We want to make sure we're not looking like *any other* home invaders." Despite such efforts, the resemblance is uncanny. Vanessa, now a widow, says that she and Jose had no idea that the people breaking into her home were connected with law enforcement.

O'Connor had a lot to say about this killing, including that the victim had "brought it on himself" by being armed when law enforcement burst through his door. This was a "high-risk" warrant service, a designation which applies to "homicide suspects...someone known to carry weapons...*narcotics* cases." All of the bullets fired into the home were perfectly according to procedure and by the book, as far as the PR flak was concerned.

Seventy rounds in seven seconds did not impress Lieutenant O'Connor as being excessive force, against a man who did not fire a single shot. "We found material that was pertinent to this drug conspiracy case. I'm not going to go into detail on what those things were, but it was connecting material..."

In other words, they either found, or manufactured, evidence that Guerena somehow knew or was involved in some way with one or more of these individuals, including his brothers and father-in-law, who lived in his neighborhood. Maybe he was mowing their lawn for extra income, or bowling on the same team. Perhaps Guerena was constantly getting the suspect's mail misdelivered to his home and he was spotted bringing packages over by the Keystone Kops running this pathetic excuse for an investigation.

The real question is, what were they doing applying military force to a paper chase? Whether or not Guerena was tied to this alleged conspiracy, what urgency brought combat troops to break in, bearing assault rifles themselves? By what right does the government send adrenalized gangs of thugs to invade peoples' homes in support of making some abstract drug case?

Guerena's guilt is highly doubtful, however. Why would someone engaged in a high-level trafficking ring be employed as a humble miner working the late shift to get by? He was at worst guilty of associating with his own relatives, and possibly being too amenable in accommodating questionable favors for them. Those who knew him find the allegations to be less than credible. What is truly incredible is the gall of the police pretending they are protecting, rather than menacing, public safety, when bringing an elephant gun to hunt drugs.

People in Arizona were concerned after SWAT mercilessly gunned down Guerena, who by all appearances had been an innocent man killed through incompetence and shoddy investigation. This is when the Copaganda machine goes into high gear, with the assistance of the local news.

A little more than a week after Guerena's death, KGUN9 (motto: *On Your Side*) ran an uncritical profile segment on SWAT, scripted like an advertorial. Well-groomed Jennifer Waddell tells us the real skinny about the elite squadron busting down our neighbors' doors. She lets us know that they are the "best of the best, responding to the worst situations in Tucson."

"Let's just put it this way," she intones, quivering with rock star awe, "when the police call 911, *they* get SWAT." Admiration dripping from her voice, Waddell doesn't let notions of objective reporting interfere with her puff piece. "Highly skilled and specially trained, to handle every and any emergency," she purrs.

"The goal of SWAT team is really to save lives," a combat-clad jackboot declares, automatic rifle hung from his shoulder.

The cheerleading report goes on to display the rigorous weight training and boot camp physical exercise regimens the shock troops must undergo before being unleashed upon residential targets. Dressed in full camouflage gear, as if the next stop is a firefight in the jungle, the heroes riddle targets with their high-powered rifles.

"With this type of specialized training, already stellar officers rise to higher levels," Waddell gushes. The emphasis, beaten like a dead horse, is on the training. "SWAT teams are highly trained and only brought in on the most volatile of situations," we are assured, as if the public might be doubting this point after the debacle at Guerena's home.

The profile goes on to highlight the rationale of SWAT: "They use the *appearance* of overwhelming force as a *deterrent*." Nothing says "overwhelming" like seventy rounds fired into your house, nothing *deters* quite like a bullet to the gut.

Next, we get to see the "emergencies" and "volatile situations" that SWAT is called out for. "On this day, detectives from the narcotics unit asked SWAT to serve the warrant."

A sweaty cop, still pumping iron, explains the investigation. "There was a coordinated effort between two teams," he said. Were they investigating cartel killings? Giant international shipments? Serious quantities of dangerous hard drugs?

"It was a search warrant regarding, uh, marijuana sales and delivery." In other words, a dime-bag bust. Large-scale dealing is charged as trafficking.

"We knew through our intel there were children involved. The search was for some specific evidence, and we did have a lot of concern about destruction." So the "emergency" SWAT was being deployed to prevent was that the marijuana, which they were so eager to remove from the street, might be destroyed before they had a chance to do it themselves. The presence of children was a motivator rather than a discouragement to employ this hazardous level of force.

The operation was a rousing success, Waddell proudly proclaims. "In this situation that lasted all of seven minutes, from entry to a secondary search, and finally clearance for the SWAT Team, no one was hurt, the true measure of success for this team."

The camera follows the troops to their next emergency. "In another 'hot zone,' another narcotics search warrant is served." A new house is rushed by a dozen jackboots screaming orders and swinging battering rams.

If it seems odd that the most pressing emergency occupying the expensive time of this paramilitary unit, is the possibility that someone may be in possession of evidence tying them to controlled substances, it shouldn't. While the popular image of SWAT is that the armored truck rolls in to handle standoffs and hostage situations, the reality is that such genuine crises are rare, and the day-to-day routine for these tactical units is primarily engaged in drug raids.

In fact, up to eighty percent of SWAT activity is in support of pharmafascism. Most of the time, the "emergency" is the urgency of a prosecutor to make yet another case stick.

"It's pretty much a complete turnaround from what you see in the movies," says a SWAT agent dressed in camo and about forty pounds of combat gear. To be sure.

"As you've heard, becoming an elite member of this team takes a lot of special qualities," Waddell concludes her Pravda report. "When these SWAT members are not on the job, a lot of them are home with their families, their kids." Unlike Jose Guerena, who thanks to these "elite, highly trained" killers will never see his family again.

"They're donating to schools and charities, in fact this summer there is a golf tournament to benefit 'Wounded Warrior,' which helps officers and their families." How generous of them to devote themselves to a grueling eighteen rounds, all in order to help other gun-toting servants of government repression. A golf tournament! What selflessness!

"What a job!" exults anchor Guy Atchley. "Incredible stuff," Waddell agrees.

"Weather is next."

The everyday activities of narcotics police represent a laundry list of felonies, from robbery to murder to kidnapping, yet are upheld by all branches of government as just and necessary sacrifices of our freedom. Imposing their narrow vision on those of us who supposedly employ them, the job of the police is to exercise the government monopoly on criminal activity.

Law enforcement is, really, the most organized of crime, that which is authorized by the State. Like other violent gangs, the police are bound by a strict internal code, are routinely armed, and generate funds through forcible abductions, extortion, and robberies. They are, as the late Dr. Tod Mikuriya frequently said, and we have taken pains to repeat, criminals under the color of authority.

It's all by the book, because *this* gang *writes* the laws, silencing anyone who tries to change them. We, the People, are ostensibly responsible for this outrage, though none of us have been asked whether we *want* the assault on millions of Americans committing no other crime than trying to feel better. We have been told how it is, and ought to be, by a thoroughly convinced cadre of ideologues.

We have seen the United States government transition through many violent and unjust campaigns against behavioral scapegoats. History teems with such unsavory episodes, from the witch trials of Salem to the witch-hunts of McCarthy.

Never has there been a more successful form of political persecution than the war on cannabis and drug users. It has been promoted at the level of world government. All the nations of the planet, with only a few exceptions, have agreed to deprive their citizenry of sovereignty over their own neurochemistry.

Like other behavioral minorities, users of illicit substances make excellent fodder for the State. Police enjoy arresting them, correctional guards like supervising them, courts find processing them simple and streamlined. They tend to be on time for their court dates. They tend to pay their fines. They tend to go quietly and take the plea without a fuss.

The crackdown on cognitive liberty has forced even the most conscience-plagued domestic soldier to participate in horrific acts of barbarism. It gives those with fewer scruples license to abuse their authority, and visit gross brutality and injustice on individuals whose only crime is preferring one substance over another. Often enough, as in the sampling of cases above, the casualties of war include those who haven't even committed that questionable offense.

Employing informants, secret police, and paramilitary shock troops against peaceful private citizens are the sort of tactics we are taught to associate with totalitarian regimes. Persuading the American people to tolerate this police incursion requires a multimedia smokescreen, which generates the illusion that these crimes against humanity are in fact the product of a lawful government.

Copaganda speaks in generalizations, conflating concepts which do not equate, leading to absurd results. A plant growing on private property is converted into an emergency, a threat somehow to the community. Fundamentally, what is more dangerous: individuals wanting to modify their own consciousness, or those striving to modify everyone else's?

This book will examine the verbal tricks, culturally-implanted memes, and false premises employed in the promotion of government repression directed at pharmacognitive sovereignty. Most importantly, we shall carefully weigh the cost of this domestic war in human terms. We shall confront and document the patent madness of protecting people at gunpoint from the largely phantom menace of their own choices.

We shall also explore the many ways various controlled substance statutes and enforcement are at odds with the plain language of the Constituting document under which the land is allegedly governed. Here is why it evidently does not apply to you.

ARTICLE II:
Prisoners of War

"Welcome to hell. A hell erected and maintained by human-governments, and blessed by black robed judges. A hell that allows you to see your loved ones, but not to touch them. A hell situated in America's boondocks, hundreds of miles away from most families. A white, rural hell, where most of the captives are black and urban. It is an American way of death."—Mumia Abu-Jamal

Every person incarcerated for a controlled substance offense is a political prisoner. There is no logic to the equation between possession of unauthorized mind-alteration agents, and the draconian sentences dispensed for having them, other than to fill needs of the State.

No matter how many voices are raised against these unreasonably harsh prison terms, they continue to be dispensed at all levels of jurisdiction and in every State of the Union. It is quite common for a drug sentence to outlast that for a manslaughter or even murder conviction. When sizable quantities are involved, mandatory minimums and multiple-count indictments magnify the penalty far beyond the horizon of reason. Some convicts are condemned to effectively pass their natural lives behind bars for playing an incidental role in the trade of unauthorized chemicals or plants.

The vehemence with which the governments of the world persecute the neurological underclass—and yes, virtually all them participate—is reminiscent of many sordid affairs, past and present, now condemned as intolerable abuses. Whenever a group is rounded up and interned, blamed unreasonably for all the ills of society, and stripped of their rights, we call this tyranny.

Over 1.6 million Americans were arrested for possession of illegal substances in 2009. Over half of these were for possession of cannabis. One might be inclined to assume that most of the arrests were dealers or manufacturers. Busting the big fish.

Think again—the court system is slurping down the minnows, feasting on the easy catch of small fry. Nearly nine out of ten of these arrests were for simple possession. By contrast, just over a third as many, five hundred eighty thousand, were arrested for *violent* crimes. Drug busts are the bread-and-butter of the modern prison-industrial complex.

Sixty-seven percent of felony drug convicts are sentenced to some form of confinement, despite a popular impression that probation is usual. In the Federal prison system, just over half are doing time for controlled substance offenses.

Being brought into jail, even for a night, is a traumatizing descent into a world where you are not free in the least and no one who cares about you exists. Rights you have depended on your entire life evaporate, as you unwillingly exchange your street clothes for the uniform of a captive.

Those who are fortunate enough to have someone on the outside willing and able to post bail can see the light at the end of the tunnel. Everyone else—the poor, those arrested while traveling, or who have a hold based on long-forgotten warrants—are transferred to longer-term housing.

The inmate in jail faces a state of constant abuse. Subject to arbitrary commands and unremittingly supervised by angry cops, being in custody rapidly drains the soul. Stripped of all personal belongings, the inmate is forced to wear ridiculous striped pajamas or colored jumpsuits.

No lip service is paid to the possibility of innocence. There is an absolute presumption of guilt by guards, who know nothing of any individual case and couldn't care less.

Simple choices, such as what to eat, or whether to take a walk outside, are now subject to approval by a grim, silent staff, which responds with hostility and petty brutality to the most reasonable requests. Medical complaints are generally viewed as malingering, and ignored or even punished.

Shackled during every one of the many random transfers that transpire in the course of a typical pre-trial incarceration, each step is a punishment, as the chains and cuffs pinch and bruise unprotected ankles and wrists. Naturally, begging for the bonds to be loosened is likely to bring the opposite response.

All cell phones are immediately confiscated upon booking, so if you tend to depend on technology to stay in touch, and store all contact numbers in your phone, you may as well be on another planet. Telephone books and directory assistance are alien to this world. Pay phones may be available, but only if you are able to reach someone who accepts unexpected five-dollar collect calls from jail. The TV trope about a cop handing you a quarter so you can notify your loved ones is antiquated myth. Unless the key numbers are committed to memory, there is no hope of acquiring them inside lockdown.

On one hand, the isolation from the outside is nearly absolute; on the other, exposure to dangerous social conditions in jail is unavoidable. Racially-based gangs aggressively recruit fresh fish immediately upon arrival, and target for harassment those who dare refuse.

Some inmates may be comforted by the unity of racism, but for those who value openness and diversity, the enforced segregation is a nightmare. For example, a Jewish inmate may be approached for recruitment by the Aryan Brotherhood, creating quite the dilemma. Revealing an ethnic ineligibility for membership is sure to make matters worse.

Non-violent offenders are at risk for extortion, assault, and rape, from both gangs and individual thugs. In close quarters, perhaps for the first time, with larger, stronger and easily agitated individuals, the peaceful pothead is under constant pressure and threat.

Conditions of hygiene in a county jail are abysmal; an overnight lock-up can expose you to staph, hepatitis, tuberculosis and other air-or-skin borne diseases, which will stay with you long after release. For example, the Hepatitis C infection rate is twenty times as high among inmates as the general population.

Overcrowding amplifies the spread of disease, so it should come as no surprise that a jail cell is a virtual petri dish for infections. Add that to such niceties as a single toilet serving the entire holding cell, the utter absence of soap or warm water, and the frequent refusal of guards to relocate the seriously ill, and it is a very lucky inmate, even a temporary one, who escapes catching a case with medical consequences outweighing the legal ones.

The terror of the arrest is repeated over and again, as paramilitary units, armed with tear gas and rubber bullets, raid the tiers in a fishing expedition for tiny amounts of tobacco or incriminating papers. Inmates are routinely forced preemptively to the floor, despite having done nothing to provoke these shock attacks.

Incarceration is the most serious abridgment of human rights that is tolerated in this society. Short of execution, no form of penalty approaches the total loss of freedom that is the fate of everyone behind bars. When politicians banter about getting "drugs off the street," they are advocating sending millions of people on a trip to hell.

Considering that, shouldn't we be sure that citizens subjected to this treatment have actually done someone harm?

In the neighborhood of 2.5 million individuals currently reside in the jails and penitentiaries of the United States. Roughly one-fifth of these, about half a million, are doing time for possession offenses, not counting those locked up due to enhanced sentencing for drug priors, or probationers who failed a urine test. Millions more are on some form of community supervision, one dirty drop away from being shipped off to the camps.

No country on the planet, not even China, imprisons as many of its citizens as the United States. As we have made clear, this gigantic surplus can be accounted for by the large number of controlled substance offenders serving long terms for refusing to cede the government control of their minds.

The measure of tyranny in a government is the rigor with which police force is exerted on those whose only crime is disagreeing with official policy. By that metric, the US is leading the way as a pseudo-democratic police junta.

The burgeoning prison population is the preeminent civil rights issue of the time. Wrong-headed policies continue year after year to destroy lives in the name of improving society. The equivalent of an entire city of people is living under armed guard. So many nonviolent people languishing in a box to fulfill some misguided ideology should alarm the rest of us. The ease with which this unbridled entity, this tangled web of interconnected social and economic self-interests, reappropriates human life, is one of the more frightening realities of the world in which we live.

The obscenity of prohibition is self-sustaining. The institutions which derive power from these laws feed on the lifeblood of those caught in their net. Consigned to a cold metal cell, these millions have been forced to endure deliberately hellish conditions while unrecoverable months and years tick away from their lifespans. Converted to numbers in the system and on the bottom line, they have been sacrificed to a fate which for many is worse than death.

One might say, well, these people violated the law; and they knew they were breaking the law, so they deserve what they get. There are several problems with this perspective. First of all, there is no moral sanctity in laws; history abounds with reprehensible legislation and edicts adopted against every disadvantaged class. Indeed, the worst atrocities since antiquity have uniformly been committed under the auspices of governments, according to rigid laws.

We have not consented to these laws, nor are they the product of any truly democratic process. The doings of elected officials often contrast with the express will of the people, and we firmly believe that if current controlled substances legislation were subjected to direct public approval, as penalties stand, it would not survive a fair vote.

Moreover, even if these reactionary restrictions were to be enacted with full assent of the majority, that would still not wipe out the arbitrary inequity created when one prejudiced part of the population, consumers of alcohol and caffeine, hound and imprison the other part, who prefer marijuana, cocaine, or some other unapproved substance.

So many unjust legal concoctions have been repealed, renounced, and deemed intolerably repressive, that we have no sympathy for the argument which places bigoted social control over individual liberty, no matter what repressive statutes have been adopted in the halls of power. We hope prohibition, too, will someday fall into the dustbins of history, and we shall look back upon this time as another shameful episode of appalling marginalization and persecution of a targeted minority class.

That the hapless denizens of drug gulags may have broken some misguided regulation is no excuse for this treatment. Many governments concoct legislation to oppress elements objectionable to the elite. When foreign enemies employ such means, they are roundly condemned. The United States has led and been instrumental in sanctioning against human rights abuses, as they have occurred in other lands, and ought to be held to the same high standard in official domestic policy.

Having criminal charges pressed is arguably the most unfortunate fate which can befall an individual. Only serious medical conditions can compare to the gravity of a term in the custody of a penal institution. Unlike a terminal illness or permanent disability, however, incarceration is a wholly preventable condition, which is perpetrated not by accident or infection, but by the stubborn and deliberate actions of agents of the State.

Of course, exposure to disease is included with the sentence; for many, even a brief stint represents a death sentence. The high incidence of infectious agents in jails and penitentiaries is no accident. These institutions are maintained in such a way as to amplify the transmission of pathogens, herding prisoners together in a state of continuous crowding.

The consequence inflicted on a defendant with a tap of the gavel outweighs the damage done by the crime of any private citizen, save only murder. Being killed is a very real risk attendant to being hauled off in shackles. So far as we know, literal executions by guards are rare. But confining nonviolent, often defenseless substance offenders in close quarters with dangerous and predatory criminals creates more unreported and unaddressed crime behind bars than exists on the streets.

If the purpose of prison is to reduce crime, it is in that a miserable failure. The crime has simply shifted to the crucible of the tiers and yards. Concentrating violence behind barbed wires might keep it off the streets, but tossing the lambs to the lions is an outrage worse than nearly any defendant's behavior.

We are told that we must keep the police around to protect us from criminals, but that is not all they do. If they only responded to calls for help, we would have little quibble with the police. In the course of brutal application of incomprehensible rules, officers are issued lethal armament, along with a badge conferring license to menace the public more dangerously than any private lawbreaker. An arrest, particularly for non-violent offenses, is a legally authorized assault, abduction and theft all at once. Often enough, the situation erupts into a murder as well, which is normally punished with a period of paid leave.

One might say that a brutal rape is a worse fate than being processed by the criminal system and confined for years. This is a judgment call, and the two really cannot be compared, but we would submit that the constant violation of personhood, which begins when the handcuffs click shut, represents a greater loss of freedom than the temporary force of an assault by any citizen. While each is a traumatic loss of personal sovereignty, police are insatiable victimizers, not content to merely take what they want and go away. They will stalk you incessantly if you have triggered their attention.

There is no need to debate the issue, for rape is yet another aspect of the "justice" meted out in court. Rape is widely considered a women's issue, and the crime of forcible sexual entry is rightly regarded as one of the most heinous of all human acts, ranking just below murder. Women, especially prostitutes, are vulnerable to sexual exploitation by the police, and the key difference is that this type of crime is even more rarely reported.

In prison, however, rape is also a man's issue, a constant and unremitting threat for those too weak to resist. This is not to say that female prisoners are not also sexually exploited while incarcerated, both by guards and aggressive inmates, but that males in prison are exposed to, on the whole, an unparalleled level of sexual predation, which is itself perhaps the saddest of all the many evils of the war on cognitive liberty.

This feature of the penal system is well known, and the police are not shy in citing it when attempting to gain cooperation from recalcitrant suspects. The author knows from personal experience that police frequently threaten this vicarious rape to induce even juvenile arrestees to willingly surrender their rights.

To put perspective on the magnitude of such behavior, consider how the law regards a bystander, who neither participates in, nor prevents, a sexual assault. Such an individual will normally be brought up on charges of conspiracy and often receive a sentence similar to the actual perpetrators. If anyone outside of government were to plausibly make reference to locking a minor in a room full of sexual predators, that person would face the most vigorous prosecution. If they acted on such a threat, the sentence would likely be for many years, or even life. Yet we tolerate the offhand use of this grim and disturbing reality as leverage in a negotiation over confessions and betrayal.

This aspect of the vast and impersonal system is the subject of derisive and mocking humor in the culture about dropping the soap in the shower, or being traded for a pack of cigarettes, but the joke is decidedly unfunny to the victims of this most debasing treatment. Some individuals are subjected to repeated and sustained attacks throughout their sentence; once branded as an exploitable punk, the label is hard to shake.

By maintaining these conditions, and remanding so many individuals, who are not dangerous, to be forcibly housed in cells with those who are, the State is complicit in every assault, every rape, every contraction of incurable disease, and every murder which occurs in their "correctional" facilities.

Yet it is difficult to assign blame for this outrage; no single individual or even agency can be said to truly be the origin of prohibition. It is a monster born of fear and greed, nourished by power, which it ruthlessly wields to protect its reign.

It's not just the legislatures passing draconian bills, nor the courts contorting jurisprudence to approve them. Presidents such as Nixon, Reagan, Clinton, and the two Bushes can certainly shoulder much of the culpability for spearheading the initiative to incrementally ramp up the war on pharmacological deviants.

Historical hypocrites like Harry Anslinger worked tirelessly to bring us to this point, with the collusion of corporate interests, but even these influences fail to account for the vastness of the repression. Joe McCarthy, working his witch-hunt during the same period, was equally rabid, but his legacy has long since faded, his name and ideology synonymous with discredited and unwarranted political persecution.

It's not even the cops, and their brutal application of unfair tactics, which have brought this state of affairs. Although it is true that the imprisonment industry exerts tax dollars to ensure the unceasing flow of warm bodies fed into its maw, the ultimate responsibility for this travesty must be said to lay with we, the People, who have failed to rise up in unwavering protest against this officially sanctioned criminal conspiracy to rob us collectively of our rights.

When we look for the villains behind this shifting shell game of responsibility, the buck can always be passed. Lawmakers are just responding to the demands of their hysterical constituency, courts are merely validating the acts of elected representatives. Presidents are simply providing leadership in this misguided war, and cops, of course, are just doing their jobs.

Much ado is made of the gargantuan cost of this wasteful destructive crusade. Legalization advocates, knowing what motivates the average citizen, tend to emphasize the expense of this industry which produces nothing but suffering. The marginally successful rhetorical angle seeks to legitimize cannabis in particular, so that it can be taxed and thus enrich the State rather than bankrupt it.

The reality is that incarceration is a profit-driven enterprise, franchising a can't-lose blueprint for redistributing wealth from the public to special interests. Much of this largesse flows to the many obedient servants who constitute a standing army in the streets of every city, at a wage enviable to other jobs with a similarly low standard for education. It pays for the overpriced construction of quadruple-occupancy dormitories on undesirable real estate, for the sole purpose of accommodating the living damned, and pays for demons to torment them.

You will frequently hear law-and-order types rallying against more humane treatment for prisoners, claiming that these sprawling gulags are "country clubs." We imagine these sour reactionaries lay awake at night, preoccupied with the idea that people they hate aren't suffering enough. They call in to radio shows and write their representatives to express outrage at any small privilege or allowance granted to the unfortunate souls who must live out their days in confinement. Such sadism is beneath contempt. We have compassion for the plight of every prisoner, whether or not they "deserve" their punishment.

There are some behaviors for which confinement may be the only remedy. We have no ready alternative for the disposition of violent acts, other than some sort of remand to a facility of rehabilitation. There is no need for these places to be dungeons; but such "violence hospitals" of necessity could not be terribly pleasant. We earnestly believe that violent crime is properly the domain of law enforcement, and while corrections reform is certainly on our agenda, we are not suggesting that this function of the government be fundamentally abolished. On the contrary, it is the only legitimate reason to tolerate the State at all.

When it comes to all other criminal offenses, however, there is no pressing need for confinement as a precaution of public safety. Economic crimes would be more rationally addressed through civil remedies, which emphasize restitution rather than retribution. The current system brings no benefit to the victim, and dramatically increases the chance that more crimes will eventually follow.

Interrogation is not an honest business. The supposed guardians of society's virtue will mislead, dissemble and threaten, in order to get the words they seek to issue forth. On the other hand, uttering the slightest untruth in the face of an angry cop can trigger felony charges, even if the information itself concerns no crime, despite the right to be free of compelled self-incrimination. The police can defraud and imposture in the name of investigation, but if one of us were to assume the props and identity of the baton-bearing class, we'd be liable for serious criminal complications.

This double-standard, wherein the agents of law enforcement are not bound by law or even common decency, while citizens are held to an impossible standard concealed within a mountain of legal tomes, is the fundamental unfairness fomenting the police State.

Anything you say can be used *against* you in a court of law...but if what you say tends to *exonerate* you, your words no longer constitute admissible evidence. Although the officer can testify to self-incrimination by the subject, relating your protestations of innocence is deemed hearsay. Far from being agents of justice, their mandate is to seek only evidence of guilt.

No dirty trick is too low for some narcotics investigators. So loose are the strictures on ethical behavior, that not only will cops stoop to impersonating their prey, a form of deception which is standard practice, but some have been known to resort to practicing law without a license—giving some very poor legal advice indeed.

In Tennessee, Monroe County Sheriff's Detectives Pat Henry and Doug Brannon conspired to hoodwink John Edward Dawson, who was being held on drug and theft charges, into believing that Henry was his assigned defense counsel. After convincing Dawson to shun his actual public defender—who recommended the poor confused man for a psychiatric evaluation, due to his inexplicable contention that he was already being represented by nonexistent attorneys—and accept a guilty plea, his real lawyer became suspicious and uncovered the plot.

When the subterfuge came to light, Judge Amy Reedy denied the motion to continue the case, despite overwhelming evidence that Dawson had been maliciously deprived, in the most disreputable of ways, of his Constitutional right to legal counsel. She sent him up the river anyhow, noting that the defendant had made "a real dumb decision" to be deceived by the deputies, and that he had "picked his poison"—a pointedly non-strategic submission to an unfavorable plea arrangement.

Think of a year of your life. What is it worth to you? What does it mean to you to be able to freely associate with friends and neighbors, to indulge in hobbies or pursue the goals you have set for yourself? How much do you value the right to eat the food of your choosing, the option to live where you see fit and with whom?

What would you do to someone who wanted to steal that much from you? What if they tried to steal ten times, twenty times that much? If you are like most people, you'd fight to defend yourself from anyone who tried to do anything of the sort to you.

Yet for the most part, we placidly accept this treatment from a government which is allegedly administered at the pleasure of the people, according to the public will, in order to protect us from the evil we do to each other. Scarcely a whisper is raised against this subsidized crime spree which has plundered millions of their lives and everything they value.

So unnatural is the prison environment, the wonder is that not everyone is driven insane by the experience. These facilities represent the extreme logical endpoint of totalitarian politics; every bite of food, every voiding of the bowels, every moment of rest or exercise is at the strict command of authority.

The pathology of penal institutions and the politics of confinement were graphically illustrated by an intriguing psychology study conducted at Stanford University in 1971.

"I was interested in what happens if you put good people in an evil place," explained project leader Dr. Philip Zimbardo. He converted the basement of Building 420 into an experimental jail, calling it "Stanford County Prison."

Participants, all local students at the University, were drawn in by an ad offering $15 per day payment, and randomly assigned to the role of either guard or inmate. Barred doors were added to three offices, which would serve as cells, while the "Hole," for solitary confinement, was a converted storage closet with no light whatsoever. The guards were outfitted with beige military style uniforms, silver reflective sunglasses which concealed the eyes, and thick wooden batons to maintain order.

"When you put a uniform on, and are given a job to keep people in line, you really become that person," recounted Dave Eshleman, who had been a guard in the experiment.

Zimbardo appointed himself as the Warden. He told his staff, "We have to maintain law and order. If prisoners escape, the study is over." This would of course mean an end to their payments as well. He also told them they were forbidden to use force. "We're trying to create the impression that because of surveillance, we have all the power in the situation and they have none."

The students who became inmates were brought into the makeshift tier blindfolded. They were stripped by the guards, subjected to de-lousing procedures, and issued ill-fitting gowns along with a numerical identity, just like real inmates.

By the second day, a prisoner revolt was in progress. Denouncing the simulation in loud, pained wails, the students on the short end of the stick barricaded the cell with their bed-frames, and refused to cooperate with the experiment.

"Initially, I was stunned," admitted Zimbardo. "I didn't expect the rebellion, because not much had happened. It wasn't clear what they were rebelling against." Then he caught on. "They were rebelling against the *status*. They were rebelling against being anonymous, rebelling against having to follow orders from these other students."

In retaliation, the guards put the ringleader, who was known as #8162, into solitary confinement, and began a campaign of ritualized harassment against the others, which included late-night headcounts, forced exercises, and degrading tasks like cleaning a toilet bowl with a toothbrush.

The leader of the spirited riot had had enough and went to Zimbardo, asking to be released from the study. This was no longer play; he was scared and wanted to go home, to hell with the $15 a day.

Zimbardo, however, saw a way to demonstrate another principle of power exchange behind bars, and instead negotiated lighter treatment for this student in return for information about the other prisoners. In a short span of two days, the leader of the resistance had been recruited to become the lab prison's first snitch.

Back on the tier, he also brought back some frightening, if not entirely accurate, news from Administration. He told the others that he had asked to leave, and was not being allowed to. Zimbardo had not actually said that, employing persuasion rather than force to retain the subject, but so intimidating was his perceived power as faux warden, that his firmness was taken for denial.

#8162 told the others that they were being held against their will, and would not be able to leave. "I was told that I couldn't quit. At that point I just felt totally hopeless, more hopeless than I had ever felt before." He began ranting and raving, begging to be released, partly feigning insanity in hopes that they would kick him out of the experiment, and partly going genuinely mad. "I've never been so upset in my life. It was an experience of being out of control."

"That really transformed the experiment into a prison," Zimbardo recounts. He was forced to give in to #8162's demands, and granted clemency to the student. By day three, however, a rumor made the rounds that the freed inmate was organizing a very real rescue effort to secure release for the other subjects.

At this point, Zimbardo himself was caught up in the role. "I quickly convinced myself that my most important function was not to allow this prison liberation to occur, and what I could do to keep this *prison* going, not to keep this *experiment* going." Thrust into his social role, he converted to the authoritarian figure he originally was only posing as.

In a state of near-panic about the imminent jailbreak, Zimbardo broke down the tier, and transferred the entire population of Stanford County Prison to a new pod established in a different wing. He then personally sat vigil in the original location, prepared to confront the rabble-rouser when he appeared with friends to spring the other subjects. Zimbardo planned to tell the former #8162 that the study was over, so that he would abandon the effort to liberate his comrades.

Instead, Zimbardo was visited by a colleague, who wanted to raise academic points about the research. "I'm trying to get rid of him, and then he says, 'what's the independent variable?' I get furious, because he doesn't understand that there is a *riot* about to take place, that this prison is about to erupt. I had totally lost this whole other identity, of scientist, of researcher, psychologist."

On day four, the guards, who were frustrated by the extra work of twice transferring the prisoners and rebuilding their tier, began to ramp up the aggression toward the inmates. "They escalated the level of control, the level of dominance, the level of humiliating behavior."

A new front of resistance developed, this time from prisoner #819, who irritated the guards by erecting a barricade of his own. This time, however, instead of rallying around the new leader, the inmates succumbed to the strategy which the guards spontaneously evolved to discourage dissent. The entire pod was punished for #819's rebellion and encouraged to vent their anger on him rather than the guards inflicting torment.

"That was one of the surprising things to me," said Eshleman, who had acquired the nickname John Wayne because of the sadistic enthusiasm he brought to the role. "That there was so little the prisoners did to support one another after we started our campaign of, you know, divide and conquer."

After a stint in solitary, #819 had also had enough, and demanded to be freed as well. He was replaced by an alternate, Clay Ramsay, a long-haired hippie fellow who was to become known as #416. The first subject to be immersed in the maturing prison culture, which in five days had developed a repressive social order on par with any genuine institution, Ramsay found himself trapped in a nightmare.

"He came into a madhouse. All of us had gradually acclimated to the increasing level of aggression, increasing powerlessness of the prisoners, the increasing dominance of the guards," Zimbardo recalls. "He comes in here and says to the other prisoners, 'What's happening here?' And they said, 'Yeah, you better not make trouble, it's really terrible here, it's a real prison.' And he says, 'I'm outta here, I don't want this,' and they said, 'No, you can't leave, once you're here you're stuck. This is a *real* prison.'"

John Wayne had taken over the cellblock, amusing himself by

inventing new ways to humiliate the inmates at his mercy. "He was creative in his evil. He would think up ingenious ways to degrade, to demean the prisoners," Zimbardo recalled. Not all the guards took so naturally to the role of tormentor. "One of the best guards was also on this shift. Instead of confronting the bad guard, this sadistic guard, because he didn't want to see what was happening, he took on the job of gofer."

"We were continually called upon to act in a way that was really contrary to what I feel inside," this guard said. "Just continually giving out shit, it's one of the most oppressive things you could do."

Then #416 initiated a hunger strike. He wasn't playing at dissidence; he was actually willfully refusing food to protest the conditions. This method got under the skin of the guards, who became outraged that a prisoner could undermine them through exercising the last freedom available to him. Self-denial of nourishment is a venerable method for the unjustly confined to defy the authorities by consciously subverting their physical self-interest in favor of spiritual autonomy.

"They were pushing my limits, but here was a thing I could do which would push *their* limits," Ramsay explains. "After I had missed a couple of meals, I saw that this was not a matter of indifference to the guards. I was making headway. They were upset." In just a day inside the experiment, the whole of #416's motivation became directed at recovering the personal power he had lost to his keepers.

He was locked in the storage closet, while the other suffering inmates, punished for his intransigent posture, followed the lead of the guards in banging on the door and loudly "thanking" him for the abusive response to his behavior they had to endure.

John Wayne took all of this quite personally. "He yelled at me, and threatened me, and actually sort of smashed a sausage in my face to get me to open up, but I didn't have any intention of eating until I was out," Ramsay recounts.

"Number 416 should have been at some level a hero, for he was willing to oppose the authority of the system," Zimbardo observed. "In fact, the prisoners accepted the guard's definition of him as a troublemaker."

John Wayne agreed. "I remember some of them saying, 'would you eat, goddamn it! We're sick and tired of this.' And that was proof that there was no solidarity, there was no support between the prisoners."

Now on a personal mission to crush #416's little rebellion, John Wayne devised a way to further prove that prisoners put their own skins above the welfare of their comrades. He offered to let the inmates choose between their blankets and freedom for the rabble-rouser. Three out of four opted to betray the one who might have led them to revolution, simply so they wouldn't have to sleep on bare mattresses.

By the end of the fifth day, the experiment had so grotesquely succeeded that most of the prisoners were demanding release. A visiting colleague was so appalled by Zimbardo's social Frankenstein monster that she urged him to terminate the study for ethical reasons. The inmates were granted clemency and the guards fired. The Hole was restored to storing file cabinets, and the walls came down around Stanford County Prison.

"When I look back on it now, I behaved appallingly. It was just horrid to look at." John Wayne no more, Dave Eshleman had discovered a side to himself that had a talent and predilection for making others miserable. Such individuals rise to the top in the context of the prison industrial complex, exulting in work which others literally cannot abide.

"I think I tried to explain to him at the time, that what you experienced, what you hated so much, that was a *role* that I was playing, that was not me at all." Like so many in law enforcement, John Wayne was merely doing his job.

Ramsay wasn't buying it. "He tried to dissociate himself from what he had done. That did make me angry. *Everyone* was acting out a part and playing a role. It's when you start contributing to the script...that's *you*, and thus it is something you should take responsibility for."

For his part, John Wayne thought it was everyone else's job to set limits on his power trip. "It surprised me that no one said anything to stop me, they just accepted what I said. No one questioned my authority at all, and it really shocked me. Why didn't people stand up to me? When I started to abuse people so much, I started to get so profane, and still people didn't say anything."

Zimbardo observed, "There were a few guards who hated to see the prisoners suffer, they never did anything which would be demeaning of the prisoners. The interesting thing is none of the good guards did anything to intervene in the behavior of the guards who gradually became more and more sadistic over time."

We find this experiment to be fascinating and revealing about the psychological factors at play in a penal institution. Particularly remarkable is the ease with which all these individuals settled into the social roles they were arbitrarily assigned, even though they had gone in with perfect awareness that they were acting out a scenario.

Some inmates instinctively reacted against their inhumane treatment, resisting exactly as their counterparts in actual institutions, while alienating the majority who preferred cooperation to punishment. The guards spontaneously fell into a pattern of abuse, although they knew their inmates had committed no crime, simply because the lure of power was so great. Those who were bothered by their conscience sought out duties which took them away from contact with the prisoners, leaving the sadists in charge.

In each case, the setting and internal identity overwhelmed whatever personal traits the participants had brought into the study, including the researcher who initiated it in the first place. Although none had been on either side of this most inequitable situation previously, all assumed behaviors which reflected the imbalance to be found in any jail.

That the students so quickly adapted to this power dynamic in the laboratory is instructive as to the reasons why such conditions prevail in real prisons. If students at a prestigious University so easily take on these patterns of behavior after only a few days, what does this say about prisoners and guards compelled to these roles by force of law over many years?

This study has further implications with regard to the wider community of law enforcement in open society, who treat every suspect as an inmate and are driven to formalize that status. Like John Wayne, they came in to the job as an alternative to flipping burgers or whatever menial labor is otherwise available. Some had ideals about the greater good and protecting the community, just as John Wayne had ideas that fulfilling his role in a convincing fashion was beneficial to the goals of the experiment.

Just before the study began, Eshleman had seen the prison movie "Cool Hand Luke" and modeled his obnoxious character on the "Captain" from that film, played by Strother Martin, famous for drawling the line, "What we've got here is a *failure* to *communicate*."

Similarly, newly employed police and correctional guards seek role models among their elders and find that the most dynamically successful are often the most cruel. Finding this to be suitable behavior for them, the rookie adopts a bulldog persona which personally profits the bad actor bound to rise in the ranks and earn esteem from their colleagues. Those who find abusiveness unpalatable gravitate toward desk work, where they don't have to choose between the demands of their job and their inclination for mercy.

We are left to cope with the rest of them, the sociopathic personalities who derive pleasure from causing suffering. Sadists dominate law enforcement because they are drawn by the very thing which repels the compassionate nature. A great deal of this has to do with the addictive nature of success; when an individual discovers a marketable skill, even when that talent is torture, the tendency is to capitalize on it.

ARTICLE III:
A Matter of Semantics

"All laws which can be violated without doing any one any injury are laughed at. Nay, so far are they from doing anything to control the desires and passions of men that, on the contrary, they direct and incite men's thoughts the more toward those very objects; for we always strive toward what is forbidden and desire the things we are not allowed to have. And men of leisure are never deficient in the ingenuity needed to enable them to outwit laws framed to regulate things which cannot be entirely forbidden... He who tries to determine everything by law will foment crime rather than lessen it."—Baruch Spinoza

There is always some dissonance between a word and its meaning. Language represents reality; it is not reality. We have words for things which do not exist, things which may exist, or things whose existence is purely subjective. Laws are merely words, but the most powerful sort: those verbal constructions which modify and bind reality by placing limits on the content of the world. Rather than describe reality, the verbal expression of law actually prescribes it.

A word is merely a symbolic image of the idea it is intended to convey, the object or action it is intended to describe. The use of language to transmit emotional responses through pejorative terms is seminal to any system of propaganda.

Take the word, "drug" for example. At the beginning of the twentieth century, the word simply meant any health remedy, readily available at a neighborhood corner store. The 1913 Webster's defines it as "any animal, vegetable or mineral substance used in the composition of medicines."

A hundred years later, the word has taken on demonic connotations. In the mouths of politicians, it is almost invariably followed by the word "problem." Recklessly and mindlessly attributing all of society's ills to deviant pharmacological behavior, the word *drug* has become a push-button for repression. It is presumed that taking them is evil, destructive, and criminal. Yet these properties apparently only apply to certain arbitrarily assigned formulations, while other, similar, substances are barely regarded as such.

Common usage of the term "drug" is highly prejudiced, frequently resting on confusing and vague ideological conceptions deriving from a Federal law. The government's contribution to the dictionary replaces denotation with connotation: "Something and often an illicit substance that causes addiction, habituation, or a marked change in consciousness."

Webster's-Miriam now contains a definition so broad as to include everything under the sun: "A substance other than food, intended to affect the structure or function of the body." This is apparently the range of objects under the purview of State drug policy.

According to that definition, a warm bath would seem to qualify. Heated water can be medicinal for skin and muscular discomfort, soothing to the psychology, and even generate euphoria. The world is filled with incidental items which cause a positive psychoactive change, from the smell of a rose to the sound of the ocean.

Mountains have certainly been made from molehills over them, but what, exactly, is a "drug?" More importantly, perhaps, what is *not*?

Echinacea is a powerful herb, but is never called a drug. The same is true for a host of psychoactive herbs like gingko, yohimbe, or valerian root. Marijuana is called a drug, and is now recommended by physicians in several States, but it is also simply a powerful herb. Yet it is decreed a drug by the authorities, and a forbidden one at that.

At what point of potency or utility does an *herb* become a *drug*? The question is not academic. Lives hinge on the way it is answered. The government's glossing of this distinction indicates how mindlessly whimsical the official definitions are.

The word has a radically different meaning in a medical context, where a drug is considered a solution for symptoms, than in a legal context, where it conjures up a threat of unreasonable urgency, a reason to deprive a citizen of every liberty.

Affix the word "dangerous" to it, and all sorts of confusion ensues. Danger, in a drug, seems to have something to do with it being popular, enjoyable, and inviting repetition. It does not seem to necessarily have anything to do with toxicity, side effects, or physical dependency, all of which are features of FDA-approved "safe" products, provided by the pharmaceutical industry, or the legal recreants alcohol and tobacco.

The real hazard of such "dangerous" drugs has nothing to do with consuming them, but rather the draconian penalties for getting caught before having a chance to do so. There are hazards in every experience, including the consumption of legal and illegal psychoactives. The harm deriving from the latter category is no greater, on the whole, than many substances in the former.

A drug is any chemical compound which is ingested to effect a specific desired psycho-physiological outcome, to relieve symptoms or heal discomfort. In other words, a particular molecular configuration, produced and consumed with the motive of improving the mood, and general outlook, of the one ingesting it. This is as descriptive of antibiotics as of Ecstasy.

Despite the negative associations pinned to self-directed chemical enhancement, there are literally thousands of such useful formulas administered by physicians; indeed, their manufacture is among the largest industries on Earth. The majority are produced by giant corporations who aggressively market their wares to doctors and the public alike. Pharmaceutical products are invariably sold in strictly measured dosages of isolated chemical synthesis. Never is it a whole-plant preparation.

According to a 2010 study, a whopping forty-eight percent of Americans are on at least one type of prescription medication, spending a rising three hundred billion dollars annually with Big Pharma, for an incredible four billion scripts. That's a lot of sick people! The report goes on to document that the most commonly prescribed drugs for adolescents 12-19 are central nervous system stimulants. Among adults 20-59, the leader is antidepressants.

So the *problem*, whatever it is, cannot simply be that people are using substances which affect the mind. When millions of teenagers are prescribed pharmaceutical speed so they can pay better attention in class, the cries of "keep our kids off drugs!" ring a little hollow.

When it comes to danger, it is tough to beat antidepressant medications. Dispensed like candy specifically to individuals who are unsatisfied with their unmodified neurochemistry, many of these perfectly legal mood-altering substances sport impressive side effect profiles.

Cymbalta™ is a fairly new remedy for depression. It is also known as Duloxetine. Here are the known side effects:

• nausea	• stomach pain	• difficulty urinating	• muscle pain
• heartburn	•headache	• weakness	• vomiting
• constipation	• dry mouth	• dizziness	• cramps
• diarrhea	• increased urination	• tiredness	• drowsiness
• decreased appetite	• uncontrollable shaking	• sweating or night sweats	• changes in sexual desire or ability

Remember, this is something they want you to take every day, maybe for the rest of your life, in order to feel better. A recent study found that the average prescription drug warning list contains seventy possible negative reactions, with the leading two hundred brands topping the century mark.

The manufacturers of Cymbalta™ are not embarrassed by their modest list, which is, after all, quite typical of Big Pharma's wares.

They want you to watch out for these other side effects, too:

• unusual bruising	• loss of appetite	• blurred vision	• difficulty breathing
• unusual bleeding	• confusion	• difficulty swallowing	• fever
• itching	• flu-like symptoms	• rash	• blisters
• hoarseness	• fever	• hives	• peeling skin
• dark colored urine	• severe muscle stiffness	• fast or irregular heartbeat	• swelling of the abdomen, face, throat, tongue, lips, eyes, hands, feet, ankles, or lower legs
• pain in the upper right part of the stomach	• yellowing of the skin or eyes	• extreme tiredness or weakness	

Well, if that's not enough to make you think about just taking your chances with the depression, get ready, they're not done yet. "Duloxetine may cause other side effects." With such an array of drawbacks, one might expect the government to leap in and save us from this scourge, but Cymbalta™ is an FDA-approved method for treating pathological sadness, despite making some people feel quite miserable indeed.

There are, of course, a wide variety of options for addressing a clinically sour mood, with a more benign impact on the body and mind, but you won't be getting them from your psychiatrist. Only these poisonous, unpleasant medicines are available to the depressed. Don't blame your doctor; there are plenty of promising remedies that all physicians are legally precluded from offering, no matter what they might professionally prefer.

Many of the most effective and powerful of these substances are forbidden, particularly *because* they cause a desirable and positive shift in emotional disposition. No prescription pad dare speak their names. These condemned medicines appear to have little in common with each other, or distinguishing them from those which are allowed, apart from the tendency of users to enjoy their effects, with or without authorization.

People generally do not need to be forced to avoid truly dangerous products; they will do so of their own free will, out of self-preservation. There is no law, or need for one, criminalizing the ingestion of poisons such as ammonia or bleach. A simple warning suffices. Prohibition is predicated on guarding individuals from self-destructive tendencies, but the motive for crossing the line in the shifting sands is rarely to cause damage to oneself.

Datura Stramonium, also known as "jimson weed," is a powerful dissociative herb. It has never appeared in any of the schedules of the Controlled Substances Act, despite causing convulsions, days-long delirium, amnesia, and death. The reason is simple: due to the unpleasant and hazardous effects, jimson weed has been rejected by the market as a recreational inebriant, is almost never sold, and rarely used. No legislation is needed to restrain the proliferation of *Datura*; only the foolish abuse it. Highly conscious shamanic aspirers are able to safely employ it infrequently in their arsenal, without the assistance or guidance of the government.

The most widely used and abused stimulant drug in the world is produced primarily in South America, although it is cultivated in all tropical parts of the world. Its production is facilitated by a grossly underpaid labor force, working on giant plantations for powerful cartels, who ship tons to the United States each week. Although it is available virtually everywhere, use is concentrated in fast-paced urban areas, where the drug is an adjunct to both high-stress workday routines, and socially oriented nightlife.

Habitual users often consider it impossible to function without, and consume large quantities dozens of times each day. In fact, many addicts consume it continuously throughout their increasingly prolonged waking hours, gathering in places dedicated to selling it and providing a venue for its use.

No legal restrictions prohibit the use of this drug by anyone whatsoever. Any five-year-old has access to it. It is served in restaurants, workplaces, and even schools, without more than a hint of social disapproval. Both addiction and withdrawal symptoms are commonly experienced, but despite this chemical dependence, no public emergency seems imminent. Only infrequent crimes or psychological breakdowns can be attributed to it.

Caffeine, like cocaine, is a central nervous stimulant which is popular both among workers eager to accomplish more, and recreational enthusiasts who are looking for a lift in their time off. Viewed objectively, there is little difference between these drugs. One derives from a bean, the other from a leaf. The remaining points of departure can be ascribed, not to their respective natures, but to their wildly divergent legal and social status.

Unlike cocaine, caffeine is consumed quite lawfully by ninety percent of Americans. The drug appears in soft drinks, coffee and tea, with the pure form chosen only by a tiny minority. Usually it is combined with white sugar, which is called a food, because it is metabolized in cellular respiration, despite being highly addictive and mood-altering, especially among the children who consume it the most.

Cocaine, also, once enjoyed a law-abiding existence, appearing in many of the early soft-drink formulations. The evolution of such tonics, from patent medicine to recreational decadence, was perhaps inevitable, but the larger question is whether pure cocaine, and all the violence attendant to its production and traffic, would have ever come into existence had the drug simply remained an ingredient in soda pop.

Prohibitionists point to the correlation between crime and drug use, forgetting to mention that drug-related crime typically has less to do with the substance in question than the effects of black-market trade. Also conveniently forgotten in this equation is the widespread crime-free proliferation of "table drugs" which are part of nearly every diet, including those of the people lecturing us on the dangers of substance abuse.

The legal system, partly to avoid this ambiguity, prefers the term "controlled substance." This phrase, too, is an ironic misnomer. The prohibited substances may be many things, but they are certainly not *controlled*. No inspector verifies the purity or proper labeling on these products. No Department of Weights and Measures checks bags on the street to ensure that ingredients are clearly listed and that quantities are correct.

Uniquely in the economy, billions of dollars a year worth of these substances are sold *without any controls at all*, without any liability recourse for those harmed by tainted batches. No one knows exactly how many billions, of course, because there is no way of knowing.

As our politicians keep reminding us, illegal drugs are *out of control.* Of course they are. Regulations don't apply to street dealers. Amateur chemists, no matter how talented, cannot afford to submit their product to an independent lab for analysis. Research on most of these substances has halted completely.

Human beings are creatures of habit. In fact, all creatures are of habit. Life itself is an inexplicable habit, perpetuating repetitiously, for reasons which are not entirely clear. All living things are addicted to a number of widely available mind-altering chemicals. Nature is filled with them.

The gateway drug was oxygen. Oxygen addiction is a global epidemic, the junkies requiring a hit every few seconds, lest they suffer from horrible withdrawal symptoms leading immediately to death. If you don't think oxygen is addictive, see how you feel after a minute or two without it. We're also inextricably hooked on water, and to the various sugars, proteins, and fats that are the components of food.

Our species shares these chemical dependencies with all other animals. Stalking the planet in search of the next fix, life seems to consist of little more than the quest to ingest. Even the bulk of human labor is devoted to one form or another of consumption.

Consider the ephemeral language surrounding the concept of "addiction." We call some behaviors "taking medicine," while other, virtually identical conduct is denounced as "chemical dependency." The sole difference is whether the consumption of a substance meets with outside approval.

It is undeniable that addiction is a complex issue, not readily amenable to pat solutions. It is a problem of human nature; we are consumptive, like all creatures, and compulsive.

It is also undeniable that some habits are more dangerous than others, terminating some are more difficult, and that many promising lives have been cut short through overdose or other medical complications.

There is a real question, however, whether the stiff penalties associated with the possession of such substances does anything to curb their use. Indeed, sales have increased as steadily as arrests have. Production always expands to account for interdiction, and people find a way to get their medicine. After a century of prohibition, there are more illicit drugs and people using them each year.

Why do so many individuals choose to break the criminal code with regard to certain psychotropic substances? Some feel an obligation to defy an unjust law. Some are in it to relax, or to potentiate sensory input, such as lights, music, or sex. Some are pursuing a social ease difficult to come by without chemical assistance.

There are those who approach them as sacred gateways to transcendent awareness, and can't imagine letting some politician make our decisions in such intimate matters of mind and soul. We feel that the condition of our consciousness is no one's business but our own, and that laws to the contrary are an affront to the freedom of thought.

Others experience a biochemical need for a particular formula. This is the relationship which is allegedly the focus of prohibition, the sustaining justification for prioritizing the hydra-headed monster of "narcotics" enforcement.

Considering the human costs, as well as those to taxpayers, it is vital to stress this point: the criminalization of drugs dramatically increases *both* the supply and the demand of them. The legal punitive approach is demonstrably a failure in every goal, except the transfer of funds to the prison-industrial complex.

The word "narcotic" also suffers from this curiously distended official diction. The meaning of the term has expanded in various contexts to apply to unrelated substances, in ways that have nothing to do with the medical usage. Grouping cannabis or cocaine with the products of the opium plant is just part of the broad brush prohibitionists paint with to oversimplify the issues.

As Abbie Hoffman was told by his judge, after protesting the classification of his cocaine charges as narcotics violations, "If the legislature wanted to define *milk* as a narcotic, it can." Indeed, it would be more accurate to designate soporific dairy products as narcotics, than the stimulant cocaine.

Heroin is classically considered the quintessential addictive drug.

There is no doubt that some habitual users are under physical compulsion to continue their regimen. Surely the laws against such a destructive substance are justified by public safety? What else can we, as a society, do with those who refuse to cease their harmful habit? Prohibitionists cannot imagine a remedy more appropriate than forced isolation and legal abuse.

There are, actually, many promising treatments for narcotic addiction. Some of the most intriguing options are illegal. Ibogaine, for instance, is Schedule I in the United States, despite multiple reports of successful opiate cessation, following a single administration of the psychedelic. While not the solution for everyone, the curative potential of Ibogaine is unmatched.

Derived from a root in Africa called *Tabernanthe iboga*, 19-year-old addict Howard Lotsof discovered Ibogaine's remarkable effect on opiate habituation in 1962, curing himself with startling ease. The medicine was ironically swept up in drug control legislation, because of its psychedelic effects, in 1967.

The crusaders against drug abuse might be more successful if they weren't always throwing the baby out with the bathwater. The holy grail of drug treatment, relieving both withdrawal symptoms and removing compulsion, Ibogaine is simply not legally available in the United States. Citizens with the resolve to kick the habit using this quick, effective therapy must travel internationally, at great expense and risk, to utilize clinics in countries with less reactionary policies.

Methadone is available to, and working for, many opiate-dependent individuals, but there are issues with methadone substitution, including a high discontinuation rate. Several European countries have recently begun achieving superior results, by treating heroin addiction with another, more effective opiate: diacetylmorphine, better known as heroin.

A German study found that heroin was much more successful than methadone, in all three criteria quantified: an improvement in physical or mental health, patients refraining from unprescribed use, and, most significantly, a retention rate which was twelve percent greater for patients receiving injectable diacetylmorphine, versus those prescribed oral methadone. No fatalities directly attributable to the medication occurred.

Switzerland has also achieved tremendous, irrefutable progress with heroin maintenance treatment. Studies show that prescription heroin reduces criminality by about sixty percent, more than doubles rates of permanent employment, improves housing situations, and achieves penetration into a population which is notoriously resistant to other forms of treatment.

Heroin maintenance might seem counterintuitive to those who have bought into the disease/abstinence model of addiction treatment. After all, if the problem is drugs, dispensing them surely isn't the answer.

But are the drugs truly the problem? Let us consider a different point of view: that of the so-called addict. For the opiate dependent, the illness is what occurs in the *absence* of the drug. Withdrawal is called "getting sick." The habit itself becomes troublesome, with the constant chase for expensive and often impure product, the health risks associated with street use, and, of course, the ever-looming presence of the Man.

The problem isn't the drug; the problem is the *need* for it. For some individuals, this need won't go away. Whether through disposition or acquisition of habituation, real biological factors make normal life impossible, so long as this need remains unfulfilled.

The law is geared to punitively condition illicit self-medicators, in an attempt to force them to discontinue all unauthorized drug therapy under pain of prison. Legislators, with their abundant knowledge of pharmacology, have consistently decreed that enormous penalties shall befall those who are discovered to be making their own decisions about medication.

Not all kinds of addicts are counseled toward abstinence, however. Some types of junkie are given a free pass. For example, there is a wildly popular mind-altering drug which is perfectly legal to prescribe for injection, at need, up to half a dozen times daily. In fact, for this protected class of addicts, depriving them of their dope can be considered a criminal act in itself.

This drug can be mind-bending if used improperly, but the real bitch is the withdrawal. Disorientation, delirium, coma and even death can occur if the stash is cut off. So intense are these symptoms that no one counsels the users of this drug to quit. It would be fatal for many of them.

This drug is, of course, insulin. "But that's different!" you might say, outraged at such a comparison. "Diabetics need their medicine in order to live." Indeed. And the opiate addict does not? What societal ills would accompany the search for insulin, if it were banned? What crimes would diabetics commit to obtain the formula which allows them to function?

To those who dispute this equation, we point to the famous case of Jerry Garcia, widely regarded as one of the most prolific, accomplished guitarists and composers of his fertile musical era. Garcia was also known as an inveterate heroin addict, who sadly left the world when his spark gave out at the age of fifty-three.

Garcia faded away when he once again attempted to quit cold turkey after checking in to the clinic of his own creation. His untimely passing was not the result of heroin, but from the sudden deprivation of it. A medically monitored tapering program might have saved his life, and he could be gracing us with his genius to this day.

Diabetes is the failure of the body to produce sufficient endogenous insulin. It may be caused by genetic deficiency, or, more commonly, from the abuse of the white powder drug called sugar. In either event, the accepted and acceptable treatment is a life-long regimen of maintenance doses.

Opiate dependence is the failure of the body to produce sufficient endogenous endorphins. It may be caused by genetic deficiency, or, more commonly, from the abuse of opiates. In either event, the accepted and thoroughly unacceptable treatment is to threaten, bully, imprison and brainwash whoever is thought to have the disease.

Endogenous opioid deficiency syndrome is estimated to affect 2.5 million individuals in the United States. Endorphins are key to controlling the debilitating effects of pain, both physical and psychological. A person who is lacking in this area will suffer depression, anxiety, and anhedonia. There is significant evidence that this syndrome is genetic in nature, and frequently precedes any opiate use.

In medicine, drugs are routinely used to regulate chemicals in the body for which there is a shortage or pathological surplus. They operate chiefly due to their similarity to endogenous compounds, or by influencing the body's use of them.

Whether arrived at through acquisition or disposition, genetics or culture, states of neurochemical imbalances are considered to be the cause of psychiatric symptoms such as depression, anxiety, and schizophrenia, for which the preferred therapy is some chemical mimic or inhibitor, acting to restore the balance.

Demanding that opiate users quit their medicine, forcing them to struggle without supplementation for what their body naturally lacks, is cruel beyond measure. In the end, addiction is just a word. We don't usually call people addicts when a doctor states that their medical condition requires them to take a pharmaceutical. One is only an addict if making this determination for oneself.

When misguided public policy forces people to take matters into their own hands, they are stigmatized for "self-medicating." There are certainly hazards associated with varying purity and the predatory black market to which such individuals are forced to resort.

What else, though, are they to do? Physicians, hampered by the law and the perverse reversal of their role, are given the job of ensuring that those with this sort of illness do *not* receive medication.

Every consumable substance is associated with drawbacks, as well as benefits. The scheduling system employs a false standard for assessing the ratio of positive to negative effects. The desire of the user to ingest a given formula, the reason it is being chosen at all, is recast as a detriment. The potential ramifications of extreme and irresponsible chemical self-administration are counted as properties of the substance, rather than being caused by traits or ignorance of the user.

There are, in fact, a good many functional opiate users. While the image of the street junkie, committing unspeakable acts to acquire the next fix, dominates the debate, the truth is that heroin, on its own, causes relatively few side effects. The public health hazards associated with dirty needles, and varying purity, would all be readily rectified by medicalization.

The threat of overdose from heroin alone is greatly exaggerated. Despite the popular fear that one might accidentally shoot up too much of the drug, with lethal consequences, it has been well-established since the 1920s that the disparity between the active and fatal dose is up to one thousand percent. Presented in other terms, seasoned users could tolerate up to eighteen hundred milligrams before inducing terminal side effects, whereas even novices did not show lethal results, until consuming a gigantic dose of half a gram.

An Australian study found in 1992 that up to eighty percent of deaths involving heroin included either alcohol or tranquilizers being used as potentiators. One might say that these other depressants are as culpable as the demonized opiate, but most accurate would be to blame the *synergy* between these substances for the majority of such deaths. Underdosed addicts, trying to stretch their expensive stash, mix up a hearty depressant soup in their bloodstream and die from too much respiratory suppression.

The risk of overdose from legal pharmaceutical medication dwarfs that from illegal drugs. Notwithstanding the giant zero registered by cannabis in this category, even notoriously "dangerous" drugs like heroin, cocaine, and methamphetamine, cannot hold a candle to a number of drugs approved by the FDA, and lawfully prescribed each day by script-churning physicians.

Over one hundred thousand annual deaths are ascribed to these medications, according to the National Institute on Drug Abuse, an astounding figure written off as the cost of doing medicine. By contrast, less than one-fifth as many deaths, about seventeen thousand, are attributed to *all* illegal drugs, directly or indirectly. This number is compounded by the tendency of authorities to assign to this category any deaths where traces of such drugs are detected, regardless of other factors at work.

Even over-the-counter pain remedies like aspirin, which are considered safe enough not to require a prescription at all, account for seventy-six hundred deaths annually. Alcohol, pinned with eighty-five thousand deaths, is dangerous enough, but not as much as fatty foods, which claim a whopping one thousand lives each *day*, in the United States, three hundred and sixty-five thousand per year.

Driving kills more people than illicit chemicals, yet manages to remain nicely legal, while auto manufacture is subsidized in times of trouble, being "too big to fail." Let's not even talk about tobacco, whose users would surely kill for a cigarette if it were to be made illegal, and who die in unparalleled droves each year as a result of the habit.

The other primary risk associated with heroin use involves disease transmission through sharing of intravenous needles. Here, too, prohibition interferes with harm reduction, although needle exchange programs have greatly ameliorated this problem where they have been applied. A better solution would simply be to provide fresh works to those who need them, along with a short-term supply of medicine.

Prescription of pharmaceutical grade maintenance doses, under a doctor's care, might turn out to be the solution *par excellence*, not only for managing opiate addiction, but, indeed, the majority of chemical dependency problems. The singular advantage of this therapy is that no coercion would be necessary. Addicts would sign up of their own free will to be rid of the back-alley rat race.

Imagine simply if physicians were authorized to prescribe those substances which are currently Schedule I as treatment for addiction. A complete history of use patterns, no longer a confession of lifetime criminality, would help determine the optimal dosage. The full range of options, including tapering, substitutions, and, yes, even abstinence support, could be simultaneously offered for consideration. Different approaches would be explored and customized, until the doctor and patient alike are satisfied with the results.

The militant drug warriors may never be happy with this remedy to a problem they would perhaps prefer to remain unsolved. Providing truly "controlled" substances, to the millions who require them, would feel too much like conceding defeat. Prohibitionists would rather house addicts in ever-sprawling prisons, cut them off from opportunities for employment and housing, and expend billions of dollars in a futile effort to stamp out anyone unfortunate enough to be born with or develop the need for "dope."

Of course, it may be a while before we know for sure what potential the medicalization of addiction could have. Certainly the political atmosphere in the United States is not such that even limited tests, like those in Europe, could be conducted. The measure of success for any substance abuse treatment program in the US is calculated purely according to abstinence. To such a mentality, it is nonsense to talk of treating an addiction by prescribing the drug of choice.

The societal stigma and political repression of a certain class of medical patient is among the most unwholesome types of prejudice. Such discrimination would not be tolerated if it were applied to those suffering other, more acceptable, diseases, requiring different medications.

If the goal of a drug policy is to reduce the ills of addiction, both for the user and society as a whole, then monitored maintenance is just what the doctor ordered. If there is a health problem, let health professionals be the arbiter of which medications are most appropriate for the circumstances.

The most obvious benefit of this would be for the patients, who would no longer need to pass through life as criminals, sulking about for the next fix between prison stints. They could take their medicine with the minimum of hassle, and spend the remainder of their time productively, much like the millions of Americans who are already prescribed mood-stabilizing pharmaceuticals. If people weren't committing a crime simply by using a drug, there would be far less crime generated in the acquisition of it.

Less obvious, but equally important, would be the effect on the drug trade. Without addicts supporting the massive illegal import business, the cartels would begin to see the money dry up. There would be fewer casual experimenters, as many of them are today exposed to illicit substances for the first time through the social network of the underground.

Law makers and enforcers are unqualified and incompetent to make these decisions for the rest of us. Their policies have amplified the damaging effects of banned substances, while making no discernible progress toward reducing either supply or demand.

When prohibitionists challenge us to propose an alternative to jailing addicts, there are ample solutions all around us. The establishment tends not to listen, preferring to employ brute force as a tactic. Drug warriors tout "zero-tolerance" approaches, as if lacking tolerance is some kind of virtue.

Applying medical solutions to medical problems would be a beginning. Like so many of the phony justifications for the systemic punishment of users, the notion of treating addicts by arresting them is an unnecessary, counterproductive exercise in torture and futility.

ARTICLE IV:
Improbable Cause

"The right of the people to be secure in their persons, houses, papers, and effects, against unreasonable searches and seizures, shall not be violated, and no Warrants shall issue, but upon probable cause, supported by Oath or affirmation, and particularly describing the place to be searched, and the persons or things to be seized."—The Fourth Amendment to the Constitution of the United States of America

This book was born of a frustration with the judiciary, guardians of these words, who have steadfastly refused to honor the spirit and letter of them. Sitting on high, the minions of inverted Justice have gradually stripped nearly all practical meaning from the Fourth Amendment. A century of Supreme Court decisions, incompatible with the plain text cited above, have expanded police powers so greatly that today there are barely any limits at all.

In criticizing the SCOTUS, let us say that we admit to being strictly amateur as legal scholars, and that we understand that there are highly technical rationales which apologize for the Court's habit of issuing what we regard to be a veritable mountain of erroneous decisions that neutralize this essential defense of liberty. As deliberately inscrutable as the Supremes tend to be, we shall attempt to explain why the protections don't appear to apply to most of us, and why we believe they ought to.

The focus of our vexation is the unwelcome encroachment of law enforcement personnel, who can frequently be found poking about in the possessions of private citizens. These regular intrusions are instigated in hopes of making an arrest, usually for some illegal herb or drug, as well as money or property the police can confiscate. The nature of prohibition is such that only by invading privacy rights, supposedly enshrined in the Fourth, can this perversion of justice be enforced.

Those who attempt to invoke their rights in order to prevent police from desecrating their sanctuary may be in for a rude surprise. They are likely to be immediately handcuffed and helplessly watch as armed thugs swarm over their belongings anyway, creating an enormous mess and often causing significant damage. If any item of contraband is discovered, no matter how trivial, enormous, life-changing consequences ensue. If not, the subject of the search is free to pick up the pieces and go, without serious avenues of redress for their trouble.

An even greater shock is in store for those who later contact an attorney, convinced that an illegal search occurred, and that their rights were violated. They will learn that virtually any pretext now authorizes a government agent to gain entry in order to procure evidence, quite often without any tangible documentation whatsoever.

There is a legal means to suppress any evidence which was gained in an illegal manner, under the Exclusionary Rule, but this expensive and lengthy procedure is usually more odious than the penalty itself. A motion to suppress is presented before a judge, who will employ a highly abstract set of tests before generally deciding to deny it. In the event that the motion is successful, owing to some glaring defect in the police report, the prosecution is likely to appeal the decision all the way to the Supreme Court. Very few defendants can weather this expensive, time-swallowing ordeal, no matter how egregious the search which brought them into the system may have been.

Worse still, the police are usually acting within legal parameters, generously defined for them through the collusion of the highest tribunals. When it appears that an officer is conducting a search on a whim, they are often utilizing any of the multitude of excuses provided to them by the friendly black robes.

These excuses are termed "exceptions" to the warrant requirement, and we take issue—exception, in fact—with the entire concept. The Fourth is very clear. There are *no* legitimate exceptions to the warrant requirement. Every search and every seizure requires one. Even the Court has conceded that warrantless searches are *per se* unreasonable, and therefore unconstitutional. Nevertheless, a slew of SCOTUS opinions authorize what are held to be "well-defined exceptions" to the mandate of privacy.

We hold this truth to be self-evident: that every time police officers examine the belongings of a citizen without warrant, "the right of the people to be secure in their persons, houses, papers, and effects" is violated.

The Supreme Court, as an institution, has proven hostile to the protections of this Amendment. Choosing consistently to value police power over the rights of citizens, these political appointees have bent over backward to endorse and allow this behavior during the past century of prohibition. Ruling after convoluted ruling has expanded this most basic of powers, and devalued this most basic of rights.

The warrant requirement, as stated in the plain text of the Constitution, makes no provision for exceptions. A search or seizure is unreasonable, unless "supported by Oath or affirmation, and particularly describing the place to be searched, and the persons or things to be seized." This can be inconvenient for law enforcement personnel wishing to snoop for contraband, and even more so for the prosecution desiring to pump conviction rates based on questionably acquired evidence.

What has been compromised is an important extension of the principle of checks and balances on which the government is based. The executive branch, including police and prosecutors, acting at the behest of mayors, governors, or Presidents, is prone to commit arbitrary and retributive invasions of privacy. As rebels against the King, the framers where all too aware of this dynamic, and sought to guard against the development of this downside to their own government.

The Fourth Amendment guarantees that a judge must be consulted before any such possible violation of rights may occur. The people, however, should get their money back on this "warranty," so rarely is it honored.

The Founders had had enough of presumptuous King's Guards rifling through their papers in hopes of exposing evidence of their treason. They had been, after all, dangerous capital felons in the eyes of the lawful British colonial authority, risking the hangman's noose to spread ideas and organize against the occupying army. Possession of seditious documents was the primary crime for which the Redcoats invaded homes, buggies, clothing, and satchels. Incriminating papers could mean a one-way trip to the gallows.

In creating a regime of, for, and by the People, the Fourth Amendment was added, so that future generations would not have to abide intrusion from an unjust government seeking to prosecute self-serving laws. To be sure, although the Fourth is a plain-speaking dicta, the language was left sufficiently loose to allow the construction of wild rationales for undermining the framer's original intent. The protection could be perfected by the addition of the words "no search or seizure shall be without Warrant," which is implied, although ambiguously stated. Alas, this suggestion comes over two hundred years too late, and so we are left with language susceptible to distortion.

The purpose of the warrant requirement is to place a check on such abuses, by demanding that each search and seizure be authorized by a supposedly independent magistrate. Nor is it permissible for a judge to approve every such request; there must be a sworn oath that the probable cause justifying the warrant is accurate, and the place to be searched and specific objects or persons to be seized must be described beforehand. That's what the text plainly says. We hope we have made that abundantly clear.

Probable cause. Now this is a funny phrase. As noted previously, the courts have declared that a warrant is frequently unnecessary, if there is, in the opinion of the officer conducting the search, *probable cause* that they will find what they are looking for, evidence of a felony.

This may be the most wrong-headed contortion in modern jurisprudence. Probable cause is not an *exception* to the warrant requirement; it *is* the warrant requirement. Nonetheless, in combination with other factors, so broadly defined as to allow nearly all desired intrusion, the phrase has been twisted into an end-run around the limits imposed on government bodies at the inception of the Union.

The foundation of the legal theory which supports situational suspension of the warrant requirement is the concept of *exigency*. Briefly put, if it is impracticable to obtain a proper warrant prior to commencing a search, the formality may be dispensed with. The problem with this logic, no matter how eloquently presented, is that it is not reasonable to put the enforcement of criminal law ahead of the rights belonging to those subjected to it.

The result is a laundry list of excuses for not procuring the proper document prior to a search, which, in aggregate, amount to allowing free reign to snooping cops. By "skipping" the warrant, the officer does not need to establish probable cause *prior* to a search; he or she need only be able to state, *after the fact*, that it was present. This creates a dangerous incentive for perjury.

Moreover, there is no disincentive to go on "fishing expeditions." Police can search at will, knowing there are two possible outcomes. Contraband will be found, or it will not. If nothing illegal is discovered, as occurs nearly ninety percent of the time, the suspect is set free to count their blessings.

According to Bureau of Justice statistics from 2005, only 11.6% of traffic stop searches actually uncovered the contraband sought. We could want no better evidence proving the fallacy of the "probable cause" exception. If a major league batter had such a poor average of success, he'd be benched.

If fish are caught, so to speak, the seized items themselves provide sufficient support of whatever probable cause is later to be concocted. The authorization for the search is no longer the documented, sworn statement of the officer, enshrined in advance. Now, the search is justified by the recollection, *in hindsight,* of whatever sensory impressions allegedly led the officer to believe that a search might yield fruit.

So-called "probable cause" searches are unreasonable on their face, because they occur at the sole discretion of the officer. Yet the Supreme Court has expressed a definite preference for allowing police to avoid the cumbersome warrant procedure, particularly in cases involving motor vehicles.

In the real world, the failure of law enforcement to uncover contraband has no practical bearing on the existence of it. Contraband exists regardless. If some escapes by leaving the jurisdiction, it is no different than the vast majority which simply remains undetected. The only compelling emergency is in the mind of the suspicious agent on a mission to make an arrest.

The so-called War on Drugs would be virtually unenforceable, if Fourth Amendment protections had not eroded to this point. Very few other acts of law enforcement demand that so many effects and persons be made insecure.

Some may question the importance of this point. "If the cops have probable cause, then they could get the warrant anyway," one might say. "What good is it to force them to waste time putting it in writing and getting the rubber stamp of some magistrate who never says no?"

The importance is this: by swearing the officer to their probable cause statement in advance, they can be held accountable for their claims. Cops don't get to retroactively rewrite history to conform with whatever the search might have yielded. Small protection, but it is our Constitutional due, and it would mean the difference between freedom and felony for many defendants.

Furthermore, there is no reason that the system should be allowed to sidestep Fourth Amendment rights, simply because it is time-consuming to procure warrants in each instance. It is *meant* to be time-consuming, so as to ensure that if the privacy of citizens be invaded, it be for good reason.

The State often incarcerates individuals as a direct result of warrantless intrusions. It is, in fact, the most common way for a drug bust to occur. Considering the grave consequences at stake, the many years in prison that might hinge on the decision to search, ought not the police take an hour or two to procure a valid warrant in every single case?

Many may disagree with this point of view. Certainly, most of the wise sage Supreme Court Justices of the past century, who have declared new exceptions at the flimsiest of pretexts, would take strong issue with these declarations. However, we charge that warrant exceptions are a legal fiction, and that the Court, given the power to interpret the Constitution, is not empowered to *amend* it.

Many long-winded, voluminous opinions have been handed down by the SCOTUS in support of this doctrine. It makes for poor literature, and even poorer law, because the Fourth Amendment does not say that it only applies where practicable, or unless it interferes with government agents achieving their aims. Interfering with schemes by the authorities to ransack private property is rather the point of the Fourth.

The premier example of legal gymnastics which allows law enforcement into our private space is the automobile exception to the warrant requirement, which was invented in response to the needs of alcohol interdiction. Originally, the Volstead act, which defined the terms for enforcement of the ban on ethanol, actually provided criminal penalties—a misdemeanor—for any officer who conducted a search for alcohol in the absence of a warrant.

Now, the courts are very different places than the real world. In the real world, we know that there was abundant alcohol despite its illegality, and that if one car happened to be smuggling moonshine, it made very little actual difference to the total supply of bootleg liquor.

In court, the Fourth Amendment became a source of extreme frustration. Defendants were being freed, despite clear guilt. At the time, before cellular phones or even fleet radio, the possibility of obtaining a warrant during a traffic stop was nil. Smugglers could with impunity cart their goods along distribution routes, knowing that they could pass undetected.

In *Carroll v. US*, the Court decided that police could detain and enter vehicles to look for contraband, so long as they promised that they had a really good reason and thought they could find something illegal. Since then, the bright line has drifted inexorably toward the police.

The exigency of the automobile exception has long since faded, but the abridgment of rights in our vehicular property has become virtually absolute. In the twenty-first century, a warrant can be requested and confirmed electronically, while the traffic stop is in progress. Nevertheless, this outdated pretext still stands as controlling case law, giving license to the very lucrative business of highway robbery as conducted by police on the prowl.

Part of the reasoning used to sustain the bizarre proposition that we should not be secure in our persons and effects, if these happen to be capable of movement, is that occupants of vehicles should *expect* less privacy in a locked mobile conveyance, than in their homes, where warrants remain the standard, though frequently violated, procedure.

This idea, that there is a "reduced expectation" of privacy in transit, is purely the invention of the courts. We have locks on the doors, and commonly store "papers and effects" inside; one is in fact required to keep certain important documents on hand. A motor vehicle is a registered, considerable property, secured by notarized title, and protected by a special classification for theft of it. A driver, at sixty miles per hour, has no reason to believe that the privacy to which one is accustomed inside their compartment will be violated by anyone.

The only reduced expectations of privacy derive from the liberties taken by law enforcement, as they rove the roadways to score drugs. This artifact of the Court is self-justifying, as if the increased possibility of being searched in transit is itself the reason for easing the limitations on police. This extension of police autonomy includes boats, airplanes, trains, or any other means of conveyance. The very fact that cops are on the highways or high seas means that no one ought to expect their effects to be secure *while in motion*, no matter what the damn Constitution says.

When the police are given permission to commit acts which are otherwise crimes, the net effect is not an asset to public safety. When the pretext for these authorized felonies is to gather evidence of some form of thought-crime, be it sedition or psychedelia, the path to tyranny is trod.

There are many other supplemental and complementary theories on which agents of the government may forego the warrant process, all devolving around this notion that if probable cause of illegality exists, the Constitutional guarantee is void.

One such is the "plain smell" doctrine, which allows immediate entry of virtually any location or vehicle, solely on the word of an officer. The smell could be cannabis or crack, or even air freshener thought to be masking them; but in either event, a cop looking to make a drug bust need only claim that they observed such an odor. If marijuana was found, then, hey, it was *marijuana* he smelled. If there is some crack, on the other hand, then *that* becomes the pretext, retrospectively.

Of course, there might have been no smell at all. The investigation could be based on the appearance of the suspect, who might have long hair, or belong to a racial minority. The real motivation might be a bumper sticker which proclaims a political cause at odds with the personal beliefs of an officer.

This alleged odor is undocumented and undocumentable; there is no means to question the legitimacy of such probable cause in court. The words behind the badge are presumed credible, and are usually unimpeachable in the minds of judges.

Apart from corrupting the original intention of the clause, the practical result is a daily assault on the privacy of citizens in the course of routine traffic stops. One could be casually driving through a jurisdiction, pulled over for a minor infraction, and inside of an hour be on the way to jail in a strange place because nosy police located a forgotten pipe, an empty container with residue, even properly prescribed medication stored outside of its labeled bottle.

Once in a while, there is the bizarre blip of sanity emerging from the decisions of the Supreme Court, who find a particular defendant worthy of protection, and thus impose some level of constraint against searches of people in their specific circumstances. We don't know what to take from these rare court victories, except to note that at times precedent is reversed, and the bright line pushed back a meter or two. Some small cause for hope.

One such anti-search ruling was in *Arizona v. Gant*. Rodney Gant was arrested on a charge of driving on a suspended license, after exiting the vehicle. Following the detention of everyone in the vicinity, the police in Tucson initiated what is known as a search "incident to arrest."

Gant's vehicle was inspected, after he was cuffed and stuffed, yielding cocaine and a weapon. His motion to suppress this evidence wound its way to the Supremes, who decided for some reason that they would no longer tolerate these searches incident to arrest, once the defendant is detained out of reach of the vehicle's interior, unless that search could be said to be in quest of evidence related to the arresting offense.

This decision reversed the earlier ruling in *New York v. Belton*, which had governed for thirty-eight years, during which the Fourth simply didn't apply to anyone under arrest. In practical terms, *Gant* means little. Police can bypass the restriction by impounding a vehicle and performing an "inventory search," which is supposed to verify the contents of a seized vehicle so they cannot be disputed later. Of course, any contraband discovered in the course of this procedure is admissible to evidence. Another tactic is to *not* detain the suspect in handcuffs, until the search has begun, using the pretext that a weapon might be within reach, creating exigency.

On the whole, though, the consistent trend has been to whittle away at the Fourth, with the apparent goal of leaving nothing at all. Various Courts have gone back and forth, leaving an odd patchwork of precedent, but most have supported the prohibitionist agenda and expanded latitude for the police. From *US v. Ross*, which allows for inspection of closed containers during a vehicle search, to *Atwater v. Lago Vista*, upholding search and arrest for a seatbelt violation, the overwhelming tendency is to let cops treat drivers and their belongings in any fashion they please.

The most recent rulings to come out of the SCOTUS set a similar pattern of exceptions to securing a warrant for house breaches as well. The trend is not encouraging. As State-sanctioned home invasions become more common, the Court has backed away from centuries of precedent preserving the "castle doctrine," by declaring that the police may manufacture their own exigency.

In a nearly unanimous blank check to law enforcement, *Kentucky v. King* reversed the decision of the State Supreme Court, that an exigency created by the police cannot serve as justification for voiding the warrant requirement.

The case involved an apartment complex in Lexington, Kentucky. Drug task force agents were pursuing a suspected dealer, after making a controlled buy. Having lost the target, they chose a nearby door, and, based on the smell of marijuana, decided that their fleet-footed suspect must have ducked inside to take a quick toke off a joint.

After banging loudly, the officers heard reciprocating noises inside, which they took to be evidence that someone was hiding or even ditching drugs. The police broke down the door, and King's long legal nightmare began. The original subject was not inside, but the cops smoothly switched gears and proceeded to bust the randomly selected apartment. Charged with trafficking crack cocaine and marijuana, King's prior conviction enhanced the sentence to eleven years in prison.

On appeal the sole issue was disposition of the motion to suppress evidence for illegal search. In explaining why the Constitution doesn't apply to King, the Court wrote: "Occupants who choose not to stand on their Constitutional rights but instead elect to attempt to destroy evidence have only themselves to blame for the warrantless exigent-circumstances search that may ensue."

In other words, when the police knock on the door, you're supposed to go outside and calmly debate the Bill of Rights with them. It must be nice up in that ivory tower.

The principle of exigency is simple; when circumstances of sufficient urgency create the need for law enforcement presence, officers cannot afford to be "handcuffed" by abstract civil rights. The contingency of the situation must predominate.

Fair enough, although this is nowhere to be found in the Fourth Amendment. If the police want to search for a bound-and-gagged kidnapping victim, we agree that they cannot be constrained by the warrant requirement. If they find a torture room, they want to be able to admit the contents to evidence, even if it was only a hunch that led them to uncover this heinous deed.

That doesn't necessarily translate into an unmitigated license to ransack the place for drugs, although that is precisely what the Court has decreed. Nor is this type of entry a suitable reason for unrelated evidence to be sought in a location to which police have come to save the day.

The same is true for searches authorized under the "community caretaker" function, where entry is made to determine the physical welfare of someone inside. Having entered for this noble, and often vague reason, the police are then free to conduct a shakedown of the entire interior if any sign of criminality is discovered.

Yet when we move from situations of genuine danger to an idea which is itself rather abstract, the vague necessity to prosecute drug possession, the notion of exigency doesn't seem to fit. Rather, the strict warrant requirement seems to be exactly what the Constitution calls for.

In a way, all exigency is created by the police, unless they were called to the scene by a complainant or witness. The emergency of evidence destruction is not to be feared until that knock at the door, and is hardly a matter of immediate safety in any event.

Cops and prosecutors certainly consider it a matter of extreme urgency, since someone flushing their stash cheats them of their sick need to punish and plunder.

But, really, what do *their* needs matter? Who are these people? If they are part of the government founded by and for the people, why should the "compelling State interest" in enforcing drug laws subvert the primacy of the Bill of Rights?

Another problem with warrantless probable cause, is that it often consists solely in the mind and senses of a single officer. "I heard," "I smelled," even "I saw" are all unverifiable claims which are impossible to prove or disprove. There is no way of recording or documenting such assertions, and thus these impressions are easy to manufacture or imagine. Without a warrant application, this pretext can be crafted in retrospect, depending on what was actually discovered.

The "plain view" doctrine holds that if an officer is positioned in a place where they have a legal right to be, anything they see, through a poorly curtained window for example, becomes fair game. Never mind that a *private* citizen who peeks into windows is committing a crime. The error here is that, again, an officer's statements are substituting for judicial approval. While a plain view sighting might logically provide probable cause to *obtain* a warrant, under current case precedent, such a glimpse actually *supplants* the warrant.

Similarly, "plain smell" of any illegal evidence is an invitation to entry, no warrant required. This applies to homes, as well as vehicles. Your home is not your castle if a cop thinks he or she smells illicit herbs outside your door, even if they have arrived hours after it was burned. In fact the courts have extended the exigency to the odor of burning marijuana, since combustion means that the evidence is being destroyed.

An officer who is unfamiliar with burning sage might mistake the odor for cannabis, and initiate a search on that pretext. On the roadside, the smell of a skunk can fool even seasoned smokers, for a moment, into thinking a giant session or garden is nearby.

More dangerous is the deliberate misuse of this latitude: when the search is conducted, not due to any odor, but because the officer *saw* a drug arrest they wished to make. Perhaps the suspect is ethnically targeted, or appears countercultural.

Maybe the suspects are from out of State, or in a home or vehicle in such a condition of disrepair that surely they must be guilty of something. The "plain smell" exception allows officers on a fishing expedition to cast line willy-nilly into the barrel.

In *King*, the officers testified that they heard sounds consistent with destruction of evidence. What a convenient claim that is for police wanting to let themselves violently in! How could the defense ever counter such testimony?

When the Constitution was drafted, the police did not exist as we think of them. The premise that a government must maintain an organized force, so as to impose dictates on the people, was not adopted by early colonial government, or that in the succeeding States. Militias would certainly be a part of defending the young nation, but turning it on the citizenry would be reserved for extreme situations of civil revolt.

Today, every level of geographical jurisdiction operates a standing army: municipal police, county sheriff's deputies, State Troopers, Highway Patrol, even University Police. There are Federal law enforcement bodies of every stripe: Forest Service, Customs, Boarder Patrol, TSA, FBI, ATF, and of course the DEA. Even the Post Office has an impressive law enforcement division. All are targeted, to a greater or lesser degree, at controlled substance interdiction.

TSA and Border Patrol each perform routine searches at ports of entry, where, again, the Fourth Amendment is deemed not to apply. The reasoning here is some sort of mass, ongoing exigency, the possibility that a bomb might enter the country or board an airplane. Such a risk to national security is invoked to suspend the injunction against general warrants. Remember, this is why the Fourth specifies *"particularly describing the place to be searched, and the persons or things to be seized."* This clause was supposed to prevent blockade searches premised on general suspicion.

No probable cause is required *at all* to allow a thorough inspection of the belongings and bodies of travelers, since any of them might be terrorists. In practice, it is far more common for these searches to expose controlled substances violations, than any sort of weapon, although the vast majority turn up nothing at all.

There may be some who say, "If you have nothing to hide, what is your objection to a search?" This presumes that the intrusion is a mere inconvenience unless something illegal is disclosed. On the contrary, every search is a massive imposition, a theft of time, destruction of property in many cases, and a trampling of the basic right to be free of government snooping. As we have seen, people are killed by searches, frequently during erroneous ones. Tensions run high, and situations escalate quickly, when armed strangers insist on sticking their noses where they do not belong.

Nowhere is the folly of granting *carte blanche* to raiding police more evident, than when ordinary citizens run afoul of faulty investigations. We have discussed several which led to the victim's deaths. Note that Scott, Johnston, and Guerena were all of different socioeconomic classes and ethnicities. Young and old, rich or poor, erosion of the Fourth Amendment is a danger far more palpable than any crime issue.

If the police are supposed to protect us, who protects us from the police? The answer is supposed to be the courts. Sworn to uphold the Constitution, a form of treason is committed by the black-robed arbiters every time a ruling is issued which breaches the boundaries barring tyranny.

Mayor Cheye Calvo of Berwyn Heights, Maryland, and his wife, Trinity Tomsic, a State finance officer, are not the sort of people to get caught up in interstate marijuana trafficking schemes. Moreover, considering their positions in government, one might suspect that they would at least be circumspect, if for some reason they *were* living some kind of double life.

That didn't stop the Prince George's County police from violently raiding their home, when a package containing thirty-two pounds of bricked marijuana arrived on the doorstep addressed to Ms. Tomsic.

Before initiating a raid on a residence, the police are supposed to conduct a thorough investigation. Apparently this background did not include the information that the cops were tooling up to kick in the door of the Mayor.

Now, this is not to say that the Mayor should not be subject to the same standards as everyone else. In fact, had he truly been involved in a trafficking conspiracy, we'd be citing this case as an example of official corruption and hypocrisy.

But it does seem that raiding the home of the elected executive deserves a little more deliberation than the average police operation. There are legal ramifications to consider, conflicts of interest, the stability of local government.

When the target of a criminal inquiry is an elected official, there could be countercharges of politicking arrest, which is possibly the most corrupt of all police action. Such arrests amount to a virtual coup d'etat. You'd expect the stack of paperwork collected on the case to be thick, the investigation to be months long, the probability of cause to be impeccable. It was, after all the Mayor. This would be a giant scandal.

Nevertheless, Prince George's County SWAT burst through the door, after delivering the suspect package, shooting the two family dogs dead as they scurried away. The indignity continued with the raiders arresting Calvo in his underwear, and slapping the cuffs on his mother-in-law, who had initially refused to sign for the strange parcel.

The deputies did not have a no-knock warrant, but they later defended their illegal impoliteness by invoking "exigency" created by Calvo's mother-in-law. Seeing jackbooted Robocops on the porch, the poor woman screamed, which, deputies say, put them in danger. These SWAT raiders are always sensitive about the danger *they* are in. Similar reasoning explained the senseless and tragic killing of the blameless pets.

Narcotics investigators had been tracking the marijuana shipment since it entered the FedEx system in Arizona, with Tomsic's name and address printed plainly on it. The mayor and family had fallen prey to an innovative strategy, whereby homes of seemingly random strangers are unwittingly recruited to serve as drop points, taking the heat if the package gets tagged.

It turned out that a delivery contractor, along with a partner, had hatched the scheme, directing the deliberately misaddressed contraband to uninvolved parties, with significant hope of retrieving it later from their befuddled patsies. As many as six other packages were caught in this ploy, with over four hundred pounds involved. Another crew, in an unrelated case in the same county, used similar means and were nabbed bringing in about one hundred pounds.

The prevalence of this ingenious, but karmically perilous, smuggling method means that presumption of innocence ought not disappear merely because a person's name and address are clearly printed on thirty-plus pounds of brickweed. On the contrary, only a fool would have their *own* data on such a shipment.

The family was utterly vindicated, with the arrest of the actual traffickers, but the police were strangely reluctant to apologize for a traumatizing error that was decidedly more than an inconvenience. "The guys did what they are supposed to do," shrugged Sheriff Michael Jackson, who stalled the IA investigation of the case so that no charges would be filed on any of the officers.

After stonewalling for nearly two-and-a-half years, the county, on the eve of trial in January of 2011, settled for an undisclosed sum, along with promises to reform SWAT practices.

Why should it take a lawsuit from a prominent citizen before the spotlight shines on the out-of-control service of search warrants? Of course, time will tell whether Prince George's County actually reins in these abuses, or whether the department will take the usual course, grudgingly complying with the explicit letter of the agreement, all the while seeking new ways to keep doing business as always.

This is a frightening pattern we see with these "wrong-door" raids: even though the probable cause is faulty, even though the suspects turn out to be thoroughly uninvolved, even though death and mayhem intrinsically follow the deployment of SWAT on peaceful residents, the police stand by their actions and defend their right to wage war, despite this collateral damage.

What is really galling about the Calvo case is not so much that the Mayor was subjected to a violent invasion in his home—that happens every day in the police State—but that the probable cause statement was based on such a sloppy investigation that the raid party did not even realize whose home they raided.

One of the often overlooked clauses in the Fourth Amendment is the *particularity* requirement. The issuance of general warrants, those unfounded by any specific cause, was regarded as an odious intrusion into the lives and spaces of individuals who had fallen under no suspicion and been implicated in no crime.

Because of the devastating effect on privacy such blanket warrants necessarily wreaked, the Founders wisely forbade them by mandating that each warrant describe particularly the place to be searched, and people or things to be seized. This specificity is key: it protects the citizenry, at least in theory, from arbitrary interference and intrusion from law enforcement.

Pharmafascists don't see any reason to honor this necessity, believing they are above the law they claim to cherish so dearly; indeed a common predicator for shakedown is mere presence in a "drug trafficking area." Anyone found in such a zone falls under automatic suspicion, whether they are visiting an aunt or traveling to their own impoverished rat-rap.

In a way, the effort of a government to subvert the laws constraining it is the very seed of tyranny. After all, the charter which created this entity, the source of all the legitimacy behind these institutions, defines limits to the powers which are dispensed to them. A State in violation of these is rogue, and does not rule under a logic of law.

As an example of how far the cops and courts will go in bending the Fourth Amendment out of recognition, consider the unconstitutionally categorical warrant issued for an entire sixty-unit low-income housing complex in the Newtown neighborhood of Sarasota, Florida.

Responding to an alleged high density of marijuana and crack near the Mediterranean Apartments, police sought and gained a warrant authorizing a search of the entire complex, including anyone who set foot in the parking lot.

A SWAT team, along with regular-duty officers from the Sarasota police, descended on the Mediterranean, stopping and frisking anyone unfortunate enough to enter the area at that time. Although the police avowed that "no innocent person" congregated in the parking lot, only four drug arrests ensued during this typically inept display of brute unconstitutional force.

Judge Rochelle Curley, who evidently missed the section on this Amendment in law school, upheld the outrageously generic warrant, allowing for prosecution of the few netted in the dragnet. She evidently had no problem allowing the police to invade an entire residential unit and everyone in it, without particularized suspicion and without individualized probable cause. The raid was a fishing expedition, pure and simple, but the randomly selected catch of the day will not find a friend in the court by arguing that the hook was illegal. Judges also enjoy eating fresh fish.

The indiscriminate application of residential tactical operations highlights a broader crisis accompanying the virtual suspension of the Fourth Amendment. This is everyone's problem, whether you break these drug laws or not. Every day, vehicles are torn apart, doors knocked from their hinges, homes ransacked, and there is precious little recourse, even when the victim is cleared of suspicion.

On a wider level, we question whether even valid search warrants for drugs are inherently legitimate under the Fourth. Can they meet the reasonableness requirement? Is it ever *reasonable* to kick in a door with a battering ram, flash grenades, tear gas, and assault rifles, simply because there may be controlled substances inside? Where is the danger? What is the imminent emergency?

Someone being in possession of marijuana, or an illegal drug, is not an emergency. Police department PR flacks are always careful to stress the possibility that raid teams, on a mission of malicious trespass, might themselves face weapons, justifying maximum force. The firefight which might greet a forced entry is a genuine danger, one that would be thoroughly avoided by the stormtroopers simply failing to arrive.

In truth, no genuine public interest is served by these searches. It is the police and prosecutors who benefit from such Gestapo tactics. What is the public safety impact of a prosecutor's conviction record? It looks fancy come election time, but who is *actually* made safer through the relocation of any given drug violator to prison?

Because of these searches, we are all manifestly *less* safe. The danger befalls not only the victims, who lose some part of their lives each time one of these raids is conducted, but every single citizen, who could join their ranks at any time. It is as if a gang of violent criminals were loose in every city of America, unchecked by any sort of law at all, free to break into cars and homes at will, hold families at gunpoint, and abduct them for ransom. Not merely as if; it is exactly like that. Why have police at all, if we must endure such terror from them?

The highly theoretical death of some unknown consumer, resulting from ingestion of a substance like heroin or methamphetamine, often serves as a pretext to invade the places where stashes are thought to be stored. The stark reality is that no matter what law enforcement does, the supply will remain unimpeded. Other shipments will arrive to replace what is seized, and other players will step in to take over the interrupted game. There are no lives to be saved by confiscating one particular cache.

The dangers of these drugs are generally overstated, but one fact which cannot be stressed enough is that more lives are destroyed by overzealous interdiction than by any drug. In the cost-benefit analysis, one must ask: is the real emergency that someone is holding the key to some forbidden pleasure, or that the police are there to apprehend them for it?

The Fourth Amendment implications stemming from various types of drug enforcement are endless. Since every case at the minimum includes a seizure, most often following some kind of search, controlled substance detection, as a matter of routine, brushes up against this Constitutional principle. The exception has become the rule.

Courts have worked overtime inventing the legal means to circumvent this right. There is the doctrine of *inevitable discovery*, which holds that illegally obtained evidence can be used in a prosecution, so long as it would have been revealed by legal methods, if they had been used. There is the *good faith* doctrine, which holds that *erroneous* probable cause does not disqualify a search. For example, a search predicated on an arrest warrant which later turned out to have been dealt with. The theory being that, since the officer *believed* they had cause, this earnest belief is as good as the real thing. Who cares that some criminal, who obviously was not law-abiding, sits in a cell due to a mistake?

The mother of all warrant work-arounds is the so-called "consent search." The notion on the face of it is absurd; who would willingly consent to a stranger rifling through their belongings? Even those with nothing to be found should fear their possessions being disturbed, often damaged, and their time wasted by this fruitless rooting through the effects of private citizens.

The reality behind this "consent" is that it is *always* relinquished under duress, express or implied. On the stick side, grudging permission is wrangled from motorists, using threats of dogs being brought, harsher treatment, or being transported to the police station for processing. On the carrot side, police gain entry via promises to go easy on a passenger, let small amounts of marijuana slide, or to "put in a good word with the prosecutor," for being cooperative in your undoing.

Apart from frequently being untrue, such inducements put lie to the very meaning of consent. Not only that, there is just about absolutely no chance to refute the legality of such a search, or to challenge the original traffic stop, once your rights have been "voluntarily" surrendered. It cannot be stressed enough that no one should *ever* consent to these searches, even those who are confident that nothing illegal is inside. As we have seen, some police plant evidence as a matter of course, and it could be impossible to defend one's innocence in a courtroom.

Speaking of dogs, canine units are yet another way that police have of sticking their noses where they don't belong. In the case of *Illinois v. Caballes*, SCOTUS decided that dog sniffs don't constitute a search, although they *can* become instant probable cause for one. The reasoning is that trained dogs only detect contraband, and so the privacy interests of the innocent are not infringed. Notice that the rights of the ostensibly guilty have disappeared altogether.

Dissenting, Justice Souter pointed out, "The infallible dog, however, is a creature of legal fiction...belied by judicial opinions describing well-trained animals sniffing and alerting with less than perfect accuracy, whether owing to errors by their handlers, the limitations of the dogs themselves, or even the pervasive contamination of currency by cocaine..."

"In practical terms, the evidence is clear that the dog that alerts hundreds of times will be wrong dozens of times. Once the dog's fallibility is recognized, however...the sniff alert does not necessarily signal hidden contraband, and opening the container or enclosed space whose emanations the dog has sensed will not necessarily reveal contraband or any other evidence of crime."

We couldn't have said it better ourselves. Unfortunately, as is often the case, this wisdom did not hold sway with the majority. One or more Justices periodically stand up for their own odd view on behalf of freedom, leaving sound reasoning in the form of dissenting opinions which hold no legal force. The majority hastily adopt the illogical opposite position, afraid to let the genie out of the bottle.

Another danger with canine-generated probable cause is that an unethical handler can train a dog to alert, on some pre-arranged signal, opening the door for any desired search. Sometimes the signal is as simple as sitting down. Dogs have been brought into schools to scan lockers and students, are a fixture in airports, and rove the highways in SUV's with handlers who exist for no other purpose than to make busts. The hearsay testimony of such badged canines holds official weight in the eyes of the law, and thus, in a sense, these dogs outrank any human. No other being is afforded this astonishing presumption of credibility.

It is hard to imagine that this is what the framers had in mind, when enshrining protection from unwarranted government intrusion in the fundamental law of the land. The Supreme Court is nothing if not imaginative in redefining our freedom.

To get a sense of how cops feel about their might to search, and our right to be free of their hands in our pockets, think of interdiction the way they frequently do: as a business. Such a lucrative growth industry it is, that successful narcs, like Texas cop Andrew Hawkes, are offering get-rich-quick schemes based on a can't-fail system of hunting drug possessors.

Marketing his e-book like a no-money-down real estate guide, Lieutenant Hawkes promises that he holds the secret to bigger busts, rapid promotion, and the envy of your peers. Under his experienced tutelage, you, too, can "feel the rush of finding the Mother Load!"

"So why do some cops bring in huge drug hauls so easily while you struggle to find a dime bag? What if there was a way you could bring in 10 lbs, 50 lbs, even 400 lbs of dope?" He is not joking, although at first we suspected a satirical hoax.

Complete with teaser tips such as "passengers that don't know each others' names is a strong indicator of drug trafficking" (or maybe merely hitchhiking?), we can only guess whether he is hawking the real dope, or just suckering dimwitted rookies.

The guide is only available to members of law enforcement, and anyway, we don't have money to waste on such trash. Just in case we wanted to give this jerk thirty bucks, he warns that he will prosecute those who impersonate cops to acquire his information.

Just the ad, which is so gaudy we'd suspect it to be fake, is enough to send chills. His sample tips are pretty run-of-the-mill, stuff like, "be sure to turn on the A/C vents" and "always stack your dope load on the hood of your squad car so the jury gets a great picture of it from your in-dash camera." What we find scary is the idea that this how-to guide on ruining lives seems to actually be selling. "There's no better adrenaline rush than opening a trunk with over 200 lbs of marijuana!" gushes one testimonial.

The very existence of this blatant appeal to the darker nature of cops is reason enough to raise the question of whether the Fourth Amendment is an arcane relic, or whether we still have a basic right to privacy in our persons, papers, and effects in these United States.

The question is not rhetorical. Our very lives are at stake.

ARTICLE V:
Freedom is Slavery

"An avidity to punish is always dangerous to liberty. It leads men to stretch, to misinterpret, and to misapply even the best of laws. He that would make his own liberty secure must guard even his enemy from oppression; for if he violates this duty he establishes a precedent that will reach to himself." —*Thomas Paine*

Copaganda is very heavily invested in promoting weighted emotional memes in support of drug interdiction policy. Defying logic while proclaiming incredible falsehoods, prohibitionist authorities say the darnedest things.

No one could match the unbelievable gaffiness of the late Harry Anslinger, whose legacy lives on to this day in the idiocy of cannabis criminalization. The passionate crusader against joy promoted his stance with memorable misrepresentations, which still serve to illustrate the narrow perspective from which interdiction originates.

From reefer madness such as, "You smoke a joint and you're likely to kill your brother," and "Marijuana is the most violence-causing drug in the history of mankind" to the opposite contention: "Marijuana leads to pacifism and communism," Anslinger slung a lot of infertile, anal-retentive manure at the poor flower and her human admirers. No contradiction, duplicitous exaggeration, or outright lie, was too outrageous for the author of modern mind-control policy.

King George Bush II, um, that is, George W. Bush, the former Resident-in-Thief, was a master in conflating issues which have little relation. About what ordinary citizens could do to fight terrorism in a post 9-11 world, he said, "If you quit drugs, you join the fight against terror in America." The causal link is vague, but that sort of fuzzy thinking is foundational to the campaign against cognitive sovereignty.

It would be funny, if we didn't have to live under the rule of such ignorance. Today, the rhetoric spouting from the State, linking controlled substances with violence, blankets the airwaves. We hear these baseless assertions so commonly that they are taken for granted.

When announcing an arrest and seizure, there is invariably some sort of reference equating this "success" with "protecting our children" or "keeping our streets safe." One imagines a package of cocaine jumping from the table, switchblade in hand, wildly casting about for some toddler to take hostage.

More subtle is the deceptive slant woven into the nomenclature of the inevitable court process. The prosecutor's opinion of the defendant is advanced as the position of "the People," as if *all* the people, *collectively*, are against this individual, and believe from the outset in both guilt and the appropriateness of any proposed sentence.

This is a tremendous arrogation for a single civil servant to make, even an elected one, but this pretense to democracy is universal. Every defendant must combat the claims made by aggressive lawyers in the name of the entire community, who of course were not consulted.

The jury, who are at least an actual sampling of the people, if not quite representative, hear over and again in the course of a trial that *the People* favor a conviction and stiff sentence. These pejorative semantics encourage a presumption of guilt, as in many minds the mere filing of a prosecution is plenty indication of wrongdoing. Despite hollow instructions to the contrary, the average juror, who is never a convicted felon, enters into a criminal trial with a strong tendency to condemn anybody that nice DA says they should. It's what's best for *the People*.

The very language we use to talk about these practices is warped by the distorted labels conferred upon them. For example, it is uneasy to use the phrase, "criminal justice" when discussing controlled substance charges. The first term presumes the wrongness of defendants; the second presumes the moral correctness of what is happening to them.

The prosecution is referred to in speeches and legal documents as "the People," but, in fact, these lawyers do not represent the position of the electorate at all. Their view of the case is unresponsive to the will of the people. Prosecutors are but another tier of the police force that initiated the action against an individual.

The *people*, at least theoretically, are supposed to be represented by a fair and impartial panel of the defendant's peers. The role of the prosecutor would best be understood by the transposition and substitution of a few letters. Persecution, the deliberate harassment of a certain class, is the function of the State's attorney in a controlled substance case.

It is called the "Justice System," but what is happening amongst courts, prosecutors, and the police on either side of the barbed wire is actually the gravest sort of injustice. Citizens are hauled before grim tribunals to have years of their lives excised from them in retribution for behavior which is nominally illegal but in which no harm was done.

It may be impossible to discuss these linguistic phenomena without drawing parallels, well-worn though they may be, with the world of George

Orwell's *1984*. We plead the necessity of describing a mind-manipulating bureaucracy, whose leaders and minions appear to be under the impression that Orwell's cautionary tale is actually a reference manual. We do not invoke this comparison lightly.

For evidence that the Federal government mimics the machinations of Ingsoc, consider that, with the ink hardly dry on the first edition of Orwell's dystopian classic, the Department of *War* was renamed, in 1949, to the Department of *Defense*, in a brilliant example of Newspeak.

Since adopting this mantle, the DoD has waged a virtually continuous foreign combat, in what appears to be deliberate imitation of events in *1984*. And since the formation of NATO, even the tripartite division of power envisioned by Orwell became a practical reality for the next forty years.

If we replace *Eurasia, Oceania*, and *East Asia*, with the *Soviet Bloc, Capitalist NATO*, and *Maoistic Asia*, we see that this equilibrium was successfully maintained through the decades, peaking, prophetically, during the actual 1980s. Battlegrounds on the periphery of these superstates devastated poor countries caught in the crossfire, like Korea, Vietnam, Cuba, Nicaragua, Czechoslovakia and East Germany, while each imperialist bureaucracy cracked down on dissidents at home.

Similarly, in this period, we have seen the evolution of agencies whose function is opposite to what is implied by their names. The Department of Justice is in charge of hounding people, the Department of Corrections is in charge of criminalizing them. The Department of Revenue takes your money away.

Condemning people to live in foul holes, over a trivial violation of drug statutes, should no more be the work of a Department dedicated to *Justice*, than rewriting history should be the work of the Ministry of *Truth*.

Replace "Thought Police" with "Narcotics Task Force" and we see a very neat parallel to domestic enactment of psychological totalitarianism. Like O'Brien, undercover cops pose as subversives in order to entrap nonconformist elements into exposing themselves. Once discovered, the deviants are consigned to a reconditioning program consisting of confinement, slow torture, and renunciation of their former selves.

The essence of *crimethink* is the failure of an individual to respond to the conditioning and propaganda of the State. The thought-criminal places his or her own biology and values ahead of the will of the ruling class, thus breaking rules which place unreasonable restraints on the pursuit of pleasure. Unable to resist the lure of disobedience, they become a threat to an edifice which depends on each tier of the pyramid staying precisely in place.

Such people are inimical to the organizing force of civilization. As workers they can not be trusted to obey; as patriots, they cannot be trusted to sacrifice themselves for the war machine; as parents, they cannot be trusted to instill the next generation with a fanatical adoration of the status quo.

The dominant classes depend on the people redirecting their libido in the service of their masters. Piety is incompatible with orgiastic ecstasy, because the former cannot compete on an even footing. In order for an artificial value system to override natural urges, a consensus reality must be generated signifying that nature is evil.

The lure of heresy has always been a problem for empire builders. Uncooperative souls present a real threat to rulers out to exploit their subject population. Subversive self-interest disrupts the orderly direction of resources flowing toward the top. Worse still, the very presence of dissidence serves as an attractive example to those whose indoctrination holds sway, merely because they have not yet conceived of an alternative.

All governments must confront the difficulty of dealing with subversive malcontents. Most political rulers have operated as unrestrained, religiously sanctioned dictatorships, and historically used slaughter as the method of choice in controlling dissent.

This was as ever true in the regime from which the founding revolutionaries staged independence. The British Empire held property at gunpoint on every corner of the globe. The ownership of this vast holding was invested in a single inheritor, who was entitled to impose any law, and execute or imprison any real or perceived enemy.

Such was the legal legacy facing the framers of the Constitution. For all of written history, the vast majority of human beings have had the misfortune of living under the rule of one autocrat or another. Some were benign; some were bloody tyrants; but their subjects enjoyed liberty, or endured repression, at the unearned whim of a single being.

The Constitution is hardly a perfect document. Yet it sets out to create what would have been the first institution to govern collectively, rather than by caprice, and to protect the citizenry from being abused by authorities. Unfortunately, simple words on a page are insufficient defense from tyranny. Almost from its inception, opportunists of every stripe have seized upon the weakness of the ambiguous language of the Constitution to construe whichever meaning best suited whatever undemocratic scheme was being pursued.

It took less than a decade for the guarantees of free speech and press to be voided. The Adams administration and Congress, peeved at having political opposition, enacted the Sedition Act in 1798, making it a crime to criticize the sitting government. As expressing dissent would seem an essential component of any democratic reform, the Federalists made an early demonstration of the principle that the party in power need not heed the constraints detailed in the original charter or its amendments.

Wisely, Adams saw to it that the sedition law expired the same day as his Presidency, so it could not later be used by his opponents, when they gained power. The stage was set for conditional observance of the spirit and letter of what is theoretically the highest law of the land.

Although it is popularly referred to as a "democracy," and technically regarded as a "representative Republic," the modern United States Government, in form and function, might be most properly described as a *corporate bureaucracy*.

This is not merely to signify the stranglehold which private business interests have on the political process. The government itself operates as a sort of meta-corporation, specializing in the business of coercing funds. Since most of the money which flows into the coffers of the State is essentially extorted, one might equally compare it to the Mafia.

The government, when it is not providing social services, is engaged in principally destructive acts. Regulations, on the whole, increase scarcity, modify the labor pool, and manipulate the value of the dollar.

The twin towers of this demolition firm are the armed incursions into foreign lands, and the domestic prison-industrial complex. These manufacturers of misery operate in tandem to increase production, without improving the quality of the general welfare. Each is a form of wealth redistribution, from the poor at home and abroad, to the State and to the corporate entities who profit from these extensive and wasteful activities.

The prisons and the military also have a regulating effect on the labor pool. Maintaining the proper level of each skill class is critical to a healthy economy—that is, one which allows the dollar to flourish and stockholders to gain wealth. The equilibrium of the job market is a key function of government. Excessive unemployment brings civic unrest, bottoming markets, and stress on the investment in social services. On the other hand, businesses need workers to be sufficiently abundant that wages may be kept reasonable.

Wars accomplish both functions nicely. Civilians and military personnel alike, on both public and private payrolls, are absorbed into an enterprise whose product is devastation and death. Arms are constructed solely to destroy and be destroyed; armies are assembled solely to be deployed in foreign lands. War is the business of exporting suffering.

The domestic war on cognitive sovereignty is even more dynamic in removing laborers from the useful economy. It effectively brings the war home. Again, millions of workers are occupied in industries with no useful product, both in and out of uniform.

Beyond that, of course, is the trimming away from society the millions of Americans who are stuck behind bars, none of whom are competing for well-paying jobs, as well as the millions more who have been devalued in the labor market, through losing professional licenses and acquiring felonies as a result of prohibition.

Another dimension is even more sinister. Many of these prisoners *are* "employed"—for literally spare change. In fact, an inmate who makes productive use of their time on behalf of their jailers can expect to be paid less than sweatshop workers in the poorest nations on Earth. Not content to let all those idle hands and free time go to waste, both the Feds and big business are increasingly making use of the third-world conditions here at home, paying prisoners from 23 cents up to $1.15 per hour.

Don't think these inmates are living high on the hog with their fat paychecks, however; up to eighty percent is taken by generous Uncle Sam, who has after all been kind enough to feed, house, and clothe them for free. These slave wages are perfectly statutory, yet the failure to cover prisoners at work by the minimum wage represents a blatant violation of the equal protection clause in the Fourteenth Amendment. The whole business has become a gruesome cycle of exploitation. Prosecutions fill the prisons with dirt-cheap labor, which then is impressed into the manufacture of the very tools of State repression.

Over fifty percent of the goods manufactured are sold to the Department of Defense. The uniforms in which inmates live out their drab years of incarceration are made in State-run sweatshops. Even the body armor worn by shock teams when they raid the tiers is the product of prisoner toils. Under the Federal Acquisition Regulation, preference is given to bids from UNICOR, which produces its goods for a pittance courtesy of the involuntary guests of the Department of Corrections.

Naturally, these optimally located labor pools are attractive to Big Business as well. The captive workforce has been loaned out to private concerns noted for their cheapskate labor practices, such as Nike and McDonald's, but also upscale outfits like Merrill Lynch and Shearson Lehman.

When servicing these corporations, inmates are generally paid the minimum wage, regardless of what such work might have brought in a competitive labor market. Skilled prisoners often have trade qualification which might bring forty dollars per hour on the outside. The balance of these wages, too, cycle back into the prison bankroll as deductions for the costs of incarceration.

This particular system is very popular among some conservative voters, who don't see any reason why taxpayers should foot the bill for feeding and housing these reprobates. After all, they reason, why should criminals enjoy TV all day at public expense? Let 'em earn their keep like everyone else.

Corporate America is not merely in the business of grossly underpaying prisoners. The latest trend is the private prison, where punishment itself is contracted out. Captive consumers don't need to be advertised to; the marketing is handled by the police and prosecutors. The entirely involuntary nature of the transaction allows for the shoddiest of real estate to be "rented" long-term at hotel prices.

Corrections Corporation of America, which operates human warehouses at over sixty locations in the United States, is a publicly traded corporation on the New York stock exchange, with the fiduciary obligation to maximize profits to its stockholders. With assets totaling nearly $3 billion, the private prison business is a recession-proof investment in destroying futures. One of every thirteen prisoners in the US is warehoused in a private penal institution.

While the police are cuffin' and stuffin' their daily quota, legislators are harshening penalties, and judges are confiscating paddles at the mouth of shit creek, the captains of industry are there to make a buck. The expensive and unproductive corralling of nonviolent substance offenders becomes yet another level of economic reappropriation, wherein politicians receive campaign funding from these business interests, with the understanding that votes for more draconian and sweeping legislation will be forthcoming.

The very idea of a private prison, incarceration as enterprise, is shocking to the conscience. Prison ought to be a last resort, an uneasy remedy to the problem of the incorrigibly violent, who cannot safely be allowed freedom. Instead, there is a financial incentive for these mercenary firms to see that a growing segment of society is forced to live behind bars.

This business is like no other. The closest approximation is a waste disposal service for human beings. Value is created by the removal of unsightly elements from society. Since there is no end to the natural resource of people who get high, the majority of the corporate chattel are drug offenders, convicts whose sentences have been enhanced by prior drug offenses, remanded to custody over a drug-related probation violation, or serving an extended sentence for contraband violations inside.

Worse still, the supervisory staff has a profit motive in lengthening the sentences of those already in their pockets. Although the guards are no part of government, they are contracted to wield the full might of force and repression on behalf of the authorities, and have every motive to extend the stay of an inmate slated for release.

The consignment of prisoners by the State into the hands of corporate jailers is a profound betrayal of the principles behind the law. Incarceeration should be balanced by the cost to society; laws which place an undue burden on the budget ought to be evaluated in that light. With the advent of companies like CCA, the punitive function of government has been transformed into a growth industry. There is no limit to the number of unhappy souls this greed cannot absorb.

Abuse at these facilities is rampant, of course, and public accountability at a minimum. Male guards supervising female inmates have been accused in Federal lawsuit of raping them inside a Kentucky facility. At least twenty-three women have filed suit over this treatment at Otter Creek Correctional Institute in Wheelwright.

A German woman said that an internal affairs officer forced her to submit to sex acts, in exchange for telephone access to her mother, and threatened her with legal consequences if she refused or reported the incident. The threats included arranging to have her deported, so she would never again see her five children living in the US.

Breaking her silence, she said she originally hesitated to do so, because she feared it would impact her parole. CCA moved to dismiss her lawsuit on the grounds that she had not properly utilized the grievance system. This would have been useless, since all complaints were routed through her attacker.

Nor is the profiteering limited to adults. CCA operates juvenile facilities as well on behalf of the State. In December of 2000, a jury awarded $3 million to a victim of excessive force, fourteen years old at the time of the incidents, who was in custody on charges of disturbing a school bus. The boy needed the money; he spent much of the year following his release in a psychiatric institution to recover from the trauma inflicted by callous CCA minions.

If the idea of rowdy kids being incarcerated and beaten for profit isn't frightening enough, an ACLU lawsuit demanding CCA internal records revealed ten juvenile inmates were kept past their release dates in Florida. We can only wonder how frequent such incidents really are, since such documentation isn't covered by the Freedom of Information Act, and must be obtained through court subpoena.

The dirty money derived from exploiting the incriminated underclass is just one of the factors that keep the State hooked on prohibition. Unbelievable amounts of cash are squeezed from defendants in possession cases, particularly the small-time personal quantity cases, which are generally resolved by a stint of supervision by drug courts, probation officers, or case managers in their privatized cousin, known as diversion. The word "diversion" is descended from a Latin root meaning "to turn in different directions." Indeed, these programs turn some lives upside-down.

Drug courts and probation are administered directly by departments of the government, but many diversion programs are under contract to private agencies which are not a part of the official bureaucracy operating under the auspices of the Constitution, or bound to observe the rights enumerated therein.

One of these, TASC, is the standard assignment for first and second drug offenses in Arizona. Administered at the pleasure of the prosecution, charges are dropped in exchange for a lot of money and wasted time. These arrangements bypass due process entirely, discouraging even innocent defendants from mounting a challenge to their charges. The expense and length of a trial, and consequences of conviction, are such that few try.

Diversion places the individual under the direct whim of the prosecutor, who is financially enriched by this option. Whereas convicts must pay their ransom to the court, diversion conscripts make the payoffs to the very agency who brought charges in the first place. The judge plays a largely ceremonial role, rubber-stamping the punishment and processing the eligible *en masse*. It is supposed to be a privilege, as it only applies to first or second offenders, and in truth it has advantages over conviction and probation. Compared with these, it is a relatively light punishment, but it can be life-derailing nonetheless.

Terms are six to eighteen months, depending on the type of substance involved, although a problematic urine sample, including missed or "diluted" drops, can mean a resetting of the clock, or recharging of the original felony case. Even a positive test for alcohol is punished, despite its legality and the many environmental sources of ethanol. Hand sanitizer has triggered the sensitive alcohol test in laboratory experiments, but such excuses are dismissed as the lie of a substance addict.

The program consists of mandatory urinalysis and metered treatment, all of which must be paid by the "participant," who must comply or face felony sentencing. A large fee is also paid directly to the County Attorney's Drug Task Force fund, which in turn is reinvested toward dragging more people through this pointless process. There is also a mandatory "booking fee" assessed for the cost of inducting the arrestee into jail.

These expensive jail alternatives are cash cows for the courts, and law enforcement respectively. Each extracts exorbitant fines or fees, usually many hundreds or thousands of times the value of the items being charged in the criminal complaint. Kickbacks to the police incentivize the capricious and proactive recruitment of bit players into the court-mandated treatment scam.

Moreover, private businesses profit from the imposition of these forms of punishment, most noticeably the drug treatment/urinalysis testing sector. Not only is the disturbing and disgusting practice of demanding urine samples humiliating, but the hapless "patient" is generally required to pay for this luxurious ignominy. UA fees alone can run to hundreds of dollars per month in certain programs. TASC, as an example, begins new "clients" at ten tests each month and gradually reduces frequency.

The ordering of bodily fluids for the purpose of chemically detecting psychotropic substances presents a Constitutional issue as well. Of course, this hinges on whether one thinks it is reasonable to force people to submit to regular searches of their most intimate personal fluids for the sake of detecting neurochemical apostasy.

Urine testing violates the Fourth Amendment right to be free of unreasonable search and seizure. We submit, that according to prevailing community standards, one's urine is *absolutely* considered private; it is, in fact, a crime to publicly void. Since we have a privacy interest in our urine, it is unreasonable to demand it, with or without cause, absent a warrant.

We would even include employer-imposed screenings, because the Amendment stipulates that the "*right of the people to be secure in their persons...shall* **not** *be violated.*"

Nothing about this clause limits the application of it solely to the government. Rather, the implication is that the government's role is to intervene whenever unreasonable searches occur, regardless of whether it is instigated by private or public authority.

We have our opinion on this; the Court has their radically different tradition. But what is disturbing is the ease with which millions are "relieved" of their Constitutional rights, as well as enormous sums of cash, upon a simple charging for a small amount of forbidden medicine.

The word "probation" derives from a Latin root meaning, "to test" or "place under scrutiny." When one is sentenced this way, they are subject to a set of uniform conditions, as well as voluntary ones at the whim of the judge, stipulating that life shall henceforth be a limited and fairly joyless one.

One of these conditions requires the defendant to surrender their Fourth Amendment right entirely. Not only must they submit to seizure of their bodily waste, but also foreswear refusal of any search by any agent of law enforcement at any time. So extensive is the loss of this right that it can even extend to those in the *vicinity* of anyone on probation, justifying an otherwise illegal intrusion, which can then lead to further convictions and more fodder for the growing supervisory industry.

Now, it is odd that a criminal defendant, even a convicted one, should be summarily deprived of protections included in the Bill of Rights. After all, the Eighth Amendment proscriptions against cruel and unusual punishment are presumed to apply post-conviction, even to Death Row inmates. It would hardly be logical, if conviction of some offense meant that cruel and unusual punishment became permissible.

Nothing in the Constitution accounts for conditional application of these rights. Indeed, the Fourteenth Amendment guarantees equal protection under the law. Such inconvenient details have been willfully glossed over by courts who employ a wafer-thin rationale to void rights enshrined in the document they are only supposed to interpret.

Of particular moment in the enforcement of controlled substance law is the use of civil asset forfeiture to summarily plunder vehicles, cash, and homes which show the slightest taint of illegality. Such reappropriation goes far beyond the original intent of such statutes, which was to confiscate the proceeds of criminal transactions. Today, police regularly build their fleets of unmarked cars by setting up reverse stings aimed at vehicular drug *buyers*, seizing every car although the drivers are clearly on the spending side of the equation.

Because law enforcement agencies are financially enhanced by such unmitigated theft, every pretext is sought, and found, to confiscate the lawfully acquired property of citizens, who may or may not have anything to do with drugs.

The premise underlying forfeiture is that funds derived from illegal activity, or anything purchased with such funds, ought to belong to the State. Without any due process at all, valuable property rights are voided on the mere association with a controlled substance.

In addition to being a morally offensive and odious form of robbery, civil asset forfeiture manages to blatantly violate several clauses of both the Fourth, being an unreasonable seizure, and the Fifth, Amendments. To wit: *"nor shall any person be...deprived of life, liberty, or property, without due process of law; nor shall private property be taken for public use, without just compensation."*

The Fifth Amendment supposedly guarantees that *due process* shall attend any deprivation of life, liberty or property in the United States. What this means, in part, is a right to be judged by a jury of one's peers, in any procedure by which the government confiscates possessions, incarcerates or otherwise restricts motion, or commits capital execution.

Taken strictly, the Fifth would seem to preclude much of the everyday activities of the modern court system. For minor offenses, punishable by a fine, a jury trial is generally not available. But even for felonies, where many years in prison may be at stake, nearly all convictions are entered, without a single juror being empaneled, or a single piece of evidence presented in open court.

While a jury trial is still technically an option, one which has occasionally been invoked with success, the vast majority of criminal charges are settled by means of a plea "bargain" (*half off!*), or pre-trial diversion program, wherein the prosecutor names the punishment.

Although, in each individual case, the cost-benefit analysis of trial risks outweigh what the prosecutor is willing to accept, in the grand scheme of Justice, plea bargains are a bad deal indeed. Allowing the prosecution to bully defendants out of even attempting a defense may be one of the darkest subversions of genuine justice extant to this day.

To understand what could possibly be meant by this statement, think of this as a real-life "prisoner's dilemma." Each defendant knows that they have a right to a jury trial, but if they lose, the punishment will be much greater. However, if they *all* took their cases to jury, the prosecutor would be forced to drop many of them, because each jury trial is expensive, and it would clog the system to accommodate lengthy full-fledged legal duels for every case.

Rather than trying to win in the arena of convincing twelve randomly selected jurors of guilt, prosecutors pressure the defendants to surrender their rights to due process. Consequently, none of us can reap the real benefit of the Fifth Amendment: inconvenience to the State, in requiring this elaborate procedure. It is no accident that the guarantees in the Bill of Rights tend to make things tougher on the government. So important are the life, liberty, and property of each individual, that the framers intended for it to be difficult for the State to strip them from us.

The natural limitation on an unjust law, in a fair legal system, would be the strain on resources of the State to bring all the cases to trial. If a particular petty offense is too difficult to prove, or is committed so commonly that cases clog the docket, then the prosecution is inhibited from pressing a law, and it becomes unenforceable. This is part of what ultimately defeated the ban on ethanol.

The leverage of the prosecutor is so great, and the discretion so broad, that most defendants are cowed into raising their right hands and waiving their rights away. Not only are the chances of victory slim, but it is well understood that sentences are far stiffer following a guilty verdict, than a "negotiated" plea.

Another clause of the Fifth, the right against self-incrimination, is also infringed by these arrangements. By inducing defendants to plead against their innocence, prosecutors as a matter of routine compel self-incrimination. All of this meets with the approval of the SCOTUS, but how Constitutional is it, really?

Plea bargains and diversion agreements are only nominally voluntary. They are about as voluntary as the surrender of a wallet to a gun-brandishing mugger. Sure, you reached your hand in your pocket to turn over your valuables. But would anyone say this choice is made of your own free will? Threats are the essence of coercion, and no one signs a deal with prosecutors out of choice. It is a Devil's choice between bad and worse.

Of course, every arrestee is deprived of liberty, without anything resembling due process, in the hours or days preceding the bail hearing. The courts have ruled that this sort of jailing is a mere temporary hold, and therefore not covered by the Fifth. This is little comfort to the harmless citizens who find themselves abruptly cut off from the world.

Despite popular misconceptions, a drug case can be brought without any actual controlled substances being involved. One popular tactic is to entrap the gullible into phony conspiracies to arrange sizable purchases, leading to a charge of "intent to possess."

Individuals who might not normally be involved to such a degree are enticed by an unnaturally good price, usually for pounds of marijuana, and agree to much larger deals than they ordinarily would be privy to. Although there never were any actual controlled substances owned by the defendant, the mere verbal intention to acquire them is enough for felony charges and years behind barbed wire.

Another vehicle for massive sweeps, which may or may not yield any actual drug seizure, is the conspiracy indictment. This legally perilous instrument allows for the prosecution of individuals with only peripheral involvement, for amounts that they never actually owned. Such cases are frequently generated by predatory prosecutors pressuring names out of frightened bustees, who become confidential informants in order to save themselves years of prison. While this information frequently turns out to be faulty, the victims of snitches must endure jail and permanent smearing of their record, before having even the faintest opportunity to confront and discredit their accuser.

This is what happened to Regina Kelly, whose story was made into the movie *American Violet*. Caught up in a massive crackdown on alleged drug sales in the housing project where she lived, the working single mother was rounded up along with over two dozen other residents of a low-income, Section 8 apartment complex in Hearne, Texas, all on the word of a single intimidated informant.

All of the victims of the bogus bust were African-American, although John Paschall, the DA behind this racist atrocity, insisted that one white defendant *was* among them. This claim should be taken in context with the other gross deceits issuing from Paschall, in this case of prosecution gone wild. Kelley says that no white defendants were ever seen in the mass court proceedings she attended. At any rate, the Hearne case was a textbook example of why due process protections exist, and the sort of travesties which can ensue in their effective absence.

The massive raid on the project yielded absolutely no drug confiscations or caches of illicit cash, despite a comprehensive search. Nevertheless, Kelly and the others were arraigned on $70,000 bond each, an outrageous sum that was intentionally beyond the reach of the defendants.

The evidence consisted of the word of Derrick Megress, who was facing robbery charges, and an unintelligible audiotape with several indistinct male voices. This was more than enough for the secret grand jury who had issued indictments against the project's residents for crack distribution. Clearly, an open-and-shut case.

Megress came forward with the startling news that the information he'd provided against those rounded up in the sweep, under the influence of beatings and threats to his family, had been spurious, and the pending cases against all the defendants were dropped.

"The paper had a list of names," he stated during sworn deposition. "All of the people on the list were black. Paschall asked me if I could get the black sons of bitches."

Unfortunately, unable to make bail, seven defendants had pled to the charges, as the only way out of jail. Just to get a feel for how low a priority true *Justice* is within the court system, consider what happened to those left behind by the Hearne vindication. Even though the pleas were signed under extreme duress, and the charges were shown to be utterly baseless, there is no legal remedy for victims of the system like Erma Faye Stewart, who had copped a plea under pressure from her public pretender.

Branded as a felon, she came under the heavy-handed exclusions which afflict convicts for life. It doesn't help to explain that the conviction is bogus, that the case was fabricated, and the government had been successfully sued for bringing it in the first place. Once a conviction for a felony is entered, a life of struggle and desperation is virtually guaranteed.

The secondary consequences of bearing the scarlet "F" haunt every effort to survive and prosper. No longer eligible for public housing, felons like Stewart must take a chance on private landlords, who are perfectly free to discriminate on this basis, and are in fact encouraged to do so. Employers also rarely deign to hire a felon, yet public benefits, such as food stamps, section 8 housing, and welfare, are reserved for those who have not been decreed *unperson* by the courts.

Most importantly, felons are stripped for life of their vote, the only option a citizen has to change the law. When we wonder at how these politicians and their policies fare so well at the ballot box, consider the election-swinging excluded vote of the convicted felon. Those most motivated to work for change are barred, not only from voting, but running for office as well.

Even worse was the fate of Brad Boxley, who was actually remanded to the penitentiary for his involvement in this nonexistent trafficking ring dreamed up by Paschall. Threatened with *ninety-nine years*—based on the same flimsy "evidence" as the others—Brad caved into the plea "bargain," and was sentenced to eight years in Texas Prison.

No mechanism of automatic vindication exists to free these falsely convicted victims of prosecutorial misconduct. As easy as it is to incarcerate an individual on trumped-up charges, it is next to impossible to secure release for that same person, when their innocence is later conclusively shown.

Paschall, in fact, stands by his shoddy investigation, and remains convinced of its viability. "Every one of these plaintiffs are guilty," he said, in deposition for the civil rights lawsuit against him, "and every one of them should have gone to the penitentiary, by the grace of God they did not. That's my position."

Three familiar factors intersected to bring about the Hearne raid, which was distinctive in that, in this particular case, the perfidy of the State was exposed and settled under ACLU lawsuit. The rounding up of innocents is a necessary extension of a war where body count matters, and a bounty is put on each head.

First, the Federal grant money for local narcotics enforcement, a plum prime for the picking, drove this particular mass arrest, as is frequently the case. These grants provide a financial incentive for local government to railroad as many drug suspects as possible by literally paying a reward for each jailing.

Secondly, blatant racism in the Deep South, which may seem to have disappeared from the law books, but has hardly faded from the minds of the men behind the law. Under questioning about his use of despective language regarding black people, Paschall freely admitted using racist terms since high school, although he pointed out, "I'm not *saying* I use them *every* day."

Asked about judges using the same language, he said, "Let me put it to you this way. There are very few white people in Robertson County I have *not* heard use that term."

The third factor is the broad and unfettered discretion available to prosecution offices. We regard this as the most dangerous and readily abusable defect in the American legal system. The mere bringing of charges imposes a set of penalties, from jailing and bailing, to the permanent stain of arrest record, which can never be redressed by an acquittal, or even successful civil lawsuit for false prosecution.

All of this springs from the decision of a single lawyer whose mandate is to snag convictions and property for the State. Given the corrupting nature of power and money, we ought not be too surprised that prosecutors wield this authority irresponsibly.

The secret and one-sided nature of the grand jury is another tool by which the State deprives defendants of their Constitutional guarantees, including the Sixth Amendment right to confront one's accuser. Indictments often hinge on testimony from confidential informants, who, allegedly for their protection, can testify anonymously, an unnamed mouthpiece putting to paper the false and cowardly claims instigated by the prosecution.

Like the agents of the Inquisition and the KGB, the witch hunters of prohibition put a high premium on the forced confession. Confessions insulate malicious prosecutors from accusations that they have persecuted the innocent. Today, egregious prison terms and threats to family members substitute for the thumbscrews, but the truth is that all guilty pleas, with accompanying confessions, *are* forced, thereby violating the dicta against self-incrimination in the Fifth Amendment.

Courts have ruled otherwise, of course, limiting Fifth Amendment rights to a cursory Miranda notification. Beyond that, it is tough to square an interrogation of any kind by an agent of the government with such language as "nor compelled in any criminal case to be a witness against himself." Compulsion is exactly what occurs when cops and prosecutors leverage harsher sentences and heavier charges to produce a statement of guilt.

In order to understand why courts are so hostile to individual rights, when they conflict with the interests of law enforcement, consider the typical career path of a judge. Graduating law school, a criminal attorney can seek employment with a private firm, or else a local prosecutor's office.

Defense attorneys may become wealthy and prominent, but it is the other side's podium which leads to increasingly powerful positions. There is only room for one elected government attorney at each level of jurisdiction, but many seats on the bench available. Eventually, the opportunity to move to the front of the courtroom arises, and it is overwhelmingly former prosecutors who eventually become promoted to Judge.

As the Supreme example, six of the nine current SCOTUS judges have previous work experience as an attorney for the government. It is a natural progression; prosecutors are more familiar with a particular court, the internal mechanisms and personalities which make it function, than defense attorneys, who must travel around to wherever their clients are arraigned. When a vacancy opens on the bench, the applicant with the best chance of filling it will be the advocates of State policy, who have already worked in the building for years.

When such judges listen to the arguments made by prosecutors, they naturally tend to be sympathetic to the viewpoint of the State, which they themselves once put forth. When they review testimony of police, they will tend to have the same regard for their allies in uniform as they always have.

Defense attorneys do occasionally get the opportunity to serve as judge, but there is practically an open conspiracy to exclude prohibition abolitionists. One story candidly illustrates this. Marc Victor, a libertarian defense lawyer, was assigned to serve as a Judge *Pro Tem* in Maricopa County Superior Court.

Realizing a conflict between his political beliefs and the job he had taken on, Victor did what he believed to be the right thing, recusing himself categorically from all drug cases. Many defendants would have been quite happy to appear before such a judge, but not only did Victor not hear their cases, he was removed from the bench entirely, despite having been forthright about his position as well as ethical about not making rulings contrary to existent law.

Another reason judges tend to be supportive of prohibition and its works is that the highly abstract idealism of legislating behavior seems natural, to those who have devoted their lives to this work. Law is like a religion for these folk, and a judge is a priest, garbed in dark robes, attended in ceremonial ritual.

We rise when they enter or exit the courtroom, and no doubt many of them feel that they speak for God. Respect for the Law is sacred to them, and drug possessors have a contempt for what seems to most of us like an obsolete, reactionary regulation. To most judges, the defendant is a heretic who defies their creed. Often it is the defiance, rather than the offense itself, which is being punished. A suitably remorseful penitent will often find mercy from the court, whereas those who insist on their innocence are likely to be judged recalcitrant.

We ordinary people may feel that some laws are proper, while others are misguided and wrong, but the average judge feels little of this ambivalence. What is good or bad, from that side of the bench, are the *people* in the courtroom, whose value is assessed entirely in terms of whether they obey the rules. From this narrow point of view, disciplined police appear to have a glow of conformity that matches the priest of punishment's own rigid sense of propriety.

We shouldn't be surprised that law is treated as a religion by its practitioners, for the origin of the law is religious. The very notion of an enforceable code is religious.

The words *religion* and *law* share a common Latin root, meaning "to bind." The functions of faith-based conformity and judicial power have always been intertwined, from the Old Testament Judges to the Inquisitions of the classic Catholic Church, from the witch trials of Salem to the Scopes Monkey trials of Tennessee.

Not all judges feel this way about prohibition, of course. On the contrary, many fair-minded members of the bench, some quite prominent, have publicly objected to the unjust policies they have been forced to administer. Motivated by a sense of fairness, rather than devotion to a doctrinaire philosophy of serving as the State's rubber stamp, these distinguished jurists have protested the broken system they have been unable to change from their bench in local, Superior, and district courts.

Conscientious judges are also tied to mandatory minimum sentencing laws, which, while sounding good at election time, undermine the very function of a judge in adapting the punishment to fit the circumstances. Not only does this legislation, draconian in its very essence, impose undue prison time on peripheral participants, it often requires judges, who might be inclined toward leniency, to swing the gavel on sentences with which they profoundly disagree.

The operational definition of the law is that which has been adopted by a relevant legislative body, and authorized by the highest court in the jurisdiction. This is the reality that defendants and their lawyers live under; it is no use to cry "unconstitutional" when the SCOTUS has ruled otherwise.

While recognizing this, we charge that, in a more philosophical sense, this unconstitutional state of affairs is not truly the law at all, since it is plainly at variance with established enumerated rights. The rubber stamp of nine judges, or some majority fraction of them, does not convert the meaning of these protections. It only means that they do not apply.

ARTICLE VI:
Rhymes With Black

"The most potent weapon in the hands of the oppressor is the mind of the oppressed."—Steven Bantu Biko

The United States was founded as a racist polity. This shameful legacy is obvious to anyone who takes even a casual glance at the history of the nation. Institutional racism, in the form of slavery, was part of the earliest colonization, and was no less the basis of the new social order after self-determination was achieved, despite the proud words proclaiming equality of all men in the Declaration of Independence.

We all know that many of the Founders were wealthy plantation owners, whose families built their fortunes on the backs of slaves, but they were not the sole beneficiaries of this exploitation. Collectively, the resources, land and labor, which helped the US become the dominant economic power in the world, derive from a savage policy dispossessing nonwhites, and relegating them to an inferior status.

Class divisions based on birth are hardwired into European hierarchical structure. Both Greece and Rome, who contributed their political architecture to the new government, practiced slavery as well as a tiered system of privilege among their free citizens.

This successful model of organization evolved into feudalism, the dominance of the landlord. Because estates were inherited, feudal classes were genetically segregated, one's lot in life more or less permanently predestined from the moment of conception. Serfs toiled for the very ground under their feet, giving the greatest part of their harvest to the lord, while keeping just enough to subsist. The system survived because generation after generation of peasant had nowhere else to go.

The colonists were not generally landed aristocracy in their British homes. Yet after waving a few muskets at the local inhabitants, and shooting the uncooperative ones, they now found themselves masters of giant, fertile plantations in the New World.

Unfortunately, few of their fellow colonists cared to be serfs. Thus the practice of African slavery, which had begun virtuously simultaneous to European conquest of the newly exploitable continent, and was by the eighteenth century the staple of the magnificent agricultural industry now possible through the forcible acquisition of the new lands.

As today, another source of exploitable labor was the immigrant. Poor Europeans, unable to pay passage to the glorious land of opportunity across the sea, began to sell themselves into terms of servitude which would expire at the end of so many years. These workers were not so valuable a commodity, in that they were not owned for life, and their children would not become chattel. They also had the disadvantage of bearing the same genetic markers as the ruling class, making it more difficult to discriminate.

As cotton and tobacco farming grew to cover the lush soil of the South, the need for manual labor was met by conferring the legal status of animals upon individuals of African origin. While history records that the wealth of the South derived from vegetable growth, the greatest industry of all was the farming of human beings. Bred like cattle and sold like horses, the tribal people of Africa were literally converted into beasts of burden in America.

It bears mentioning that all of this was incorporated into the Constitution, which does not explicitly authorize this foul practice, but memorialized it, by including Articles which have since been amended, such as the scandalous "Three-Fifths Compromise."

No more than a glance at this thankfully deleted clause is necessary to appreciate the irony of founding a free country using slaves. Faced with the challenge of redistributing power throughout the people, the Convention arrived at the perplexing decision to apportion sixty percent of representational weight to a population which was not permitted to vote.

Not only were the slaves unable to play a part in governing this land where they were forced to live, their masters would vote at cut-rate on their behalf. The disenfranchisement of nonwhites, and for that matter women, was a conscious, and fairly unanimous choice among the delegates. So racist and sexist was the world of the Founding Fathers that it could hardly be otherwise.

The sharing of power would be among the minority elite, with Southern landholders taking the greatest per capita advantage. The vote of a Southern Caucasian was worth far more than his Northern counterparts; his congressmen wielded his vote for fewer relative voters.

To describe the United States as a democracy is historically and practically inaccurate propaganda. The nation was, upon inception, and is to this day, a plutocratic oligarchy. The wealthy pull the strings on their political puppets and often leverage their fortunes into personally assuming command. Sharing power collectively was the stated ideal, but the framers could not bring themselves to include their children, their wives, their involuntary workers, or the dispossessed natives in the scheme.

These details of history ought to be well known to most readers, and you may be wondering why we take these pages to review them here. The purpose is to illustrate the need which the dominant cadre has for an underclass which can be exploited, and to show how the Constitution has never applied to many of us.

When formal slavery was abolished through bloody war over regional power, racism did not disappear. Nor did the exploitation of the freed slaves. Many returned to the feudalistic arrangement of sharecropping, which afforded a degree of individual liberty, while preventing the economic freedom to utilize it; these people effectively became serfs to their former masters. Others went North to join the burgeoning Industrial Revolution as wage slaves.

The new manufacturing base adapted to using these workers at a cost comparable to owning a slave. By keeping pay low and opportunities scarce, it was possible to employ laborers for a cost just barely meeting the basic needs of room and board. The savings were compounded by eliminating the purchase price; these workers were not an investment, and so their nominal freedoms were more tolerable.

Slowly, the division of class based on ethnicity began to erode. Barriers to education, salaried employment, and home ownership were eventually lifted. By the 1960s, the momentum toward egalitarianism was sufficiently strong that the government officially withdrew from apartheid policies, and the majority of the public came to oppose racism in principle.

At the same time, huge numbers of young people, of all races, began a domestic revolt against the corporate war machine. Rejecting their assigned slots in the power structure, millions of middle-and-upper class youth chose to recreate the culture in their own image, taking a radical approach to politics, art, and religion.

The counterculture, which incorporated features from nonwhite traditions, was a keenly felt betrayal of the ruling class. Hawks and industrialists were horrified to discover their own children forming the basis of a new revolution against their way of life. They demanded that something be done about these damn lazy hippies corrupting the young.

The movement was threatening on several levels. First, the overwhelming sentiment among these malcontents was in opposition to the armed hostilities in Vietnam, the latest battleground in the "small-fry" war with China. Like the cold war against Russia, scuffling in these satellite nations was mutually preferable to taking the fight to the mat on the turf of either principle.

As in Korea of the previous decade, the limited engagement in Southeast Asia was intended to settle ideological scores. Communism was anathema to the industrial power-mongers in the West, a very real threat to the upper echelons of the monied class. After all, such individuals tended to be liquidated, along with their estates, when the Reds seized power.

On the whole, however, the young people weren't buying it. Many were sympathetic to the Communist viewpoint, which, at least on paper, offered an egalitarianism they were not finding in their own society. Others were disgusted with both sides, but appalled that the Vietnamese should be used as pawns in this bloody chess match using the world as its board.

The Americans with the most compelling and personal reasons to oppose the war were the millions of draft-aged men, who had attained the privileges of adulthood only to be shipped off to foreign jungles to kill and be killed. They began to flee the country, and publicly set fire to their induction papers.

All of this infuriated politicians, who were outraged at this resistance to their plans for world domination. Losing control domestically and in the foreign war, they began to crack down on the dissidents, not for their political speech, but for the personal habits that had become the central sacraments in the Age of Aquarius.

Richard Nixon, the champion of the grumpy old guard, came to power in 1968, largely as an unintentional side effect of radical politicking at the National Democratic Convention in Chicago.

The return of the Republican party to the White House, in the form of the defeated former Vice-President, heralded a return to the rock-ribbed policies of the 1950s, where witch hunts again flourished, and some very "un-American" political persecution of suspected Communists became official Congressional policy, with its own ad hoc committee.

Nixon, who would later earn the ignominious distinction of being the first US President to resign in disgrace, had no tolerance for the long-haired reprobates and their "anti-social" habit of smoking marijuana in large groups. He set out on a crusade to crush the rebellious elements among the youth and minorities.

This was the political landscape in which the War on Drugs was officially declared. The 1970 Controlled Substances Act was conceived and implemented as an attack on the unruly smart-asses who had the nerve to employ their privileged educations in opposition to the corrupt policies of their fathers.

The CSA signified a shift in the emphasis and tone of rhetoric employed by the pharmafascist element. Whereas various laws had throughout the century proscribed this or that popular vice, the sweeping legislation helped make enforcement of these trivial regulations the top priority of virtually every law enforcement agency in the country.

Moreover, the law provided a means by which new prohibitions would be enacted, the system of scheduling substances according to their "abuse potential," and whether the drug had a "currently accepted medical use." Presence in the Schedule I category would restrict research, forbid prescriptions, and result in the strongest penalties for possession, sales, and transport. These included cannabis, heroin, and all known psychedelics, all of which had demonstrable medical uses as well as popular appeal.

Passage of the omnibus drug bill marked a major shift in the criterion for exclusion and repression in the United States. No longer giving official sanction to discrimination based on ethnicity, the new law created a permanent *behavioral* underclass.

Drug enforcement perpetuates and replaces racism, now that the policy of apartheid has become unacceptable. Not that racism has disappeared, not even with the inauguration of a partly African President. Old-fashioned White supremacy is alive and well in the system, even in high places, though it is not generally considered mannerly for officials to profess it within earshot of the voting public. It would be a mistake to suggest that racial oppression is a mere historical curiosity, a blot on the otherwise shining star of America.

On the contrary, the bulk of arrests and sentencing repercussions have fallen on young Black men. While individuals of all races and both genders are eligible for the marginalization engendered by prohibition, the disproportionate rate of incarceration among African-American males is impossible to ignore.

This phenomenon had been a part of prohibition from the very beginning. Cocaine, which was first banned in 1914 amid fears that it made Black males aggressive and rapacious toward White women, has over and again become the cover under which ethnic brutality and sabotage could be conducted.

The Reagan era, beginning in 1980, brought a new level of escalation to the domestic conflict between police and the large segment of the population who chose to ignore the government's presumption of sovereignty over personal habits.

Such flaunting of the law has accompanied every version of prohibition. To some degree, the effect may be more pronounced in the poor and disadvantaged, those who feel alienated from the hierarchy of wealth and power. But this is not in itself enough to explain the enormous disparity in per capita incarceration rates among Black and White. African Americans are 3.4 times more likely to be arrested for controlled substances than Caucasians.

Under Reagan, cocaine became the drug of choice in the United States. Stockbrokers fueled wild binges of gambling other people's fortune with a discreet toot of the coke spoon. Hollywood took to it as a child takes to sugar, and clandestine forces in the government itself facilitated the transport of large quantities in support of secret Latin American operations.

Cocaine also became explosively popular in the smokable form known as crack. Smoking cocaine was nothing new, of course; sophisticated users had been getting the most out of their expensive product by converting it to the freebase form for years, and even the commonly available salt form could be smoked, albeit ineffectively due to low combustion temperature.

What made crack different was the marketing. Packaged for the inner-city streets and distributed through tribally organized gangs, crack was targeted specifically at the African-American population.

Crack was also the subject of a media frenzy, which simultaneously promoted and condemned the rebranded drug with sensationalism, inspiring fear in parents and curiosity among the young. The little white rocks were cheap, abruptly omnipresent, and instantly addictive. And it rhymed with black.

New Coke got you higher quicker, seduced your daughters, led your sons into lives of crime. One hit and you were hooked for life. *Threatening our children. Endangering our neighborhoods.* All spread by the biggest free ad campaign ever to launch an empty-calorie product.

The airwaves were filled with reports about this new epidemic, aggressively marketed to children by pushers willing to pass out samples so as to hook a customer for life. Women sold their bodies for it, teenagers stole their parents' jewelry, strung-out addicts robbed liquor stores. Greedy drug dealers were out to get your children, and turn them out to the street.

Or so the hype went. The Reagan administration was clearly hooked on the money and power to be had by politically posturing against crack on one hand, and actively trafficking in it on the other. We'll get into *that* later.

The crack explosion certainly presented social problems, but these were largely attendant to the rising cost and increasingly violent gang domination of the urban market. The evils of crack have more to do with its legal status than the nature of the substance itself. In fact, had cocaine not been illegal, this form of it would likely never have been developed.

Furthermore, the claims of widespread proliferation turned out to be wildly exaggerated. While the sale and use of crack were highly visible in the Media—appearing on shocking news segments practically every night—in real life only a small and declining percentage of the population was actually consuming it.

A 2009 study by the Substance Abuse and Mental Health Services Administration found that only about one in thirty Americans over the age of twelve had ever tried crack, nearly three decades after it appeared on the streets and television screens of the nation.

Of those lifetime users, just over one-tenth had used it in the past year, whereas just over six percent reported use in the past month, let alone the last hour. If nearly ninety percent of those exposed to this menace were able to avoid smoking it in the past year, how "instantly addictive" could it really be? If only two of every thousand individuals are using it on a monthly basis, where's the epidemic?

By comparison, around 36 percent of those who had ever tried cigarettes had smoked them in the past month. From these numbers, it would seem that tobacco is six times as addicting as the crack cocaine the cops are beating down doors to get at.

This is not to minimize the genuine dangers of crack addiction. Some individuals clearly become dependent on the drug, desperate to acquire it, and maddened by binges exacerbated by inconsistent access to it. All in all, few lives are demonstrably improved by the addition of crack cocaine, although there are doubtless people who are satisfied with their relationship with it. For those who consider their lives unmanageable, help is hindered by zero-tolerance policies. This is a health problem to be best addressed by voluntary treatment options.

As with opiate dependency, any successful therapeutic approach will recognize the importance the drug plays in the psychology and neurochemistry of the user, and account for it, at least initially, by replacing the street product with a cleaner, more dose-reliable form at lower cost.

It is indeed difficult to imagine crack as a pharmaceutical product, but perhaps cocaine vaporizers could fill the niche for maintenance/weaning programs. Incremental replacement strategies have the immediate effect of controlling drug use, legitimizing it, and minimizing health risks. Instead of exacerbating the conditions of limited opportunity which helped bring about the habit in the first place, humane maintenance would ameliorate it. If the concern is over the harm resulting from chronic crack use, more carrot, and much less stick, would meet with greater success at luring addicts from the back-alleys into the clinics.

The government has had very little evident interest in harm reduction, however. Crack has provided a pretext for the militarization of the inner city, fattening enforcement budgets which fund the terrorization of poor communities with brutal raids.

Far from hiding the aggressive posture narcotics agencies assume to destroy lives and property over an inanimate substance, the Media celebrated the violence. The battering ram, followed by swarms of shouting Kevlar-clad shock troops, became the symbol of official policy on crack. Even bulldozers were employed to effect forcible entries.

As police took pride in beating up people who had crack, politicians conspired to remove them from society altogether, some prominent members of Congress going so far as to propose the death penalty.

At the Federal level, stringent mandatory sentencing laws were passed amid mass hysteria, once again in response to this mythically addictive drug sprouting up in the ghettoes. Crack cocaine now carried a penalty one hundred times greater by weight than the powdered form.

One way to look at this is that the corner crack dealer, holding fifty grams when busted, would get the same sentence as a mid-level cocaine distributor who is caught with over *two kilos* of powder. Neither is exactly getting a break, with a mandatory term of ten years hard time for their miniscule role in the proliferation of this global market. Yet the unfairness of this legislative inanity descends to a much greater degree on urban small-time dealers.

The disparity in sentencing falls directly on the street-level soldier, who is punished as a kingpin, despite playing a relatively minor part in the availability of the drug. These prosecutions rapidly filled the Federal prisons with low-level offenders, who had taken advantage of the only economic opportunity available to them.

By 2011, the outrage at this bizarre discrimination had reached enough legislators that reforms were finally adopted. Twenty-five years of public uproar had finally moved Congress to address the inequity of the crack double-standard, just in time for some of the first victims of it to be released.

The forces of intolerance would not give up entirely, though, so a compromise was reached. The long-awaited reform reduced the disparity to a mere eighteen-to-one ratio. Obviously, the champions of law and order felt it necessary to continue locking up small-time crack dealers for terms equivalent to those doled out to murderers.

The ghetto increasingly moved behind bars, as gangs fluidly distributed power between both realms. More and more young African-American males were processed into the system, felonized and for all practical purposes criminalized for life.

People of all ethnic backgrounds suffer from drug persecution, but the distribution is pointedly uneven. Whereas use is fairly consistent across racial categories, prosecution is not. Many civil rights groups and authors have drawn attention to this unfairness, but little progress has been made in redressing it.

While African-Americans represent about fourteen percent of all users, in line with that ethnicity's share of the general population, they are subjects in over a third of all drug arrests, and receive nearly two-thirds of the prison sentences stemming from controlled substance charges. Thanks in large part to uneven enforcement, a young Black man has a one in three chance of being incarcerated, over five times the rate of White males. More African-American males are penned in California's prisons than that State's colleges and universities. What kind of education are people of color receiving from all this?

These statistics are even more shocking in light of studies showing that rates of abuse for all forms of illicit drugs, including crack, are *higher* among Whites than Blacks, according to the SAMHSA 2009 report of household use. These figures may be dulled by the exclusion of the homeless and respondent deceit, but there is no reason to believe either factor affects the relative use data between ethnicities.

Lifetime use of powder cocaine is nearly double among Whites, at 17.1%, than the rate among Blacks, at 8.8%, while for crack, the rates are closer at 3.6% and 3.4% respectively. And the overall use of illicit substances is decisively higher among Caucasians, at 51.2%, than among their African-American counterparts, who are relatively restrained at 43.5%.

If similar proportions of each group are partaking in forbidden pleasures, why is the Black community absorbing the brunt of enforcement effort? The answer is complex, but in any event it boils down to conscious or unconscious application of racial bias on the part of police, prosecutors, and judges.

President George Bush I was no less invested than his puppet predecessor, Reagan, in casting the crack smokescreen. In a moment of classic Copaganda, the President, on national TV, openly displayed in his hand a large bag containing three ounces of crack, committing a fairly high-class felony right there in the Oval Office. Naturally, no one suggested that Bush should be hit with the same ten-year minimum any citizen would receive, for merely being associated with such a quantity.

So pervasive was this drug scourge, Bush told a worried nation, that *this very bag* of rock cocaine had been purchased in LaFayette Park, just across the street from the White House. So alarming was the accessibility of this terrible menace near the seat of power, that new enforcement initiatives would immediately commence. Orders were issued from the very top, promising to get to the bottom of this pernicious conduct under the government's very nose.

The backstory was a little more complicated. In conceiving the stunt, the President's team thought that it would make their point best if the crack were acquired nearby, as if Bush himself had stumbled on shady dealers while walking his famous dog Millie.

Unfortunately, the thrust of the entire message was jeopardized by the absolute absence of any kind of dealing in the park, which was considered low-quality turf by District of Columbia street entrepreneurs. Constant police presence made open-air sales unattractive, and the crowd, which tended to consist of students on class trips, elderly tourists, and government workers, were evidently poor customers. Therefore, a buying operation had to be concocted.

Through much dint and effort, the DEA finally managed to entrap a target into making the sale at the desired location. The hapless dealer, high-school senior Keith Jackson, was not in the habit of pushing rocks in the President's 'hood; he had to ask for directions. Nor was he up to date on the politics which were about to change his life.

When the location of the White House was explained, Jackson said, on tape, "Oh, you mean where *Reagan* lives." His DEA handler admitted, perhaps too candidly, "We had to manipulate him to get him down there. It wasn't easy."

Aside from the workers in the industry, the Media became fixated on another kind of crack demon—those users unfortunate enough to become mothers while using the drug. The specter of millions of infants born with crack pipes in their mouths was even more fuel for what had become open combat in the inner city.

As with most crack myths, this one was largely without substance, and misrepresented to cull support for harsher legislation. Despite initial predictions of mental deficiency, inherent dependency, and physical deformation, there developed very little evidence that prenatal exposure to cocaine was particularly harmful, compared to the other environmental factors of poverty, malnutrition and lack of care which also afflicted these mothers.

Of course, that didn't stop prosecutors from constructing novel legal theories, under which these mostly impoverished women could be deprived of their liberty, as well as custody of their newborn offspring. One woman, for example, was charged with delivery of a controlled substance to a minor, for passing the drug through her *umbilical cord*, and given fourteen years of probation following a year in jail.

Another was charged with assault with a deadly weapon on her fetus, due to the cocaine in her bloodstream, and sentenced to *twenty years* hard time. Yet another, in South Carolina, caught a murder rap when her baby was stillborn, and was put away for twelve years.

A Florida study found that while Caucasian mothers were testing positive more frequently, at 15.9%, than African-Americans, at 14.1%, Black mothers were nearly *ten times* likelier to be reported to law enforcement and face such criminal charges.

While no one seriously doubts that a habit so ingrained as to endure all nine months of pregnancy is likely to inhibit positive parenting practices, punishing the problem, instead of fixing it, appears to be the priority. Many treatment facilities have traditionally refused service to pregnant women. One study found that over half of drug treatment programs in New York City categorically denied admission to the segment of the population arguably in the greatest and most immediate need for help.

To be sure, the other side of the argument has supporting data as well. In 1985, the New England Journal of Medicine reported, based on a small sampling of twenty-three women, who were both pregnant and using cocaine, that there was a higher rate of miscarriage in such women, based on the four which occurred in the course of the study. This flawed and limited research became the scientific foundation for the crack-baby myth.

The study allowed, however, that no correlation could be shown linking cocaine to premature birth, low birth weight, cranial circumference or size. By 2004, the author of this study, Dr. Ira Chasnoff, became a signatory among thirty leading pediatric and obstetric physicians in denouncing the entire concept of the "crack baby" as a medical syndrome. In an open letter to the Media they collectively stated:

"Throughout almost 20 years of research, none of us has identified a recognizable condition, syndrome or disorder that should be termed 'crack baby'. Some of our published research finds subtle effects of prenatal cocaine exposure in selected developmental domains, while other of our research publications do not. This is in contrast to Fetal Alcohol Syndrome, which has narrow and specific criteria for diagnosis."

Going on to debunk the myth of the newborn entering the world hooked on crack, the letter went on to say, "By definition, babies cannot be born addicted to crack or anything else."

There are literally dozens of ways that misinformation, governmental impertinence, and public gullibility combine to scapegoat people of color under the pretext of drug interdiction. From crack house laws, penalizing landlords for failing to play cop against their tenants, to disturbing incidents of brutality and police murder, the racist character of prohibition is so obvious that it deserves mention solely by virtue of its pervasive effects on those least equipped to challenge it.

Not only has the War on Certain Drugs created a new "criminal" underclass which serves the utility previously filled by the racial underclass, slanted enforcement and judicial inequities help ensure that many of the very same people continue to be fed to the machine.

ARTICLE VII:
The War on Flower Power

"That is not a drug. It's a leaf."—Arnold Schwarzenegger

In reality, there are two distinct inanimate "enemies" against which the war of affliction is waged. Each is fought with the same tools, repressed with the same arguments, and prosecuted under similar legislation. The establishment uses Copaganda to confuse the issue, lumping substances of wildly disparate character in the same class.

On one hand, there are actual *drugs*, which are isolated chemical compounds of human manufacture with the unfortunate side effect of causing an improvement in mood. Some of these have dangers associated with overuse, much like their legal counterparts; unlike them, they also bring risks of impurities and the perils of negotiating underground markets.

On the other, we have the peculiar and offensive laws purporting to ban an entire species of plant from the face of the Earth. The virtues of cannabis hemp are well documented, and we won't dwell on them here, but suffice it to say that it is the most valuable and versatile vegetable species on the planet, capable of yielding food, fuel, fabric, paper, building materials, and, of course, medicine for literally hundreds of illnesses. It has been for many thousands of years, and is to this day, a central sacrament in religions around the world.

The movement to legalize cannabis is rightly the focus of reform efforts. Whereas drug prohibition presumes government dominion over chemistry, the eradication of marijuana is an assault on nature.

Marijuana is not a drug. It is a medicinal herb. There are dozens of such herbs available, without any legal restriction whatsoever, generally in health food stores. Some, like chamomile, ginseng, and kava, are known to have subtle and psychoactive effects. Nature abounds with vegetable-derived remedies, but only a handful have, by virtue of their power and that of their detractors, been reassigned as drugs.

The laws prohibiting cannabis are the least defensible of all. It is by far the most popular illegal substance. According to SAMHSA's 2009 household study, 41.5% of the US population admitted to using it at some point in their lifetime. Considering the hesitancy people have in reporting illegal behavior to government agencies, one might conclude that the actual percentage is probably higher. The past three Presidents have admitted trying it, although all have acted to fight legalization and medicalization.

No other illegal substance is publicly used at large gatherings dedicated to the practice. For that matter, no other illegal act regularly draws tens or hundreds of thousands of people to show their faces, and be counted, as do cannabis enthusiasts engaging in enjoyable civil disobedience. While there are no conventions for murderers and thieves, or even users of meth and crack, marijuana smokers have been unafraid, and unashamed, to say that the laws making us criminals are unfair and undemocratic.

Hempfest, in Seattle, has for the past two decades held ground to become the largest event of its kind. Over three hundred thousand individuals gather annually in a city park to demand reform. Can we imagine a crowd turning out in that size to demand the changing of *any* other kind of law?

Police are invariably present, and occasionally flex their muscle on protestors, as they did in 1997, issuing about fifty citations and making three arrests in Myrtle Edwards Park. For the most part, however, the cops tend to understand that they are outnumbered at such events, content to simply observe what are notoriously peaceful demonstrations of the harmlessness of cannabis culture.

When we examine the typical criminal code, we realize that there are essentially three distinct types of acts which are prosecutable by statute. There are violent crimes, such as assault, rape, and murder; these are invariably offenses against specific victims.

There are property crimes, such as theft, burglary, fraud, or vandalism; these may be violent or not, but also are defined by harm to a particular individual or institution, who are generally relieved of some object having value by means of stealth or guile.

When it comes to substance abuse laws, there is no discernible victim. No one who is directly involved has any objection, other than the authorities. Those rare busy-bodies who do complain are in no way injured; at the very most, they have been offended, perhaps by the odor. No material or physical damage is inflicted on anyone else in the commission of what are popularly termed "victimless crimes."

For this reason, it is strange to call such behavior a *crime* at all. Pharmafascists, defending the nanny-State, may retort that the *user*, or the user's family, is the victim in such cases, and with this we wholeheartedly agree.

In an arrest for possession, the only party being assaulted, abducted, and relieved at gunpoint of personal property is the defendant. Whatever damage one might do oneself in a life of using illicit substances, it generally cannot compare to the penalties for even the smallest quantities of marijuana.

When it comes to cannabis, that damage is virtually nil. In fact, marijuana, apart from the consequences of prohibition, has a remarkable safety record when compared, not only to legal recreants such as tobacco or alcohol, but ordinary daily activities, such as driving to work.

For purposes of criminal prosecution, the role of "complaining witness" is often played by the arresting officer himself, in a curious inversion of reality. After all, the defendant is the one with a valid complaint against the cop who brought force into the occasion. Often enough, this person is a professional con artist, who obtained through subterfuge the evidence for which the defendants stand to lose years of their lives.

Why is the testimony of this deceitful impostor accepted as reliable evidence, when whatever contentions the defense wishes to make are generally dismissed as the unreliable excuse of a criminal? Take away the badge and who is more credible? Every word coming from the lips of an active undercover agent is a lie; why should these individuals be believed when they mount the stand to seal the bust?

Dihydrogen monoxide, commonly known as water, is far more deadly than marijuana, or for that matter, any illegal drug. Over four hundred thousand people worldwide are killed by an environmental overdose of water each year, a condition otherwise known as drowning. An estimated 1.8 million more die from consuming the tainted product. Thousands more perish from withdrawal effects of water deprivation, a condition known as dehydration, which besets the hapless addict within mere hours and becomes lethal in a few short days.

Of course, there is no global campaign to ban water, or even discourage its use. A critic might suggest that we are born with a need for water, and this is certainly true. It is also true of cannabis, which is the only naturally occurring endogenous source of certain molecules for which our bodies and brains already have receptors.

Here the metaphor breaks down, for cannabis causes no deaths, either in deprivation or administration. The wholly voluntary association between plant and human is precisely what allows it to be persecutable.

If marijuana is illegal for the sake of public safety, then a better policy would ban the hundreds of things human beings do every day which actually result in their deaths. Marijuana is not among them; it is practically impossible to die from cannabis, unless a ton falls on your head.

The issue of marijuana law reform raises many issues. Should possession be a misdemeanor, rather than a felony, or an infraction payable with a fine, as has been achieved in a growing number of jurisdictions; legitimized through permission of a medical doctor, as has been adopted by a growing number of States, or shall the laws prohibiting possession simply be unwritten entirely?

Further questions arise with regard to cultivation, intent to distribute, and sales, all of which continue to be charged as felonies everywhere, unless covered by a medical exception. Is there any logical reason to have a limit on how much cannabis one might possess, or to legally prefer consumers over producers?

Should possession be legal if adopted as a sacrament, as by believers in Rastafarianism or Shaivism, as well as several newer faiths, such as THC Ministries, or the Church of Cognizance? After all, even at the height of the ban on alcohol, a necessary religious exception allowed congregations based around the ethanol sacrament to enjoy a certain regulated immunity from the law.

The use of cannabis in religion is arguably more venerable than alcohol, even in the Judeo-Christian tradition, which now generally embraces only the latter. The famous anointing oil, with which all priests and kings of Israel were consecrated during the period recorded in the Old Testament, has recently been shown to be a hemp product. The formula is included in the Book of Exodus, and the Hebrew University in 1980 declared that the ingredient called "ken-ah-bosom" is indeed cannabis.

We would clearly like to see the immediate abolition of all laws forbidding cannabis. The world would be a far freer and more enjoyable place to live, had the notion of criminalizing a plant been dismissed at the outset. Unfortunately, the struggle for a freer society is a war of gaining inches from rulers, with some people and places benefiting from hard-fought reforms, while others continue to be sacrificed to the economic needs of the prison-industrial complex.

Given the enormous edifice of laws which criminalize psychotropic materials, abolishing all statutory penalties and enforcement related to them may not be an attainable goal in the near future. To be certain, it would require a virtual revolution to overturn the conspiracy by all three branches of government to arrogate dominion over the chemical and vegetable content of the world.

Indeed, the prohibition is a matter of international law, as several treaty agreements require the US, along with other 170 signatory nations, to maintain laws against possessing any of these substances, specifically including cannabis. True legalization would mean withdrawing from these

UN conventions, which were after all instigated by the leaders of the United States.

Until there is a radical shift in the political landscape, we may have to settle for half-measures and work toward goals of harm reduction. By far the most successful approach has been medicalization. Beginning in California with Proposition 215 in 1996, it became possible for physicians, rather than law enforcement, to make decisions on the appropriate use of cannabis. The vehicle driving change has been voter initiatives, passed in response to the failure of legislatures to heed the will of their constituency.

The Federal government, to date, has not recognized the primacy of such State referendums, which represent the only examples of truly democratic legislation adopted on the topic, in that they were voted on directly by the people.

Part of the reason the laws against cannabis are so noxious, is that the herb is so innocuous. Discerning consumers choose marijuana, instead of competing products like alcohol and tobacco, partly because it *is* so safe. Unlike these legal recreants, which kill a small city each year, not one single death can be tied to cannabis use.

Prohibitionists allege that the danger is more subtle, that cannabis harms the mind, causing shiftlessness, memory impairment and inhibiting the development of the brain. Users, they claim, lose motivation and are doomed to failure. Belying this myth is the significant number of highly successful individuals, particularly in the entertainment field, who openly endorse cannabis and regularly enjoy it. Whatever one might think of musicians, actors and comedians, they are all engaged in a highly competitive and intellectual sort of work, which makes incredible demands on memory, and where only the driven achieve. Marijuana doesn't seem to have set back the career goals of these individuals.

Another bogus claim about cannabis is the "gateway" myth, the logically fallacious notion that smoking marijuana leads to hard drugs. Based on the overwhelming history of drug users having also smoked marijuana, this theory persists in the councils of the State, despite having been thoroughly debunked. Nothing about cannabis itself predisposes anyone to try any other substance, except perhaps oily food, although of course the same people who experiment with drugs frequently had their earliest opportunity to try marijuana.

One might equally claim that alcohol, tobacco, or a bevy of pharmaceuticals, would qualify as "gateways" under the same criterion, considering how the illicit use of these are also commonly cited as having been the initiation into the world of forbidden habits.

The reality is that by drawing this arbitrary line in the sand, prohibitionists are daring young people to cross it. Part of the intriguing social structure attending any illegal recreant is the underground nature of the associations one must form to participate. Outlaw groups develop insular customs and revel in alienation from the mainstream. What really hooks people to the drug-related cultures is the absolutist choice one must make to defy the State. If marijuana is a prelude to wider experimentation, part of the reason is the finality implied by that first toke.

The "gateway drug" rationale has long since been disproven, but it still lives on in the minds of pharmafascists who can't imagine discerning between a natural herb and synthetic chemicals. The idea of the gateway is that marijuana use predisposes one to try other, more dangerous drugs. It's a short-circuit to the counter-argument showing the non-lethality and remarkable safety profile of cannabis relative to, well, almost anything.

Even if marijuana itself is not a killer, the rhetoric goes, using it *leads* to drugs which are deadly. Look! Most crack users smoked marijuana first. Therefore, once your kid puffs their first toke, they are already lost. You may as well familiarize yourself with the local gutters, because one day that's where you'll find your kids, if you let them get away with smoking marijuana.

Once again, we see that the prohibitionist spin is based on anything but science. The argument confuses correlation with causation: if crack users tend to have previously tried marijuana, all this really shows is that people who tried crack had an expansive propensity for experimentation, as one would expect.

Here, too, the effects of the law become the justification for it. If indeed marijuana use is a precursor to harder drugs for some, this is because it is lumped together with them by propaganda messages and in the criminal code.

This is a common feature in the flawed theories underlying prohibition. The ramifications of the illegal trade in substances are mistaken for properties of the substance itself. The pairing of cannabis as a product with other illegal goods in the market may lead some individuals to try harder drugs as well. This grouping would disappear with legalization. It is wholly disingenuous to ascribe this association to the nature of cannabis itself. The real gateway is prohibition policies.

The inverse causation between criminal penalties for marijuana possession and use of hard drugs was amply demonstrated in a 2004 study, comparing the cities of San Francisco and Amsterdam. Each represented a specific policy approach to the prosecution of marijuana.

Not only did the study find that suspending marijuana interdiction did not lead to significantly greater use of cannabis, despite the corner availability of the commodity in legal venues, the statistics dramatically showed the real success of the Dutch policy: Amsterdam showed a much *lower* rate of lifetime hard drug use across the board.

Despite having the "gateway" to drugs for open sale in their city, the participants in Amsterdam showed a reduced likelihood of using cocaine, heroin, Ecstasy and speed during their lives. The rate of lifetime crack use was over four times greater in San Francisco.

When it comes to opiate use in the past three months, San Francisco had a rate five times higher than Amsterdam, which perhaps also reflects the benefits of the more rational policies with respect to heroin harm reduction approaches and maintenance programs.

Another myth repudiated by the figures in this study is the inevitability of addiction. In both cities, the number of lifetime users in each category dwarfs the percentage consuming in the past three months. While not all recent users are habitual, one might logically infer that all habitual users, other than those in recovery, would be counted in this category.

In San Francisco, one in ten lifetime users of powdered cocaine reported recent use, while only one of eighteen lifetime crack users were addicted enough to have recently partaken. Around eight percent of lifetime opiate users reported current use in San Francisco, but in Amsterdam the rate was an astoundingly low 2.2%.

At stake with these figures is a central premise of the prohibitionist rationale. These substances and users must be suppressed, drug hawks say, because anyone who even tries them is guaranteed to be trapped in a lifetime of addiction. As true as they claim this to be under zero-tolerance, surely the problem would worsen if enforcement were laxer.

The numbers, in this particular study and many others, simply don't bear that out. Even for drugs with a reputation for agonizing addiction potential, the rate of "discontinuation"—the metric indicating onetime users who are no longer doing so—is in the ninetieth percentile or higher.

What the high rates of quitting, in this and other studies, do suggest, is that addiction is not so much a property of the drug, as a property of the user. While it is certainly true that some substances seem to foster more severe dependence syndromes than others, the propensity for this may be neurochemical or psychosocial in nature, rather than a result of exposure to a given drug.

In one sense, one could argue that all cannabis use is medical, or at least medicinal. Certainly no one takes it to feel worse. When one smokes to "unwind," isn't that a way of saying the intent is to relieve stress, that root cause of so many ailments? Is it necessary to already be sick, in order to improve mental and physical health preventatively?

Why is cannabis so versatile as treatment? The short answer is that delta-9-THC activates particular neuronal receptors, which are responsible for the state of contentment called "a sense of well-being." However poorly one may feel, marijuana is likely to improve matters.

The long answer remains to be understood by science. As we emerge from the Dark Ages and out from under the rule of reactionary elements, we will come to understand more fully why a single herb controls seizures, relieves pain, and even reverses some tumors.

From depression and anxiety, to multiple sclerosis and AIDS, the relief offered by cannabis is unparalleled. Dozens of common and rare afflictions submit in some degree to cannabis, especially those characterized by nausea, pain, seizures, or mental health issues. Whether used as an analgesic, anti-emetic, anti-convulsant, or anxiolytic, cannabis compares nicely with pharmaceutical competitors. In terms of every kind of drawback associated with medication, physical, mental, and even economic tolls are reduced with a reliance on herbal healing.

The considerable evidence that cannabis is incredibly therapeutic, while relatively devoid of toxic side effects, is not to be ignored. If we are to triage prohibition reform, there is no doubt that the chronically ill deserve top priority.

At the same time, shifting to medical models of prohibition creates other problems, not the least of which is maintaining the excessive cost of medical marijuana. Of greater concern is the surrender of personal liberties, in what is fundamentally a struggle over the right to choose.

Medically-oriented reform to some extent begs the real question, which is: why should anyone need a prescription for cannabis at all? Does the sanction of a physician magically confer legitimacy on a practice which needed no authorization for thousands of incident-free years? Does the fact that the herb has ameliorative, or even curative, powers necessarily put it under the control of a medical profession, which tends to be insensitive to the needs of patients?

Progress toward a drug-law free America is hindered by public prejudice against what is often disparagingly referred to as "getting high." The moral condemnation of ingesting for pleasure is a hypocritical, and largely implanted philosophical viewpoint, similar to the Puritanical suspicion of sex, which once crafted the now defunct sodomy statutes.

Simple-minded folk tend to take the proclamations of leaders at face value, although famous drug warriors, such as the late Ronald Reagan, are prone to make ridiculous comments like, "I now have *absolute proof* that smoking even one marijuana cigarette is equal in brain damage to being on Bikini Island during an H-bomb blast."

If Reagan didn't know the difference between a joint and a hydrogen bomb, how much more frightening it is that for eight years his unsteady finger controlled the launch button for the world's largest nuclear arsenal!

Or the equally bombastic Harry Anslinger, who contributed such inanities as, "Marijuana is an addictive drug which produces in its users insanity, criminality, and death."

The more intelligent segment of the populace learns to disregard the ignorant opinions of these buffoons. Unfortunately, such ideological monomaniacs seem always to find themselves in the seats of power, with plenty of support from special interests.

To accommodate this mindset, it seems a necessary concession to show a doctor's note. Yet even this won't do, for the entrenched pharmafascists who oppose marijuana for everyone, including terminally ill patients. These doctrinaire ideologues are saying, in effect, that dying people should make do with the synthetic concoctions Big Pharma has patented, or they can end their days in the clink like the rest of the criminals.

Reagan, whatever else he may have been, was at least forthright about his insane views. More disappointing has been the performance of "liberal" Presidents, such as Bill Clinton, and, more recently, Barack Obama, who each abandoned their considerable pro-cannabis constituencies by continuing the trend of increased enforcement, exactly in the manner of their conservative predecessors.

Bill Clinton, the saxophone player who famously claimed not to inhale, so as to reassure the voters that while he may have participated in the subversive ritual of the smoking circle, his brain was not damaged thereby.

In handling the controversy with this sidestep, he showed that it is more acceptable for a leader to be a liar, than a smoker of the Devil's Weed. He was either lying at the time, in college, feigning inhalation while bogarting the doobie, or, more likely, prevaricating roundly to the American people, while running for the most powerful office on Earth. Unafraid to be painted a philanderer, he balked at seeming soft on drugs, and proved to be an utter coward when it came to pulling the reins on police power. During his eight years in office, annual arrests for marijuana doubled.

Clinton ended his administration on a typically hypocritical note, using the power of pardon on behalf of his brother, to wipe away a fifteen year old cocaine conviction, while signing a bill that promised to put a hundred thousand more police on the streets.

When Barack Obama was elected, he invited electronic "town-hall" input from the general public. This would be the People's administration, he promised; he was listening. "Federal resources will not be used to circumvent State laws," he promised, seeming to endorse this sensible interpretation of the Reserved Powers clause in the Constitution.

Medical marijuana, at least, would be hands off. Raids take resources, so, based on this post-election promise, one might believe that law-abiding medical patients and dispensaries would finally be safe from the harassment of the government. A major milestone in the recognition of human rights embodied in the democratic will expressed through Statewide initiatives.

Questions were taken on both the Change.gov and Change.org websites. Over seven thousand queries were submitted, on a broad spectrum of policy issues. A nation eagerly awaited the responses of the new leader to their concerns. Change! What a welcome concept after eight years of Bush neo-fascism!

The number one question presented to the new President-elect was in regard to legalization of cannabis. To the chagrin of many optimistic voters, he dismissed this concern with a single terse sentence indicating, without reservation, that Obama did *not* favor legalization.

No reason was given for opposing the demonstrated position of the people, nor any willingness to discuss reform. Just a flat denial which let it be known that we were fools, if we thought this man actually meant what he had said in 2004: "The war on drugs has been an utter failure. We need to rethink and decriminalize our marijuana laws."

Apparently, having rethought matters, he did not care for the political baggage of being soft on cognitive liberty, or being the President who finally brought sanity to Federal policies. The law remained unchanged.

Later, he actually mocked the tenacity and seriousness of that part of his constituency showing concern with this grave issue, by tossing off an unfunny one-liner: "I don't know what that says about *those people*," he commented. Obama thus waved away the solicited advice from voters about how to do the job for which he'd been sent to Washington, incidentally employing a form of dismissive speech once denounced when applied to African-Americans.

A large class of marginalized citizens were standing up for their rights, and once again an elected official betrays their wishes, insulting them in the process. Here's what it says about *those people*, Mr. President: it says that marijuana smokers are a large proportion of society, that supporters of legalization even larger, and we want to stop being treated as second-class citizens for making choices about what goes into our own bodies.

Soon, even the softening of policy regarding legitimate medical distribution, in States which had chosen to have it, fell by the wayside. By

2011, Federal raids on dispensaries resumed, as if they had never ceased. Just ahead of the Ides of March, the DEA raided twenty-eight such facilities within a single weekend.

One common objection to all this argues that the Federal override of State law is un-Constitutional, in that such control isn't an enumerated power listed in the actual text. Nor is any part of current controlled substance legislation enshrined in Amendment, as was done when alcohol was forbidden.

Banning ethanol, this line of reasoning goes, was so far outside the perceived scope of what could be dictated to the States from on high in Washington, that the Constitution needed to be modified in order to accommodate it. Why, then, was a similar measure not required, in each of the succeeding phases mounting assault on other substances?

Good luck trying such an argument in court, however reasonable though it may seem. Courts, and especially the Supreme Court, have a way of misunderstanding even the most explicit language and reaching the strangest conclusions.

At most, one could say that the Commerce Clause grants Congress authority over interstate trade, which at one time meant actually exporting products across State lines. This was considered necessary, so as to mediate differences in State law in whatever conflicts would inevitably arise.

The notion that interstate commerce would actually involve *two* different States, or even economic activity, was tossed out the window in 1942, with a seemingly small-time Supreme Court case known as *Wickard v. Filburn*. At issue was a recalcitrant farmer, one Roscoe Filburn, who had annoyed the Feds by growing extra wheat for personal consumption. This, in the minds of his prosecutors, somehow interfered with a scheme the government had cooked up to boost the price of grain by restricting production.

Although Filburn argued that the wheat, intended for his own family's use, did not fall under the rubric of interstate commerce, the court unanimously agreed that it did. The logic, if it could be called that, was that had Roscoe not grown the extra wheat, he would have been stuck buying it from, presumably, the same grain distributor he had already sold his market crop to.

This is a little like saying that you're stealing from the supermarket by growing your own tomatoes. In this case, it wasn't necessary for the farmer to export his produce, or even sell it locally, in order for the Feds to stick their noses in. This goes beyond the theory that some of the unauthorized crop may eventually be resold out of State. It isn't necessary for it to ever leave the farm to be covered under this awful ruling.

Cases like this spelled the end for presumption of limits to Federal powers. Indeed, *Wickard v Filburn* is to this day cited in Supreme Court decisions, permitting Washington to override State laws such as medical marijuana initiatives.

To recognize the extent of government subversion of the democratic process, it is instructive to examine the case of Marc Emery, the so-called "Prince of Pot." Marc, a Canadian citizen, is currently a political prisoner, a martyr to repression of the legalization movement. He is serving five years in Federal prison after a long extradition fight, despite a request from his home government that he be repatriated under international treaty.

Marc was prosecuted for selling cannabis seeds, which he did prolifically, leading the market in share. This business was perfectly legal in his home country, and Emery used the profits to fund legalization campaigns. He has invested over four million dollars in a freer future by donating to the legalization cause, as well as founding a magazine celebrating the herb.

The First Amendment, unlike several others, remains a fairly well-protected bastion of rights, at least theoretically. Underdog court victories continue to be predicated on claims of free speech, despite occasional anomalies. In a democracy, or whatever the United States is, public discourse, particularly that which is critical of government policy, is and always ought to be sacrosanct. Free expression and political activity is the essence of liberty.

It is a point of perhaps unjustified pride that the US professes not to jail political dissidents. To do so tends to galvanize public opinion and foment popular unrest. Such tactics are the tools of totalitarian regimes, which govern by forcing the consent of the people. Emery was charged with selling cannabis seeds, but the motivation for pursuing him so relentlessly, across national borders, was pure politics.

As Karen Tandy, DEA Administrator, put it in a gloating press release: "Today's DEA arrest of Marc Scott Emery, publisher of Cannabis Culture Magazine, and the founder of a marijuana legalization group—is a significant blow not only to the marijuana trafficking trade in the US and Canada, but also to the marijuana legalization movement...Drug legalization lobbyists now have one less pot of money to rely on."

The gross impropriety of using drug laws to suppress political causes is a reversal of the democratic process, on which hinges the question of who actually controls this government "of the People, by the People, and for the People."

When the State acts to restrain the debate which might reform it, the resulting policies are anything but democratic. Instead of the people dictating to their representatives, the executive closes the debate by eliminating opposition. This is the very definition of a police State.

ARTICLE VIII:
Suffer the Young

"Whenever is found what is called a paternal government, there is found State education. It has been discovered that the best way to ensure implicit obedience is to commence tyranny in the nursery."—Benjamin Disraeli

The first thing we all learn about democracy is that it doesn't apply to us. To be sure, there is a Flag in every classroom, to which each schoolchild recites a daily loyalty oath. Most can't even spell "allegiance," let alone tell you what it means, but from the earliest age we are collectively forced to pledge our subservience to the colors of the gang with the most guns in the whole world.

We are taught that this is the freest nation on Earth, extending suffrage to all citizens, founded uniquely on principals of popular rule and fair elections. We are taught that our armies only march to war for the best of reasons, that our proud forces are always victorious, defeating dictators and bringing nothing but self-determination wherever they invade. It is easy to impose such ideas on children who have recently abandoned a belief in the Easter Bunny, but the brightest students, destined to be troublemakers, are suspicious of the State version of events from the start.

Nevertheless, when it comes to the ritual where citizens obtain their marginal voice in the way government is constituted, that great grand play in which we choose politicians from column A or B, children are excluded. For the next dozen or so years, a parade of figures will appear in current events lessons, as leaders are periodically emplaced, without any input whatsoever from the younger fifth of the population.

We all start out our lives as second-class entities, under the rule of a power which has untrammeled access to our minds. The marginalization of the young is so deeply embedded in the culture that it is rarely brought into question.

The government isn't interested in the input of young people, but it certainly is heavily invested in trying to control their views on history, morality, and the necessity of conducting military exercises in the name of Freedom.

Age discrimination is among the last refuges of fully official State-sanctioned discrimination based on "inherent traits"; that is, factors relating to the condition of birth, rather than behavioral choices. Disenfranchisement is just one of the ways in which "minor" citizens are afforded secondary status and relegated as non-persons.

A separate legal code governs everything related to the young, from the requirement of compulsory daily education to evening curfews. Indeed, it would be absurd to grant full powers and privileges to infants, who lack the linguistic and motor control to even comprehend, let alone exercise, freedom of choice. This presumption of incapacity carries all the way to the gradated assumption of rights and responsibilities which are withheld, pending the eighteenth birthday, and even the twenty-first.

But this rationale, that developing humans are impaired, does not justify withholding the vote. Literacy, which Constitutionally cannot even be tested as a prerequisite for voting, is widespread among seven-year-olds. The ballot box is a simple device which is often located in the school itself. It would be an easy matter to march the class, in a single-file line, down to the booths to participate in democracy.

One might question the fitness of children to be a part of the voting process. It isn't any more complicated a procedure than most lessons which make up the daily activities of a student; and while the sophistication of such voters might not lead to nuanced decisions, it is an open question whether the empowered electorate's "mature" perspective has led to rational governance, either.

Depriving the elderly of their voting rights, on the basis that their minds are declining rather than developing, would hardly be tolerated. The very old and very young are each disadvantaged, in terms of being able to fully care for themselves. Yet only the young are disenfranchised under the Constitution.

In traditional cultures, predating the twentieth century, the rights and responsibilities of maturity are simultaneously assumed, normally in some kind of ascension ritual which is contemporaneous to puberty. The modern trend has been to delay the social trappings of adulthood, until several years after Nature confers the physical transformation.

No other class is subject to as much governmental control as the underaged. Laws restrict employment, residence, associations, hours of free travel, and require compliance with daily education. Moreover, voluminous statutes regulate their interactions with those who may be only a few years older.

Like most forms of formalized discrimination, this one is wholeheartedly endorsed by the unaffected class. The rights of minors get very little play in the halls of government. Usually, when such phrases are employed, they refer to harsher penalties for adults who have in some way empowered teenagers to practice personal power, rather than debating expanding liberties for the youth.

Without a vote, the contentions of the underaged hold little interest to politicians. Except for the rare successful child actors, who lack legal access to their own fortunes, they control no funds, make no campaign contributions, and thus can be freely ignored.

As a result, disaffected adolescents are prone to flee the constricting social order, creating an emergency among their masters. Runaways are hunted as criminals, with wanted posters and arrest leading to incarceration, simply for choosing to reside away from what is likely to be an intolerably repressive home.

Adults, as the class in power, tend to find such notions frivolous. Juveniles are considered incapable of making competent choices, and must be tightly controlled lest they permanently ruin themselves. Many parents regard child rearing much as a lab experiment on which they will be graded. Such individuals become unreasonably defensive at the idea or implication of misbehavior by their offspring. After all, the job of discipline, and social brainwashing, is considered the responsibility of the parental units.

The general consensus seems to be that it is both right and proper to withhold freedom pending chronological attainment. Minors are expected to wait for their rights, as everyone has had to do. In fact, this is the only sense in which this kind of marginalization is equitable, in that we all experience it during the first part of our lives.

Compulsory subjugation by government institutions, without access to the most minimal means for determining the policies under which one must live, is contrary to democracy. Such an existence is not participatory; it is totalitarian.

The growing minds of tomorrow's adults are fiercely contested turf in the war on cognitive sovereignty. Prohibitionist arguments are strongly rooted in an emotional appeal directed at parents, who are pelted with unsubtle messages that in order for them to be able to control their children, they must allow the government to control everybody else.

Under the current legal system, parents do indeed have a powerful motivation to subscribe to the State's mangled vision of pharmacology. The consequences of a teen drug bust can fall as heavily on the adults who failed to exercise sufficient supervision, as on the young experimenter.

The expenses of bail and an attorney will likely tax the pocketbook of the parents, if they are compassionate enough to provide them. Many do not; counseled by the "tough love" school of selective abandonment, collect calls from jail are refused, leaving juvenile drug defendants to fend for themselves.

Furthermore, the parents themselves can face prosecution for certain actions of their offspring, especially if such activities are conducted partly under their roof. The family home can be seized under forfeiture statutes, if a large enough stash happens to be stored there, with or without the knowledge of the mortgage holders.

Such repercussions are rarely the main concern of prohibitionist parents, however. More compelling is the notion that all their efforts to produce a model worker ant will be squandered, on what the Media makes clear is the fate-determining choice to "get wrapped up in drugs."

The danger is the attraction, and the attraction is the danger, that drives many parents to support the gun-toting nanny-State in its quest to suppress psychotropics. The enemy is pleasure itself, that rival which conformity cannot match. So great is the fear that the investment in social grooming will be wasted in unproductive pursuits of happiness, that some doctrinaire parents go so far as to turn in their own children, believing somehow that this will restore them to the path of obedience.

A more common reaction is to enroll the experimenting teen in rehab. The monstrous substance abuse treatment industry thrives on involuntary commitments, and specializes in accommodating parents of troubled youngsters at imparting the conditioning they have evidently failed to instill. Institutions such as psychiatric wards and "scared straight" camps also make impressive profits, selling their brand of prophylactic incarceration as the solution to the overly independent adolescent.

Teenagers, like everyone else, have psychological issues, and this can include an unhealthy relationship with substances. Instead of providing harm reduction information, models of positive and moderate interactions with mood-altering recreants, young people are doused under a steady stream of inaccurate scare tactics that rightly inspire doubt in the truth of anything authorities have to say.

These days, most of us are turned on to drugs, not by pushers or peers, but by the cops. Seeking to shape rather than be shaped by public opinion, police begin to instill their version of moral pharmacology on placid children, who have no idea what the hell these scary men are talking about.

By the time the indoctrination is over, the kids are able to pass a test on the different major illicit substances, information and misinformation they will soon bring to their inevitable experiments with them.

Indulging a pathological obsession with the consumption habits of the population, the pharmafascist power structure has mounted a massive brainwashing campaign aimed specifically at reaching youth *before* they have a chance to form their own opinions on recreational drugs.

Faced with the difficult decision of whether to staff this program with psychologists, social workers, or even inspirational speakers, the State chose uniformed police to deliver stern lectures to the young.

The DARE program, administered by local law enforcement in three-quarters of all United States school districts, strives to have the first word on the issue of proper drug use. An exercise in unabashed police propaganda, DARE consists primarily of presenting scare tactics and the agenda of abstinence to those least able to resist cultural conditioning: grade school children.

The motive for targeting students is no mystery. Founding director and president Glenn Levant stated, "You have to have programs like DARE in place so police aren't viewed as an occupying army."

The architect of Copaganda 101 was none other than Los Angeles Police Chief Daryl Gates, who later became world famous as head of the department responsible for the Rodney King beating. In addition to causing the city to erupt in flames by defending the brutality of his officers, Chief Gates held a deep and abiding hatred for all users of banned substances.

Testifying before the Senate Judiciary Committee, Chief Gates claimed that casual drug use constitutes treason, and that users "ought to be taken out and shot." This bizarre and draconian stance is reflected in what has become a billion-dollar dupe, draining time and resources from school systems unable to effectively teach math and science.

One might expect a high-ranking official to be fired in reaction to advocating the death penalty for a misdemeanor, but Gates and his ideas have proven to be bulletproof. Although he is now in Hell for his many crimes against humanity, his program of indoctrination continues to be implemented in not only three-fourths of the districts in the United States, but forty-four *other* countries.

A certain class of parents also share this unhealthy preoccupation, obsessed with persuading their children to embrace the bland path of the straight and narrow, leading to a corner office and 401K plan. Terror-stricken at the thought of competing with the far more interesting unauthorized world of sensation from which they have been struggling to shelter their offspring, such parents welcome and gleefully fund this programming.

Indoctrination typically includes demonization. DARE presumes and seeks to establish a prejudice against "the bad guys" who flaunt the system, teaching youngsters to shun the "wrong crowd." Not only does this shield their delicate minds from alternate viewpoints, but it infuses them with a categorical hate, which is very useful to the police State.

Unfortunately, for those who are kept up at night by the thought that teenagers, somewhere, might be smoking marijuana, the program is an abysmal failure. Several studies have shown, in fact, that DARE actually increases the use of cannabis and drugs wherever it is applied.

One such investigation, conducted by the City of Austin auditor, concluded, "Our analysis revealed that no relationship exists between exposure to DARE and a reduction in referrals to TCJC for drug and non-drug-related offenses. Of the non-DARE students in our sample 3.1 percent had contact with TCJC for drug-related offenses compared to 4.9 percent of our sample of DARE students."

For those of you who ditched math, that means that around thirty-six percent *more* juveniles exposed to DARE in Travis County were busted for drugs than their unindoctrinated counterparts. Perhaps it is because more DARE students are turned in by their "friends."

The authors of such reports have met with intimidation and attempts to suppress their work. For example, there was the contentious Research Triangle Institute analysis, which found that the only change DARE seemed to bring was a slight increase in marijuana use.

The real controversy surrounding that study was not the modest finding that the program was ineffective and that kids hated it, but the great lengths to which its administrators would go to cripple the release of such damaging data. A campaign of harassment befell those attempting to publish it.

The inability of DARE to pressure kids away from experimenting with their minds is emblematic of the larger scale zero-tolerance position of law enforcement, and its inverse impact on the problems it purports to solve.

The dirty secret is more than a resolution to an ideological debate. Even those who support the aims of DARE tend to get squeamish about the well-documented failure of the expensive program to deliver on its promises. If it isn't keeping kids from trying drugs, if it actually seems to *encourage* them to do so, what the heck are we paying all of these hundreds of millions of dollars for?

Any bright child exposed to the programming could tell you why the course is ineffective. By placing so much emphasis on the features and slang associated with the various street wares, DARE glorifies what it purports to dissuade. Forbidden fruit is fascinating, and the more the cops drone on and on about how you shouldn't do this or that, the more desperately young rebellious souls will yearn to taste it.

Officers typically bring their egos into the classroom, hoping to impress the children with their tough talk and awe them into line with outrageous fear-mongering. Some kids go ga-ga for the clown with a gun, but the brighter ones see right through it.

For all their talk, most police are startlingly ignorant about drugs. It's not their fault; police departments insist that applicants reveal their experimentation history, and only hire those who have hardly any real-world experience at all. As a result, they tend to share all the misconceptions of those who depend solely on word-of-mouth for their knowledge. They are passing on a mixture of party line and their own off-the-cuff inventions.

When a typical DARE presenter discusses the effects of "hallucinogens," he or she is most likely guessing. You'll hear balderdash about people thinking they can fly, or seeing purple dinosaurs, or hallucinating insects crawling on their bodies. Meanwhile, harm-reduction education, such as proper dosage, or how to manage a freak-out, is left for the drug culture to promote. In theory, no one may become a sworn officer after admitting to ingesting many of these substances. There are, of course, those who break such rules, but there is a more serious issue than mere ignorance with such hypocrites pushing the zero-tolerance agenda.

Not only are the Copagandists spreading laughable misinformation, they are creating dangerous expectations that could create panic, when these children get older and actually encounter someone using these substances.

DARE cops tend to make simplistic, wildly erroneous declarations regarding slang terms that are frequently several decades out of date. One officer claimed that LSD was called *acid* because it eats holes in the brain—rather than because the unwieldy chemical name, *lysergic acid diethylamide*, contains that word.

Often they come off as uninformed assholes, and succeed only in discrediting the prohibition model. Even fourth graders can tell that the dangers are overblown. The slow ones tend to catch on after a few years. There is one lesson getting through, though: hypocrisy. Not all DARE officers practice what they preach.

Pineville, Louisiana DARE Officer Eli Smith was multi-tasking at Lessie Moore Elementary School, taking a break from spreading the gospel of resisting drugs, in order to arrange the transport of multiple kilos of cocaine.

Unfortunately, the person he was working out the deal with was also playing on both sides of the fence, and the shady travel arrangements were broadcast over the police scanner. Smith was arrested and suspended with pay.

Then there was Jim Trimble, a cop and head of the local DARE program in Urbandale, Iowa, who was pulled over with nearly half a pound of methamphetamine, which had been gaffled out of his department's evidence lockers. He was given the inconceivably light sentence of two years probation and a thousand-dollar fine, for stealing twenty grand worth of "controlled" substances from police custody.

The theft charge was dropped as "overkill." Let's just never mind tampering with evidence, either. Strangely, police, invested with the public trust, who go on to betray it by committing crimes under color of authority, are more gently treated than the many civilians they had jailed for far less.

Judge Oxberger, who had recently transferred from the Twilight Zone Superior Court, justified his wrist-slapping treatment by pointing out there was "no evidence that Trimble had bought or sold drugs." One might wonder what else he was planning to do with several hundred grams of meth, if not sell it, or why the judge thought that stealing confiscated contraband is morally superior to paying for it with cold hard cash. Gullible judges are apparently part of the benefit package, for solid members of the law enforcement community like Trimble.

Compare this to the usual treatment for a private citizen found with the same amount of methamphetamine, which would be charged under Iowa statute as a Class B felony, punishable by up to twenty-five years in prison. Possession of more than five grams is not normally probation eligible.

The sympathetic Judge Oxberger, ignoring all evidence to the contrary, gave Trimble a mile of slack when he stated, "I'm sure this is a one-time incident for you." Obviously, Oxberger had never seen a DARE presentation, or he would know that *one* time is *too many* when it comes to drugs.

Trimble was immediately fired, but the judge also "sentenced" him to one hundred hours of community service, incredibly, to be served back in the classroom, lecturing kids once again about the evils of drugs.

DEA agent Lee Paige was not actually working for DARE, but his amusing tale is nonetheless symbolic of what's wrong with using cops to educate children. During a youth group demonstration on drug and gun safety in 2004, the dreadlocked undercover agent literally shot himself *in the foot*—immediately after boasting that he was the only person in the room "professional enough," to handle what he *thought* was an *unloaded* Glock 40. The gun fortunately was aimed toward the ground, and Paige was the only one injured by this criminal negligence in a roomful of families.

As if that were not enough of a reason to cut the show-and-tell short, Paige, courageously walking off his gunshot injury, continued his speech. Incredibly, within a minute of shooting himself, he reached for the next gun in the demonstration, this time a semi-automatic assault rifle, while parents nervously grabbed their children and headed for the door. Fortunately, the chorus of protest from the frightened crowd prevented this maniac from proceeding with his all-too-real demonstration.

The video of this ironic episode aired widely in the Media, prompting Paige to sue the DEA for not squashing it. Although he had been publicly humiliated for all the right reasons, his inflated opinion of himself did not diminish. In his *pro se* complaint, demanding money from his former employer for engaging in some rare transparency, Paige heaped praise on himself, claiming that he had been "very effective" and "one of the best undercover agents, if not the best."

Perhaps the most offensive feature of police-run education is the attempt of these officers to capitalize on the naive youngsters in their care, by grooming them to spy on others and turn snitch. Many DARE classrooms are equipped with a box where tattle-tales can leave tips for the cops. They've even reassigned meaning to the traditional "three R's": now they are "*Recognize, Resist, Report.*" The basic skills of a good citizen in a totalitarian State.

Children are encouraged to become informers, even against their own parents. Eager to please the authoritative adults, inductees into the cult of DARE are taught to innocently notify the authorities of the private vices of others.

Darrin Davis, aged nine, took the cops' word for it when he called them to report a small quantity of speed he found while snooping in his parent's bedroom. "I thought the police would come and get the drugs and tell them drugs are wrong. They never said they would arrest them...I always thought police were honest and told the truth. But in court, I heard them tell the judge that I wanted my mom and dad arrested. That is a lie. I did not tell them that."

He certainly didn't expect his parents to lose their jobs and home, his father to serve three months in jail, or his parents to divorce over the aftermath of his playing at cop. So traumatized was he by these real-world consequences of allowing himself to be used by the authorities, that he eventually set fire to a house, in hopes that he could be in jail with his Dad. Sadly, the poor boy so misunderstood the system which had used him to destroy his family, as to believe that a father and son would be housed together behind bars.

The way children are programmed to react to the option of psychotropics is one of the many shameful excesses of prohibition. The outlandish and highly unscientific representations of illicit substances in the Media is one of the most disturbing examples of collusion with the Thought Police.

One notable example was targeted at very young children indeed, the infamously hideous animated feature billed as *Cartoon All Stars to the Rescue*. Funded by McDonald's, a company which does wonderful things for children's health, this piece of overblown trash was simultaneously broadcast as part of Saturday Morning cartoons on *all three* major networks and several minor ones.

The marquee was impressive enough; an unlikely convergence of cartoon worlds as diverse as the *Smurfs, Baby Muppets, Bugs Bunny, Chipmunks*, Disney's *DuckTales* and even the animated version of *ALF*. The event was billed, Trojan Horse style, as a sort of Grand Unified Theorem of ultra-juvenile entertainment.

Instead of entertainment, a nation full of stunned, pajama-clad prepubescents clutched their cereal bowls in horror, as they were treated to a full-on video indoctrination on the evils of marijuana.

So important was this moment in the lives of the little ones, that President Bush I, along with his grandmotherly First Lady, personally introduced the special. After a brief platitudinous lecture in creepy scripted monotone, recorded in what appeared to the annex of a retirement home, the elderly rulers turned the brainwashing over to the animators.

The story begins with the theft of a little girl's piggy-bank by her out-of-control brother, so he can buy marijuana. While such atrocities no doubt do occur, they are hardly the inevitable result of moderately costly cannabis use. Such crimes, when they are in fact motivated by the high price of contraband, are of course the result of prohibition in the first place, but have more to do with some individuals' propensity for larceny, than the particular influence of any drug. Others, the vast majority, deal honestly with their substance of choice and prefer to finance their indulgence with their own hard-earned cash.

The following half hour is a panorama of all the usual staples: the overbearing peer pressure which pushed the poor boy to puff his first toke, irrevocably transforming him from a preppy geek, with school spirit, to a soulless marijuana junkie who robs from his sister; the grotesquely personified demonic spirit of the devil weed itself, who lures children to evil ways; the stern lecture from Bugs Bunny about drugs ruining your life; and bizarre and highly unscientific illustrations of the damage they can do to one's brain.

For this extremely odd half hour of broadcast television, the range of options was narrowed to one: this horrible misappropriation of entertainment to push a political agenda, on an audience which was poorly equipped to apply critical thinking to the Saturday Morning Fantasy.

Children don't normally question the authenticity of what they watch during this time. They don't frown at the Smurfs, changing the channel while muttering "how improbable!" They don't question whether Daffy Duck as a psychic would really be able to see your loser future in a crystal ball, or whether marijuana actually causes brain damage.

The camouflage provided by the cartoon characters hides from children, but reveals to us, the underhandedness of the prohibitionist mania. The production was deliberately aimed at a demographic that typically has not yet begun experimentation, and contains the message that a loving sibling will tell mom and dad about any shenanigans. Thus there are spies everywhere.

Another, more pervasive, manifestation of the Media pushing the Statist agenda are the omnipresent ads from the partly government funded Partnership for a Drug-Free America. This improbable appellation has several fairly obvious flaws. First, it is as if these people, despite all evidence, truly believe that through enough propaganda, and enough brutal law enforcement, drug use could actually be abolished. History has amply demonstrated that this simply is not the case.

Secondly, the goal, as stated, would hardly be desirable. Drug-free? As in no medicine? Only the religious fringes would support a policy like that. For that matter, what about the pharmaceutical speed and other mind-altering prescriptions being issued like candy to an estimated *six million* young people between the ages of six and eighteen? According to Shire Pharmaceuticals, manufacturer of the amphetamine called Adderall™ (maybe because it helps with math?), on the order of *36.5 million* prescriptions are written annually to supply juvenile patients.

Is the doping of problem children by psychiatrists less of a crisis than self-directed illicit use? Most of these prescriptions are for Attention Deficit Disorder, an affliction whose rise coincides suspiciously with the advent of video games and cable television.

It would be off-mission for the ads to criticize this sort of thing, however, since a great deal of the funding for the Partnership for a Drug-Free America comes from, you guessed it, drug companies. Pharmaceutical giants, including Johnston & Johnston, DuPont, Bristol-Myers Squibb, Merck and Hoffmann-La Roche all made significant contributions during the first few years of the PDFA campaign, as did tobacco and alcohol merchants Philip Morris, RJ Reynolds, and Anheuser-Busch.

The "partnership" turns out to be a collaboration between the corporate interests protecting their monopoly on the legal drug trade, and the Federal government guarding their interests in promoting prison-filling hype.

Although their website is quick to emphasize the "science-based" nature of the information with which PDFA bombards the public, their ads are anything but scientific. Lacking in nuance and balance, the ads epitomize the broad brush of pharmafascist rhetoric.

Again, the strategy is usually to make unsophisticated generalizations about the evils of illicit consumption. Marijuana is frequently the focus, either as target of unproven claims about harmfulness, or in her supporting role as a purported "gateway" to the world of hard drugs like crack.

Best-known, perhaps, is the frying-egg metaphor. In the 1987 debut clip from the newly formed propaganda mill, an egg, representing the viewer's brain, is broken and dropped in a frying pan to dramatically sizzle away. The announcer matter-of-factly identifies the crackling albumen with the normal pharmacodynamics of "drugs." No mention is made of any specific substance or class of drug. Apparently this is a side effect of all of them.

It's a good thing PDFA showed up with their "science-based" perspective, since most people did not know about drugs raising cerebral temperatures to 350 degrees Fahrenheit, or the structural similarities between unfertilized chicken embryos and the human brain.

Such blatant distortion is typical of the messages spread by this organization, which obviously had as much contempt for accuracy as for the intelligence of the viewers. Yet PDFA would for the next two decades represent the gold standard in manipulating the minds of both parents and children, on a subject about which the ad's creators clearly knew nothing.

Over the years we would see a virtual blooper reel of embarrassing, unrestrained nonsense, replete with non sequiturs and featuring some the strangest faces we never expected to see lecturing us on pharmacology.

Pee-Wee Herman was recruited to deliver a *very serious* message, about crack, to the children of America. For those who don't remember this marginal character, he was at one time a quite popular, although somewhat creepy, figure in children's entertainment. Thin and pale, with a bow-tie and a suit fashioned in the 1950s, Pee-Wee was played by comedian Paul Reubens, whose shtick consisted largely of pretending he was a hyperactive five-year-old.

Unfortunately, he ran into some legal trouble for indecent exposure in a porn theater, which created a setback to his career in preschool-oriented entertainment. While we fully support Pee-Wee's right to pull it as hard as he wants, surrounded by consenting adults in an environment having no other purpose, the plea arrangement put him to work in one of the most ludicrous pieces of distorted fear-mongering to hit the airwaves yet.

During fifty-six very long seconds, Pee-Wee, under twin spotlights in a darkened room which could be the interrogation chamber of the Gestapo, holds up a vial of supposed crack. Wearing a red bow-tie and a hanky peeking out of his pocket, the paragon of style informs us that crack isn't *glamorous* or *cool*, and that it could kill you every time you smoke it.

Of course, poor Pee-Wee was not the first celebrity to deliver the State's anti-drug rap under court order, nor the last, but his appearance in this ad represents a low point in the history of propaganda. Even the vial of crack looks embarrassed to be seen with him.

These "public service messages" don't merely seek to shape the debate on illegal drugs; they aim to squash the debate entirely. The campaigns, which innocently pose as a project to deter drug abuse, represent a smear campaign, particularly against the users of marijuana.

No other class would tolerate such a vicious portrayal in government-funded advertising. Cannabis users are presented as chronic losers, suffering from brain damage, stealing to support their habits, and inevitably crack addicts as well.

Under the Fairness Doctrine, legalization groups should also be given airtime to show the many successful and prominent individuals who proudly enjoy cannabis, the physicians who point out that the toxicity of marijuana compares favorably to nearly all pharmaceutical products as well as alcohol, and the many medical patients whose welfare is visibly improved by the ingestion of the herb.

Unfortunately, the Fairness Doctrine was abolished by the Reagan administration in 1987—the same year that the PDFA launched its one-sided campaign.

The insertion of prohibitionist programming isn't limited to ads and specials, which for all their inanity, at least are clearly marked. Sometimes, the brain soap comes unlabeled, embedded into the scripts of shows whose only agenda is supposed to be entertainment.

Beginning in 1997, the Office of National Drug Control Policy, under Czar Barry McCaffrey, expended over one billion dollars, to promote the official position that drugs are just awful. That wasn't the scandal; everyone is used to seeing TV reality purchased in thirty-second increments, in support of all kinds of absurd, simplistic view points.

The average American is only dimly aware that the illegality is a State invention, some apparently embracing the idea that criminality is a property of the substances themselves. So it seems natural and good that airtime is bought at public expense to stop this scourge. If drugs aren't so bad, why are they against the law?

It is quite another thing when the State directs the creation of popular culture. It is there, for some, that the line is crossed from education to mind control. We confess to being unsure where exactly that line ought to be drawn, but it must surely be to one side of the government ordering the content of comedy.

Under a Faustian arrangement uncovered by independent online magazine Salon.com, the major broadcast networks accepted government funding in exchange for script approval on such popular dramas as *Beverly Hills 90210, ER, Chicago Hope,* as well as comedies like *Home Improvement, The Wayans Bros.,* and the *Drew Carey Show.*

With all major broadcast networks participating, the payola scheme seems to have come about through the marriage of circumstances. The ONDCP had pre-purchased the ad time at cut rates, which interfered with new opportunities to ride the dot-com boom then just underway. The bargain which was arrived at gave government agents final say on the content of mainstream television.

The precedent is a frightening one: if the State can secretly manipulate the masses by way of embedded messages beaming from the ever-present TV screen, where does it end? How often do collusions like this occur without being revealed at all? What does it mean for the politicians to be literally programming the voters who elect them?

Will networks take money to promote an unpopular war? Will sitcom families sit around the breakfast table praising the latest corporate bailout? Worse, will courageous anti-government plot-lines be edited out by the Ministry of Truth, before ever being seen by the actors? We have no way of knowing how much of this is already going on, but it is clear that the Federal government and corporate Media conglomerates have many mutual interests, as well as powers over each other.

ARTICLE IX:
The Nightly Newspeak

"Whoever controls the Media, the images, controls the culture."
—Allen Ginsburg

The mass Media is often a willing accomplice in the War on Certain Drugs. No, that is not entirely accurate. The problem is not truly with all manifestations of collective communication. When we mention "the Media," we almost unconsciously refer to a single form of it. So domineering and definitive is broadcast television, beaming Copaganda into living rooms under the guise of news reports, that Big Brother's screens seem more real to entranced viewers, than the material world directly accessible through their eyes and ears.

One might compare the macrocosm of a social culture with the microcosm of a laboratory culture; in each case, the medium dictates the nature of the content consumed by the sample, and in each case influencing the end result. A social culture fed on a steady stream of audiovisual conditioning can be predicted to respond in a particular way. We all get the same bits of packaged information, selected content, and slanted viewpoints, millions of viewers at a time.

We are of course free to deactivate the enslaver of senses, unlike the poor denizens of Oceania, or even exclude it from our presence. Very few do, however, as there are not many drugs which can match the addictive power of pixels changing colors at two dozen frames per second. With no input from the spellbound viewer, other than occasional phone-text votes for the next new singing star, the medium, specifically, which is most frequently complicit in bending reality toward the government's desired viewpoint is the omnipresent screen, inserting electronic paradigms into the very open minds of the viewing public.

Strictly speaking, the other media tend not to have a particular slant. Music, if anything, has historically been a refuge for free-thinkers, whose practitioners are likely to be firmly pro on the issue of free drugs. Musicians, in general, tend to have a positive attitude toward mood elevation and write passionately in favor of lifting restrictions. Films, too, tend to show recreational use in context, and not necessarily tout an over-the-top prohibitionist perspective. There are notable extreme exceptions, but overall these tend to swing fairly equally to either end of the spectrum.

Even print publication, taken as a whole industry, tends to be more or less balanced. The spectrum of periodical reporting represents a wide variety of positions, and even frequently preserves the quaint notion of journalistic objectivity lost to their counterparts on television. One is as likely to encounter stories which are critical of drug policy as supportive of it. This reality is also reflected on the internet, where both viewpoints are to be readily found.

Television, though, is different from all of these. Visual programming, which itself functions as an electronic depressant, is dominated by a Statist mentality, showing itself in every nightly news edition. Stories about drugs—large busts, new products hitting the street, new appropriations to law enforcement—are dutifully reported as the positive actions of a well-run and well-justified campaign against a vague, but definite, menace.

There is a constant presumption, that we, the viewers, *want* these arrests to occur, that we *want* contraband destroyed, that we are out there in TV Land applauding these efforts to rid our society of pernicious influences. Spokesmen for police and prosecutors appear on podiums, congratulating themselves and validating their budgets. Legalization groups, in general, are not invited to share their viewpoint.

Absent is the alternate perspective: that with these arrests a terrible tragedy has occurred, individuals who were previously free and pursuing happiness will now serve many years in prison. There is no mention of how much it will cost to incarcerate these non-violent offenders, or the consequences to their families. Instead, there is vague blather celebrating yet another futile act of brutality in the name of saving society.

News, in print or on screen, consists primarily of reporting the activities of government. Whether it is covering the campaign of some politician, a speech by an elected official, or a report on some criminal apprehension or trial, the essential function of the evening and nightly news is to communicate the perspective desired by the State.

So it should come as no real surprise that the slant is toward the official position. Access to the space in front of those podiums is granted, with the understanding that reporters will apply the specified focus and scope to the resulting story. Police reports are vital to the news effort, and are indeed the bulk of what constitutes local news.

As the clock pushes forward, the programming shifts to action-dramas, in which police protagonists hunt down the bad guys. Over two hundred series of this nature have been broadcast since the inception of television.

The portrayal of police on such shows is alternately comical, stereotyped, or heroic. While the vast majority of the scripts center on the classic homicide detective, a righteous figure dedicated to pinning down the worst criminal acts, during the 1980s police dramas appeared celebrating the work of the narcotics officer.

One popular cop drama was *Miami Vice*, starring a stylish, hip Don Johnson, who maintained a suave ladies-man presence while hunting the villains of the drug trade. Over the top and filled with gratuitous gunfire, the marine atmosphere and glimpse into the glamorous lives of the cocaine cowboys who would be dead by the hour's end, *Vice* transformed the work of prohibition agents into a hit.

Another was *21 Jump Street*, which debuted in 1987 on the new Fox network, featuring the even more dashing Johnny Depp as an undercover cop. Depp and his co-stars infiltrated high schools, looking for trouble and invariably finding it. Geared toward the young people who were the fictional targets of these sting activities, the show always had a Statist moral, which was generally spelled out in a brief aftershow lecture from the cast on what to do if confronted by illegality.

The police drama is standard fare on network and now cable listings, for several perfectly good reasons. Police work, especially when fictionalized, makes for a lively, fast-paced story. There is the struggle between good and evil, intrigue, and violent action. Almost any situation can turn into a car chase or gun battle. Subplots can be generated between maverick cops, and uptight administrators furious at the expensive side-effects of reckless vigilance.

Popular as these shows have been, there are disadvantages in producing them. In a fit of Spartan creativity during a writer's strike, Fox created the reality cop show, using no scripts, no actors, and no narrator. The set would be the streets of cities across the land. Gone was the time-filler drivel about the aging detective's empty personal life and the improbable repetition of the whodunnit.

Cops has been bringing the raw reality of street-level arrests to nightly TV screens for over twenty years. The show is stark, action-packed, and shows the daily routine of an officer on patrol. At least once per episode, that includes wrestling with suspects over drugs.

The acronym stands for *Carefully Orchestrated Propaganda Syndication*. Well, not really, but it would be accurate. Patrol cars are sent out on the night's duties, to chat with camera workers, light up a traffic stop, and often enough chase down a fleeing suspect, who is perhaps more frightened by the cameras than the cops chasing them.

Part of the message, implied in the show's catchy reggae theme song, is that there is no escaping the police. Overwhelming force will be brought down on the heads of anyone who attempts to run or divest themselves of incriminating evidence.

Brutality, judgmentalism, bristling contempt for the people they're stuffing in the back of their cars—the fifteen-minute stars of *Cops* let it all hang out. To be sure, you'll never see cops administer beatings on the air which are so egregious as to be prosecutable, but the standard of acceptable force is quite high. Any viewer of the show knows that resistance will be met with a slam to the ground, a knee on your neck, and three or four firm grips on your wrist, twisting your arm roughly into place.

The dozen or so shows using this format, and that of the closely related jail reality subgenre, are like watching a succession of car crashes. Even though you are watching the filmed destruction of a human being suffering one of the worst of all fates, being safely on the other side of the television screen imparts a sense of security.

Shows like these desensitize us to the cruelty of arrest. Much like the meat-eater who doesn't think too much about where dinner came from, the average American is programmed to associate the cuff and stuff routine with the resolution of the drama, and tune out the painful prosecution ahead.

In contrast, reality court shows, which actually appeared first, with an entire cable network dedicated to live trial broadcast, have been a dismal failure. The dronings of lawyers have proven unpalatable fare for the American couch potato. Fictional court dramas are watchable by virtue of artistic license and judicious editing, but the real thing is pure torment for most viewers.

This to some degree reflects the disconnect between popular culture and the law. Consumers of tele-reality are dazzled by the gruff power of the cops, the grim tension of the jail yard. Not quite so interesting is how they go from one to the other.

The shoe is on the other foot, though, when an uninvited camera arrives to document possible police misconduct. Big Brother does not like his unedited actions broadcast to the Outer Party, much less the proles, and lashes out with handcuffs when the eye of the beholder is turned on him. Civilian watch groups are frequently intimidated, ordered to surrender their recording devices, and threatened with arrest. Sometimes these threats are carried out live on digital file.

That's what happened to young rabble-rouser Robert Wanek on May 6, 2011, when he approached a canine unit outside the Whapeton, North Dakota Police Department, camera in hand, to report on Fourth Amendment abuses for the MNChange.org website with which he was affiliated.

When the officer, a K-9 operator named Dustin Hill, noticed the teenager filming him as he casually conversed with some unknown party through the passenger window of an unmarked vehicle, Wanek stated that he had come to ask the police about unwarranted drug raid practices.

As soon as he mentioned the purpose of his investigation, he was hastily handcuffed for "interfering with a police investigation" and detained inside the station for over an hour, until it was determined he had broken no law.

In fact, the precocious filmmaker activist wryly observed, "I told him that North Dakota law, United States law, and the First Amendment gives me *every* right to film *anybody* in public."

Upon his release, Wanek posted the video online, with a plea for a call flood to the Whapeton police. Hundreds of outraged callers tied up the switchboard at the police station, preventing the department from conducting business and prompting an investigation. Hill was suspended without pay for five days and required to take classes on proper arrest procedure and Constitutional Law.

Hill isn't the only cop who fears being taped on the job. As technology improves, more and more citizens are capturing their own arrests, or someone else's, on cell phones or hand-held cameras.

Despite a clear and unambiguous right to a free press, which must certainly entail documenting the activities of public employees, prosecutors are more frequently applying wiretap statutes, intended to limit police surveillance of citizens, to criminalize the opposite behavior.

That police are generally hostile to cameras when conducting unscripted activities is understandable. After all, such exposure of routine curtailment of civil rights can have negative personal consequences for them, including loss of their job, civil penalties, and, all too rarely, criminal prosecution. Even if their department supports them, a video of outrageous misconduct can so focus public outcry that their firing will be forced.

The first major public explosion of unrest stemming from a citizen recording of unsafe behavior by public safety officers occurred when George Holliday turned his camera on a police riot in progress. Four Los Angeles police officers, pumped on adrenaline following a high-speed chase, were caught on tape administering what would become the most infamous example of police brutality around the world.

A total of fifty-six metal baton blows can be counted on the grainy Holliday recording, treatment hard to square with the LAPD motto *"To Protect and Serve."* They served King the beating of his life as he struggled to crawl away and pled for them to stop. According to the civil lawsuit he later filed against the city, King suffered eleven fractures of the skull, a broken ankle, shattered teeth, kidney and brain damage, and the considerable emotional weight of such a traumatizing assault.

Without the video, this would have been just another incident of violence in the course of law enforcement, the sort of thing one should expect to happen when cops are issued weaponry and a license to perpetrate whatever barbarity can be concealed under the color of authority.

The gratuitous display of force by the LAPD was too much ugly reality to keep the lid on. For many, the Rodney King case became a symbol for a kind of abuse which usually was kept under wraps. His case became a lightening rod for the numerous groups calling for racial justice.

Rodney King being black doubtless had something to do with the angst from which the officers attacking him were seeking cathartic relief. The LAPD in particular has a distinctive reputation for abusing arrestees of color. Less frequently mentioned is that, apart from being African-American, King was also a drug suspect, falsely as it turned out.

In the police report, and later at trial, the officers would claim that they believed King to be under the influence of PCP, which as every DARE kid knows confers superhuman strength and instigates crazed violent behavior. It is telling that police officers are trained to respond to such delicate psychiatric situations with skull-cracking brutality.

Toxicology later revealed that King was not under PCP, but the idea that he had been was at the forefront of the officers' defense when they were brought to trial for excessive force. The proceedings were an utter farce. The defense was permitted a change of venue to sunny Simi Valley, where none of the jurors would be themselves African-American. In a verdict utterly blind to the self-evident criminality of the beating, which even President Bush denounced, this jury acquitted the three officers who had actively participated, and deadlocked on Sgt. Stacey Koon, who had supervised the assault.

Los Angeles and other cities burst into full-scale civil riot. Fifty-three people died and thousands more were injured, in a revolt not only against police power, but the mechanism of society itself. Over a billion dollars of property was destroyed, and more than three thousand businesses damaged. Some seven thousand fires were set over the next six days, overwhelming the capacity of emergency services while a horrified nation watched its second-largest city apparently being burned to the ground.

The blowback was highly regrettable, and King took to the airwaves to meekly beg for order. The riots became an outlet for social and economic grievances that had been building for decades. Most of the victims had no real complicity in anything being protested, but a powerful statement was made to the ruling class that the population would not tolerate such impunity and brutality in silence.

As police become edgier about being filmed on duty, citizen activists have found the camera mightier than both pen and sword, in bringing accountability to supposed public servants. The largest such organization, CopWatch, was founded in Berkeley, California, to monitor police abuses against the homeless population along Telegraph Avenue.

New Haven CopWatch member Luis Luna, armed with his iPhone, transformed from observer to subject when he happened upon an arrest outside a Crown Street nightclub. Observed by Assistant Chief Melendez to be taking video, Luna was told, "You can join them" and that he could watch the incident "on the six o'clock news." When he protested that he was only taking pictures, Melendez retorted, "*You* don't take pictures of *us*." Then he grabbed the phone, and ordered Luna's arrest for interfering with police.

This is a common pattern; the cops, who are actually the ones interfering with citizens exercising their Constitutional right to document police actions, turn their focus on the video observer, levying charges of hindering, or, ludicrously, violating the privacy rights of on-duty law enforcement operating in public space, as if any such right could exist.

Luna, faced with the expense of mounting a defense, opted to accept the plea deal offered by the prosecution rather than take his chances in the courtroom. The sentence for the reduced charge of creating a public disturbance was only a fine, instead of jail, but what galled him was trading his dignity for his freedom.

When asked by the judge if he was guilty, Luna hesitated, rightly feeling himself innocent of any wrongdoing. "He explained I have to plead guilty," Luna said, or the deal would be off. "At that moment, when I said I'm guilty, I felt like I was going against myself."

Another CopWatcher arrested in the line of duty was Jacob Crawford, who was one of hundreds in attendance at the first annual Cincinnati CopWatch block party in 2003. The revelers were literally minding their own business, community organizing, when speeding patrol cars dropped in uninvited. The units, who were responding to a cancelled call for backup nearby, turned their gatecrashing into an object lesson on why the organization exists in the first place.

Barreling past the barricades at full speed, the police cars transformed a peaceful assembly into a hazardous situation. Crawford was unfortunate enough to be recording the festivities while standing in the middle of the street, which had been closed for the permitted event. "It all happened so quick," he recounted. "The next thing I knew, I was on the ground."

Screaming hysterical obscenities and accusing Crawford of somehow endangering the police, who were the ones recklessly and unnecessarily speeding down a closed thoroughfare, the arresting officer did not apparently realize her harangue was being recorded by Crawford, even after he'd been stuffed in the back of the cruiser.

"You put *my* life in danger, my *partner's* life in danger, and everyone on this street in danger. There're cops getting their asses kicked by *drug dealers*, and you fucking blocked us from getting to them!"

Of course this last bit was poignantly untrue, as the suspect in question, whose apprehension was also digitally captured by well-equipped CopWatchers, had offered little resistance, and was truly the one getting his "ass kicked" by two stout, armed cops. He was more interested in swallowing his stash, than fighting back against the two-on-one assault.

Moreover, not only had the assistance request been terminated, moments after being placed, they had obviously found time to stop and arrest a pedestrian. When onlookers demanded to know what Crawford was being charged with, she curtly bellowed, "I'll figure it out." Arrest first, find the crime later.

Between themselves, the two officers looked up the law, trying to find something to pin Crawford with, discussing his fate as if he, and the still undetected camera, were not listening. "That's a *misdemeanor*," one said, rejecting a charging suggestion. "I want to charge him with a *felony*."

"What's the other felony, what's the other one?" her partner asked.

"I don't know, I'm going to try to find one."

Despite having done nothing but wielding a camera, and nearly getting run over by a speeding cop car, Crawford was charged with felony obstruction, and took his bogus charges before a jury, who acquitted him.

In South Miami Beach over the 2011 Memorial Day weekend, the unmitigated might of the armed police was turned squarely to bear on several civilians, who had been recording them fiercely pumping buckets of lead into the vehicle of a suspect.

Narces Benoit and his girlfriend Ericka Davis happened to be equipped with a video cell phone, when all Hell broke loose on Collins Avenue. Officers were violently apprehending Raymond Harice, who was wanted in an earlier incident involving reckless driving and fleeing police, allegedly injuring one. Surrounding the stopped vehicle, the dozen cops or so rained bullets on Harice, perhaps in retaliation for the trouble he'd earlier given them.

The couple, spotted by police documenting the massive spray of bullets, were aggressively approached by a bicycle cop who, with gun drawn, demanded the recording device.

Benoit, following orders after seeing this brutal slaying, carefully exited the vehicle with hands up, while the cop placed his firearm against Davis' head. Cleverly, Benoit palmed the memory chip, hiding it in his mouth, while his camera was confiscated and stomped on by the jackboots. He was then handcuffed, released, given his phone back, taken in for questioning, and then forced to hand over the broken phone again.

"They just wanted the videos," Davis said. "That's all they were concerned about."

Lest one think this is some concoction of anti-police zealots, Davis' own mother works in law enforcement. "I'm used to dealing with police. I have never had a view like that of an officer in my life. I mean, I'm shaking just thinking about it."

According to Benoit and Davis, they were not the only citizens filming the event to be shook down by the police for their video. They say the cops also took other people's cell phones, and smashed them as well. The hasty cover-up was not enough to keep unauthorized camera viewpoints from the public eye, but the intent to do so was clearly the top priority for the swarms of police at that dangerous moment.

Nor do the top brass of law enforcement brook defection in their own ranks. In an episode torn from the playbook of Soviet Stalinism, NYPD officer Adrian Schoolcraft was taken in handcuffs to a psychiatric ward, after he went public with secret recordings and other documentation showing his department was engaged in manipulating crime statistics and enforcing quotas on officers.

Schoolcraft, a model cop at the 81st Precinct in Brooklyn, who had received a medal for meritorious service in 2006, and an award for his dedication to the department in 2008, says he originally began packing recording equipment to protect himself from complaints by the public. As he expanded his recordings to also guard against any possible accusations from his superiors, he began to realize that he was inadvertently collecting evidence of corruption that was endemic at his precinct.

Among other irregularities, the video showed a widespread practice of falsifying training logs, so that they would show officers receiving instruction that they had not; downgrading robbery and assault crimes so as to make the precinct seem more successful than it really was; and illegal pressure on cops to bring in a specified number of each designated type of offense, or face transfer or firing.

The practice of quotas is contrary to New York statute, not because it violates the rights of civilians to be free from institutional harassment driven by numbers and revenue, but because it infringes on the State labor code, which prohibits retribution against officers who don't write enough citations.

After providing substantiation of these practices to internal affairs, Schoolcraft became the focus of hostility from his supervisors and colleagues. He was assigned to desk duty and forced to surrender his firearm. Plagued by stress, he saw a department psychologist with complaints of insomnia, as well as stomach and chest pains. She advised him that his problems were medical and cleared him as mentally fit for duty.

Just four days later, when pressure at work reached the boiling point, Schoolcraft clocked out an hour early, following an upsetting clash with his lieutenant. That's when the Thought Police showed how they react when one of their number fails to toe the line.

Although Schoolcraft says he was given permission to go home sick, several hours later his residence was entered by the Emergency Services Unit, the elite tactical squad used to subdue the most dangerous suspects.

With all he knew about hanky-panky at the "Eight-One," Schoolcraft was apparently considered threatening indeed, especially to Deputy Chief Michael Marino, who had already run into trouble over quota enforcement in 2006.

Using a key obtained from the landlord, Marino led the raid. After a brief standoff, Schoolcraft's boss had him declared EDP, an emotionally disturbed person, and transported to Jamaica Hospital to be confined for six days.

The involuntary commitment raises a number of issues, not the least of which is why police, rather than mental health professionals who are actually trained in making such a determination, are granted authority to declare someone sufficiently mentally ill that they be confined without any criminal acts or charges. More importantly, if this is how police departments treat whistleblowers in their ranks, what other corruption is being successfully concealed?

Propaganda is often as much about what information is restricted, as that which is promulgated. In a society with a free press, the government is frequently unable to control the flow of news, which today can spread through informal but wide-reaching channels of the internet.

It is thanks to this freedom, such as it is, that events like those in this book are not completely hidden from the public eye. Journalists and citizen documentarians face repression and arrest, but the story emerges often enough that an inquisitive soul can piece the puzzle together. That doesn't stop the State from trying to kill inconvenient stories, however. Because of the nature of such behind-the-scenes censorship, we may only be infrequently aware when such manipulation of collective reality occurs.

So it is not a surprise, although it is a disgrace, that pharmafascists work their retrospective editing on agencies devoted entirely to health. One recent and obvious example occurred when the National Cancer Institute, in an historic move, indicated on its website the data demonstrating that cannabinoids exhibit anti-carcinogenic properties.

After eleven days, though, the politically sensitive, but medically sound, assertion was altered to remove references to the value cannabis shows in reducing tumors. Instead, the new language put forth the notion that the benefits of medical cannabinoids were limited to symptom management and palliative care.

In fact, the news that cannabis may contain the key to controlling, or even curing, some cancers is not news at all. Medical documentation that THC curbs growth in at least three kinds of tumors has been available since 1974, when the DEA shut down a study at the Medical College of Virginia finding that lung, breast and viral leukemia forms of cancer responded to THC in lab rats, prolonging life by as much as thirty-six percent.

Efficacy in treating autoimmune rejection syndrome related to organ transplant was also shown. The study which was called, "Antineoplastic Activity of Cannabinoids," appeared in the NCI Journal in 1975, but has since more or less disappeared down the memory hole.

The Ford administration in 1976 put a kibosh on independent medical cannabis research, by universities or Federal health agencies, despite such extremely promising results during the previous decade. And in September of 1983, the Reagan/Bush administration ordered that evidence of such research be quietly destroyed.

Copies were apparently so rare, that when Spanish researcher Dr. Manuel Guzman set up a similar study in Madrid, the legendary Virginia paper was nowhere to be found. He finally obtained a copy which had been buried in the UC Medical School library in Davis.

"I was aware of the existence of this research," he told the resourceful soul who supplied it to him. "In fact, I have attempted many times to obtain the journal article on the original research by these people, but it has proven impossible."

The Madrid study reported similarly spectacular results: not only were there no harmful biological or neurological repercussions from the large doses of cannabis being applied, but eighty percent of the THC-treated rats injected with brain cancer cells lived longer than the control group. Three of fifteen rats, twenty percent, had their tumors eradicated entirely.

It bears mentioning that virtually all the broadcast Media in the United States are owned by six corporate conglomerates which are interdependent with the government, are licensed by it to operate, and hold a group monopoly on free information by virtue of connivance within it. The intersecting values of government and television make the latter the perfect venue for the former to push its version of truth on the citizenry, and manipulate our views on crucial matters of policy.

Time Warner, General Electric, CBS, Walt Disney, News Corp, and Viacom control the hive mind. Even if you don't subject yourself to their simplistic packaging of reality, the majority of your neighbors do. Ultimately, the context and slant of any major news coverage, or conspicuous absence of it, is defined in the boardrooms of these companies who traffic in the human mind.

Orwell envisioned screens that won't shut off, but in practice that just makes the mind tune out the undifferentiated patter. It's hardly necessary to force people to watch and listen; most households willingly pay a monthly fee to access America's true drug of choice.

All the arguments prohibitionists apply to marijuana are more appropriate to a criticism of television. TV makes you unmotivated, dulls the memory, reduces cognition, limits vocabulary, produces obesity and mindless spending, and fills the brain with useless bullshit.

Television also opens the mind, though not in a manner conducive to critical thinking. The sights and sounds emitting from the boob tube dominate the senses, implanting content deeply into the subconscious. Mimicking perceptual cues, the viewer is apt to respond physiologically to the world in the box, just as they would real life. Action scenes, like car chases and shootouts, stimulate an adrenaline response. Death of a beloved character brings on a pang of grief.

Even when not actively watching TV, chronic viewers are absorbed in it, comparing notes with other viewers about whatever meaningless sitcom or sporting contest last evoked a peak experience. Speculating about the destiny of scripted people is more than an idle pastime; viewers become emotionally involved, and even obsessed, with the fate of people who do not exist, as well as unhealthily fixated on the actors who play them. That this adoration is unrequited, or that the objects of their devotion are unreal, ceases to matter. Lonely addicts lose track of the fact that these simulated people are not real, and don't care at all about them. Most are only dimly aware that the entire world in which they have become absorbed exists as a thinly veiled pretext to expose them to advertising.

If we were to objectively assess the harm to human bodies and spirits, and eliminate unhealthy practices on that basis, television would be the first staple of culture to be forbidden. TV is an insidious addiction for many, who passively sink into the infinite options of vicarious reality as default. The waking dream is captivating, even when the programming is dull. The bar can always be lowered. Americans are content to watch cooking contests, dating games, and battles of wit pitting adults against ten-year-olds. Late at night, hardcore junkies will stare drooling at half-hour uninterrupted advertising which cycles through the same material every six minutes.

The ban-hammer, though, never swings on things which are truly damaging, like war or corn syrup. So long as the people are kept miserable and misinformed, they can be permitted the liberty of choosing which number to punch on the remote control.

ARTICLE X:
Throwing the Baby Out With the Bath Salts

"The prestige of government has undoubtedly been lowered considerably by the Prohibition law. For nothing is more destructive of respect for the government and the law of the land than passing laws which cannot be enforced."
—Albert Einstein

At the same time that crack was sweeping the ghettoes, upscale neighborhoods were starting to feel the magic of Ecstasy. Appearing first in Texas nightclubs and California therapy retreats starting in the late 1970s, the drug was not new; it had been patented by Merck in 1914, but had escaped notice due to the confusion of World War I.

Rediscovered by psycho-chemist Alexander Shulgin in the late 1960s, it was first popularized through the evangelistic zeal of Dr. Leo Zeff, who in 1977 transported the wonder drug to psychologists across the nation, in order to introduce them to the potential of what at the time was being called, "Adam."

MDMA was exciting for therapists, who saw that the empathogenic effects could catalyze breakthroughs, that otherwise might take months or years to achieve. Couples who had been struggling found affection and passion rekindled, or else discovered that the relationship had run its course, parting friends. Lovemaking tended to be more tender and enhanced, but the real peacemaker is the emotional openness and forgiveness, qualities enhanced by the drug.

One might question the value of couples counseling, in the overall scheme of health care. While it is admittedly a luxury to have professional help in healing a relationship, being deeply entrenched in an unhealthy union can bring about the same consequences as any other mental health issue. People go quite crazy, and sometimes violent, when unresolved resentments and dysfunction boil to the bursting point in the home.

Perhaps more significantly, the compound showed special promise in treatment of PTSD and depression, especially end-of-life crises for the terminally ill. Like many anti-depressants, MDMA's mode of activity involves regulating the neurotransmitters serotonin, norepinephrine, and dopamine. Unlike them, it is not necessary to prescribe daily use over long periods;

a handful of sessions, or even a single administration, can be sufficient to bring lasting results.

Daily use is not recommended or useful, as the effects of MDMA are strongest with the initial dose, rapidly declining with repetition. This feature, rapid short-term tolerance, makes the potential for addiction, in terms of compulsive daily use, quite low. The magic quickly wears off with such abuse.

Like LSD before it, MDMA had properties which could unlock the potential of the mind. Whereas acid brought about a cognitive revolution, evoking untapped perceptual dimensions to reality, Ecstasy was the key to the emotive structure of the soul.

The initial press was positive, as it had been when LSD surfaced. *Good Housekeeping* had stamped its famous seal of approval on acid back in 1960, gushing over Carey Grant's enthusiastic endorsement of mind-expanding experiences. Popular figures stepped forth in droves to extol the virtues of the transformative catalyst. Even Bill Wilson, founder of Alcoholics Anonymous, promoted the idea that psychedelics could be the answer for slaves to the drink.

When the government decided enough was enough, and converted psychedelia to a crime, the mass Media became mute on the benefits offered by the forbidden fruit. Relegated to an historical curiosity, the bountiful research generated during the period of legal exploration is wasted. Prohibition has cut off the potential to cure pathological criminality, chronic neurosis, and substance abuse issues. Worse, LSD has been miscast as a substance of abuse itself, for which "addicts" are forced into treatment.

Today, of course, LSD is the most overcharged category of possession offense, owing largely to draconian weighing guidelines, which include carrier mass of the medium in the sentencing assessment. Thanks to mandatory minimum sentencing, even bit players are remanded for a decade or more to the penitentiary, frequently outstaying those convicted of rape or manslaughter.

Early coverage of Ecstasy was, overall, fairly balanced. While prohibitionists predictably voiced vague concerns, the preliminary evidence showed that MDMA was safe and effective. Phil Donahue introduced the underground sensation to middle America with a jubilant giddiness: "It's called Ecstasy. Now, who doesn't want to take *Ecstasy*?"

The answer, of course, was the DEA, who felt certain that anything which felt so good must necessarily be bad. Dr. Charles Schuster, who would later serve as head of the National Institute on Drug Abuse, presented an alarming study, purporting to document brain irregularities developing in megadosed rats. The data was later revealed to have a basic flaw in methodology: the rats had been injected with unlikely doses of, not MDMA, but MDA, a related substance.

Nearly two decades later, a similar error would haunt the author of a primate experiment, Dr. George Ricaurte. Inexplicably, monkeys injected with MDMA kept dying, going psychotic, showing disturbing markers of brain damage, and symptoms related to Parkinson's. This was strange, because the great many humans who were consuming it regularly did not reflect any such symptoms.

After getting the misinformed public up in arms about the previously unknown dangers of Ecstasy, helping to pass stringent legislation against it, the bad science was retracted, with an explanation that, due to poor labeling practices, *methamphetamine*, rather than MDMA, was responsible for the results. Under further investigation, hints emerged that Ricaurte, who was widely regarded as an expert on the dangers of MDMA, had deliberately made the switch, in order to justify his unproductive research. The supplying laboratory ran an audit, reporting that the shipment had been properly sent and labeled.

This theme has always been a part of Ecstasy's image problem. While boasting a superior safety profile to most approved drugs, the baggage associated with other pleasurable chemicals has dragged popular perception into the gutter. To prohibitionists, "designer drugs" were simply another masturbatory pleasure to distract citizens from their assigned joyless routines.

In 1985, the DEA made the unprecedented move of placing MDMA in Schedule I, over the protests of mental health professionals who had been finding it powerfully therapeutic. Impatient with the laborious process of hearings on efficacy, safety and potential medical uses for the drug, the DEA terminated its investigation, and summarily ended all legal access to MDMA forthwith. The pretext was the burgeoning popularity of Ecstasy, which by then had been confirmed to be available in twenty-eight States.

This move represented a fundamental shift in the way newly discovered molecules were added to the list of completely forbidden compounds. Previously, the decision to ban a substance, misguided as it may be, had been made via the legislative process. A bill would be presented in committee, be voted on by both houses of Congress after the requisite debate, and only become law if signed by the President.

Thanks to new powers conferred in the 1984 Comprehensive Crime Control Act, "emergency" scheduling of MDMA bypassed this process entirely. From now on, the executive branch, in fact the very agency responsible for enforcing such laws, could internally decide to target any substance they chose. Not one elected official need take responsibility for a policy which, once again, criminalized medical practices some were already describing as "life-changing."

Now the cops were calling the shots, determining the law as well as enforcing it. This would become the Constitutionally troubling pattern we continue to see today. Predictably, the effect of this action, which was part of the Reagan era strategy of demonizing drugs, was to create an instant demand. The profits to be had in the underground manufacture and transfer of what were being called "designer drugs" proved irresistible to many who developed a lifestyle centered on maximizing the effects of Ecstasy.

One could no longer be sure the pill they bought was actually MDMA. On the most part, pills were of high quality and authentic. But given the "risk tax" that drove the price to $20 a pill or higher, there was tremendous incentive to substitute inferior, even lethal chemicals. When this happened, such as the infamous double-stacked Mitsubishis which were actually made from the more dangerous PMA, Ecstasy took the blame.

A phenomenon developed—a new counterculture, centered on electronic dance music. Taking elements from the acid rock and disco scenes of earlier decades, the rave was not quite like either. It had a flavor all its own, the religion of candy.

The rave turned out to be infinitely reproducible. All that was needed was some space, some turntables, speakers and lighting equipment, DJs who brought their own records and made an art form of keeping the music fresh. The rest would inevitably follow. Worshipping technology and indulging in hedonistic saturation of the senses, the rave scene grew during the 1990s, each weekend breaking ground in the science of pleasure.

Until the Media showed up.

As network Media continues on with what is aptly termed "programming," the bias persists. By nine o'clock, the major networks are airing their newsmagazines. These shows feature "in-depth investigative journalism" and promise to be hard-hitting.

When these shows, such as NBC's *Dateline*, cover drug-related stories, they don't merely parrot the official line. The guiding esthetic principle of *Dateline* is to run segments which raise the blood pressure of parents and highlight the perceived potential threats of these alien substances under the guise of information.

Dateline fell in love with the love drug, when it rang the alarm on the growing culture surrounding it in 1997. The story had everything the producers looked for in a good drug scare: vivid visual clips revealed by hidden cameras probing the rave scene, gigantic piles of multicolored pressed pills embossed with cryptic logos, a lurid sexual element hinting at teen orgies, and of course wild speculation from government sources as to the various dangers inherent in any drug this popular.

The most frightening feature of Ecstasy was the possibility that a viewer's teen—the one who disappeared to the bedroom after a silent mandatory meal—might be exposed to it. *Sex! Drugs!* No parent could hope to compete for affection or obedience with a pill that made their teen love everyone, especially the flashy underground element adult authorities so adamantly warned against.

Not content to report the news, *Dateline* ventured into the realm of law enforcement, most notably with the famous statutory rape stings known as *To Catch a Predator*. Taking a page from the police manual, producers hit on the winning formula of posing as an underage girl, who acted as a honeypot for those unfortunate enough to fall for the ruse.

But the undercover Media as a cop programming model reached fever pitch when John Larson made it a mission to uncover an underground Ecstasy guru known as "Strike."

The investigation was set off when a tape surfaced of some very blissed-out ravers in Flagstaff Arizona. Unwisely, they had documented both the racy rolling parties at the core of their scene, and the group's ambitious yet sadly ill-fated Ecstasy homebrew project. Instruction manuals, authored by the mysterious Strike, were discovered among twenty thousand dollars worth of lab equipment.

Founder of the internet forum called "the Hive," and author of a practical guide to MDMA synthesis, the elusive figure had remained anonymous to cops and fans alike. Unfortunately, he left a trail which lead directly to his grey-market chemical supply business, linking it and him with the Hive, as well as Strike's several books on practical synthesis of MDMA.

Strike turned out to be Hobart Huson, a pleasant, bright young man who wasn't alert enough to smell a trap. Not content that anyone would have a secret, or publish sensitive free speech under a pseudonym, Larson and his team tracked their suspect to Huson's chemical supply house, and there lured their hapless target into making a taped and broadcast confession of his clandestine identity.

The *Dateline* investigation, which we must admit was some fairly clever detective work, led to his indictment, arrest and imprisonment for eight years.

Further backlash against the conspicuous freedom exercised by the electronic music subculture progressed, as the movement grew and spread to every major city. The grumpy bipartisan anti-fun caucus generated the RAVE (Reducing Americans' Vulnerability to Ecstasy) Act in 2002.

Sponsored by Senator Joe Biden, who has since become Vice-President, the legislation was remarkable in that it explicitly targeted a specific youth subculture in its very name. The new law would make venue owners liable for any drug transactions occurring on their property, virtually crippling the rising promotion industry.

The regressive law, which had the potential to devastate nightclub owners as well as those who rented out commercial property for raves or even homeowners hosting a house party, failed to pass in two successive tries. Renamed as the less activism-inspiring Illicit Drug Anti-Proliferation Act and attached as a rider on the Amber Alert authorization, the measure finally passed without much public notice. The pharmafascists had broken out an old tactic: attach unpopular legislation to something which can't lose, and watch the *yeas* roll in. No representative of sound mind wanted to be on record voting *nay* on toughening the law against child abductors and molesters.

There are several problems with both emergency scheduling and the Analogue Act. Most troublesome is the notion of an executive branch agency making the laws it will then proceed to enforce. The Constitution is built around the separation of powers, and for good reason. This safeguard is to prevent the unbridled abuse of the executive, the corruption of the legislative, and the subversion of the judiciary.

When Congress ceded emergency scheduling authority to the DEA, it did so unconstitutionally. One session of Congress, absent an Amendment, lacks the Constitutional standing to permanently cede any of the lawmaking mandate to the executive branch.

Moreover, this convenience overrides the procedural protections of the people, the legislative economy of time that naturally limits the rashness with which bills are passed. Whereas a Congressional act requires debate, committees, staffer briefings, political tugging-of-war, hearings, testimony and roll calls, which may be contentious in future elections, a unilateral dictate from the DEA dispenses with nearly all of this.

Remember, these measures are not only against certain drugs, but also the as yet unidentified individuals who will eventually be caught possessing them. Their rights are at stake with each new ban, so bypassing the legislative process is a violation of them.

The ban on Ecstasy was peremptory and premature, but utterly predictable. The pattern had little to do with the merits of a given substance;

it was the economics which would easily fit into the program. People would pay for that which made them feel good, and pay all the more for that which is criminally good.

MDMA made people feel wonderful, which according to the warped mentality of the prohibitionist, is sufficient reason to wipe it from the Earth. With fewer side effects than pharmaceutical antidepressants, and a much shorter course of treatment, a sane society would hail the appearance of such a miracle drug, putting it firmly at the forefront of research.

By 2010, we would see the DEA wield emergency powers again, this time in suppression of the hydra-headed class of anandamide receptor agonists, also known as synthetic cannabinoids. Vaguely similar to marijuana, and sold as herbal incense, the new craze became an object lesson in how inept the "war on drugs" truly is.

Popularly called by the trade names "Spice" (from the Frank Herbert classic) or "K2" (because it takes you to extreme altitudes), the syncan blends were the best thing to hit the market since marijuana.

Spice itself was an anti-prohibitionary innovation; the value lay, not necessarily in the unique high, but in the way it was invisible to urine screens, law enforcement, and the law itself. The odor, which varied according to the base herbs used, was not well known to authority figures as a sign of illicit behavior. It looked like tea.

The Media called Spice a "drug," but, of course, this is an oversimplification. It was not one drug at all, but one or more of many, and only the manufacturer knew for sure what the ingredients truly were. Blends were made by impregnating herbs with any of a number of synthetic cannabinoids, most of them created by NIDA researcher John W. Huffman, in order to study the systems of anandamide reception in the brain.

Huffman identified several hundred compounds in this class, each bearing his initial and a three digit code, dozens of which produced a high roughly similar to THC when smoked in the low-milligram ranges. Each was indexed according to the affinity the compound had toward the CB1 and CB2 receptor sites, creating a virtual roadmap for enterprising souls wishing to manufacture a legal alternative to cannabis.

Stories began to regularly make the rounds about this "synthetic marijuana" widely available at the head shops. Every incident vaguely related to Spice became newsworthy. Naturally, the stuff was just plain awful; it caused panic attacks and some hospitalizations.

One popular technique was to cite the rising calls to poison control, neglecting to point out that this was due to the exponential growth in use that followed every Media spotlight cast on the novel notion of a legal substitute for marijuana. How many of those calls were precipitated, not by medical emergencies, but by snooping parents who found a mylar ziploc in the dresser drawer after watching too much news? Or simply wanted more info?

Parents were alarmed, police were indignant, and legislators in States across the country broke out the ban-hammer. But they quickly discovered a problem: since there were so many variations which could replace whatever configuration was added to the controlled substance schedule, the new laws were ineffective. As soon as a State banned the most popular syncans, which were JWH-018 and 073, the blend manufacturers would switch to JWH-250, JWH-122, or others like CP-47947, the WIN series, or yet still more obscure chemicals.

Oregon solved the problem neatly, imitating the Feds by passing the buck for the ban to the Board of Pharmacy, a seven-person committee, which, like the DEA, makes law under the auspices of the executive. Without voter input, and with no accountability whatsoever, the BOP adopted the most comprehensive ban imaginable. The new emergency rule placed any cannabinoid receptor agonist into the State Schedule I, making instant felons of the store owners and staff who had been carrying the popular wares.

The blanket ban, which was the product of some fancy lawyering, included an exception for FDA-approved items, in order to avoid covering the many food products containing anandamide itself, present in trace amounts in chocolate.

The same issue hampered development of a urine test. The labs had little trouble bringing the test for JWH-018 and 073 to market, after identifying half a dozen metabolic products to be found in urine, but by the time it was available, these particular substances had mostly disappeared, due to pending Federal bans. The chase began again; first the labs had to figure out what was in the new formula, develop a test to detect it, and watch it become obsolete as attention drove yet another change-up in the recipe.

Late in the year, the issue of Spice peaked, with an announcement from the DEA that the agency would be using its power to implement an emergency ban. The announcement drove the five listed substances from the market, while bringing onto the shelves a whole new wave of unknowns.

This move brought objections from a new special interest: the retail shops which had been raking it in hand over fist, supplying the explosive demand for Spice. The emergency ban could not go through, they argued, because it would effect more than one hundred million dollars in annual commerce. The industry was currently valued at over one billion dollars.

A bigger issue, and one virtually ignored by all sides in the debate, was that some of these chemicals could have important medical value which had nothing to do with getting high. JWH-200, included in the proposed ban despite being relatively rare in Spice-like products, showed pharmacokinetic properties as an analgesic, due to a high degree of affinity toward CB2 receptors.

Like cannabis itself, some of these chemicals also had a broad scope of potential for treating a wide variety of illnesses. Some have demonstrated anti-carcinogenic properties as well. JWH-015, which also seems to modulate the immune system, reduced tumors and inhibited cancer cell division in lab rats, making it a candidate for the treatment of prostate cancer.

The potential of these chemicals as medicine has only begun to be explored, and in light of impending blanket bans, it is unlikely that further research will be forthcoming. Like a bulldozer smashing through the rain forest, prohibition may irrevocably destroy nature's cures still undiscovered.

This creation of analogues highlights the futility of interdiction. Instead of ridding the world of enjoyable substances, a whole new class of chemicals appeared with the primary virtue of banning the illegal version. One wonders what success the Spice phenomenon would have seen had cannabis simply been legalized. What market would there be for an expensive chemical substitute, if people didn't have urine tests to foil? They would have remained a curiosity, restricted to a small class of enthusiasts, and never have fallen into the hands of the unwary.

Urinalysis is primarily successful at one thing—utterly frustrating the cannabis smoker. Other substances can be detected, but not reliably, since the window for most water-soluble drugs to disappear is the span of a weekend. This is not a failure of the lab; most chems are naturally purged within seventy-two hours. The metabolites of THC, however, are fat-soluble and remain detectable for up to thirty days, making it hazardous indeed to cheat on a urine test with cannabis.

Apart from being invasive of privacy rights, one problem with these tests is the way the casual marijuana user is far likelier to test positive than those using cocaine or methamphetamine. Hard drugs, being toxic, are given a higher priority by the body's excretory system, and so are purged more quickly than benign herbal metabolites. Screens designed to identify substance abusers chiefly impact those who are arguably making the least harmful choice.

Besides the syncans, many of the most exciting research chemicals derived from the extensive and laborious work of Alexander "Sasha" Shulgin, who had conducted research on psychoactive compounds since the 1960s. He identified hundreds of viable configurations, testing them on himself, wife Ann, and friends, publishing the results in a books called, *PiHKAL* (*Phenethylamines I Have Known and Loved*) and the sequel *TiHKAL*, dealing with tryptamines.

Tryptamines are a class of molecules which are interesting by virtue of their similarity to serotonin, which is 5-hydroxytryptamine. Psilocybin, the visionary component of magic mushrooms, is 4-hydroxyl-dimethyltryptamine. Synthetic variations like 4-HO-DiPT, 5-MEO-MIPT, and 4-ACO-DMT have in the internet age become available for international and domestic order, pending the inevitable ban.

Various configurations yield a range of potency and effects spectrums. In nature, closely related N,N,DMT and 5-MEO-DMT appear in both plant and animal sources. Hundreds of vegetable species for some reason produce these substances, which are among the most powerful mind-alteration agents known to humankind. They have been used indigenously for thousands of years as a sacred tool of shamanism.

In fact, we literally have DMT on the brain, which, due to the legal status of the substance, renders every human alive a constant drug felon. The notion of criminalizing a component of the brain might seem odd, but the long arm of the law is all too willing to reach around our minds.

The next round of Media outrage, parental hysteria, and legal rush to judgment came with the realization that not only were the head shops selling faux marijuana, they were also increasingly carrying faux cocaine, faux ecstasy, faux methamphetamine, whatever this stuff was, it was scary and flying off the shelves.

Bath salts were made of any of a number of research chemicals, variations of the many molecular structures still unscheduled, despite having psychoactive qualities on the order of listed drugs. The commercial lines generally contained stimulants, such as MDPV and mephedrone. Out came the broad brush and oversimplification. The televisions flashed with the five-minute hate directed, this time, at the new enemy driving their neighbors crazy and sending kids to the ER.

The labeling of research chemicals as bath salts was a clever expedient to get around the "human consumption" clause of the Analog Act, which intended to except from prosecution substances which might have industrial uses, in addition to psychotropic effects. Also sold as plant food, these chemicals had been making the rounds on the internet for several years, with few repercussions, until operation Web Tryp netted ten vendors for violation of the Analogue Act. Fatalities were rare, and warnings went out whenever one occurred. The scene policed itself, establishing ratings websites to identify bad vendors.

When research chemicals began to hit the liquor stores, head shops, and even gas stations, under brand names such as Ivory Wave and Vanilla Sky, the alarm bells rang all over America's neatly landscaped subdivisions. As usual, the television news Media could be counted on to proclaim the falling of the sky.

Here was an end-run around prohibition never imagined by legislators. Retail shops were openly selling powdered stimulants with no ingredient listing, and there was no applicable law against it. Because they were not intended for human consumption, according to the omnipresent disclaimer, there was no need to say what the "bath salts" actually contained.

Chris Hansen, who seems to relish the morally freighted exposure of thought-crime in our midst, went undercover to again play Media narc. The *Dateline* segment, aired on May 23, 2011, exemplified the confrontational and biased approach to journalism adopted by this "investigative reporter."

The piece begins with the dramatic tale of Jarrod Moody, a twenty-nine year old who by all appearances had become a bit of a troubled slacker. Hansen refers to him as an "All-American guy," while a dozen dated photographs of Moody, posing in his high school football costume, flash before the screen.

Jarrod's glory days were obviously long past, but the implication is clear enough to the frightened parents gathered before the boob-tube in order to be informed about the latest drug epidemic threatening to transform their perfect children into tragedies overnight.

Invited over to play video games, Moody asked to clean his friend's gun and shot himself in the face. The death was ruled a suicide, but might well have been an accident. Either way, with no note and no apparent warning, we'll never really know what was going through his mind. Perhaps he was clinically depressed. Maybe he was just sick of a dead-end life with no clear prospects.

A little digging around the local Media coverage of this highly hyped death reveals a tidbit Hansen forgot to mention about this Jekyll-and-Hyde story. Bath salts were hardly Moody's first flirtation with drug abuse; in fact, he was just coming off a stint of rehab for prescription drug issues. The All-American guy had clearly developed a craving for mind alteration long before discovering Ivory Wave.

Nonetheless, Jarrod's father and Hansen know where to pin the blame. It turns out that in the weeks leading up to his death, Moody had started using these baths salts. In fact, the *Dateline* producers obtained and included a clip showing Moody stealing some from a convenience store, hours before his death. The conclusion is obvious: bath salts cause suicide. Case closed.

This is a favorite logical fallacy which marks a great deal of Copaganda, the confusion of correlation with causation. Anyone who has studied formal deductive reasoning is aware of this flaw and the pitfalls which come from it, but don't expect pharmafascists to steer clear of drawing guilt by association.

Instead of seeing a troubled individual who may have used bath salts in addition to shooting himself, Hansen wants us to believe that suicide must have been caused by the drugs. Otherwise, why would someone who is nearly thirty decide to end it all?

The causative link is fragile at best, but there is no doubt in Hansen's mind that someone who got high, and then died, must have been murdered by drug dealers.

Conspicuously neglected is the more reasonable theory that Moody, being under the weather psychologically, experimented with the bath salts as an attempt to treat his discontent before possibly resorting to suicide. Or just plain stupidity, in playing with a loaded gun.

Repeatedly referring to bath salts as if it were a singular drug, rather than a diverse class of substances with varying effects, more clips are shown pushing the agenda of linking them to suicide. In the next segment, we see an interview with Jimmy Harris, who in harrowing terms describes his single experience with a bath salt product of unknown composition.

Harris' story is scary all right. He recounts taking an unmentioned quantity of an unidentified substance and immediately commenced hallucinating law enforcement officers and government vehicles. Ironically, the night ended with Harris' arrest for public intoxication, so one wonders if he were not experiencing precognition rather than delusion.

Well, he clearly took too much of whatever it was, which is part of the problem with the charade of mislabeling products to evade the Analogue Act. One of the legitimate dangers of these head shop products is that dosing information and cautions cannot be printed on the packaging, lest it become illegal by admitting human consumption.

We are only speculating when we suggest that Harris may have been talking to *Dateline* as part of negotiations with authorities to reduce or drop his charges. We have no evidence of this whatsoever, but he would hardly be the first to be converted into a tool for disinformation, in exchange for leniency. However, the extreme effects he claims to have experienced could only have come from an enormous overdose. If his experience were typical, considering the massive quantities involved, there would be more than a handful of such cases.

Fans of Chris Hansen's style of cop journalism could easily predict the next phase of the story. Infiltrating a local headshop with a hidden camera, viewers are treated to a lurid display of paraphernalia, which is commonplace enough to the average college student, but reeks of insidious alien criminality to *Dateline*'s straitlaced and sheltered audience.

Hansen isn't here looking for bongs or rolling papers, though. He's on a mission to catch head shop employees bending the rules about the newest wave of what he menacingly describes as "designer drugs."

First, his producer goes in and entraps the employee showing him the bath salts, by asking if you smoke or snort the white powder, to which the clerk reluctantly replies, "Basically."

Another clerk is less restrained, more or less spilling the beans; yes, the white powder you buy in the head shop gets you high.

Returning the next day, Hansen walks in with a video player to challenge the manager, proudly bearing proof that bath salts aren't for bathing by showing the hidden camera footage of some very incriminating words unwisely uttered by the staff.

Having penetrated the veil of secrecy at the undisciplined head shop, Hansen announces that the crew is ready to tackle the big fish, to go up the ladder and snag a wholesale vendor for your viewing pleasure.

The set-up is familiar and according to formula. The next step is to send in a wired crew to pose as potential large purchasers of bath salts. The unfortunate victim of this ploy, a repackager and distributor who was to find his face splattered on broadcast television, invited the narcs in, and proceeded to brag illegally about his product. He'd have probably been more subdued, if it were clear that the DEA and the country would be viewing this conversation shortly.

The *coup de grâce* is when Hansen, in disguise, arrives at a hotel meeting with the vendor, purportedly to close the deal. Instead, he begins to make insinuations that get the poor man squirming. Realizing what is happening to him, the hapless vendor scoops up his canisters, making a break for it, but it is already too late. Some lucky prosecutor has his case made, with videotaped evidence it would be tough to refute, and not one hour of police time logged.

"Don't you have a conscience?" Hansen demands of the sweating distributor. "I mean, is it really worth selling a product like this to make money?"

One might just as easily question and judge Hansen's willingness to cross the boundaries of journalistic objectivity. Does *he* have a conscience? Is it really worth playing undercover detective, entrapping people, possibly ruining their lives, just to get ratings?

ARTICLE XI:
Sex and Drugs

It is possible to read the history of this country as one long struggle to extend the liberties established in our Constitution to everyone in America.
—*Molly Ivins*

The authority of any governing institution must stop at its citizen's skin.
—*Gloria Steinem*

It is perhaps a legacy of the Puritanical roots at the heart of American culture that the legal system is so preoccupied with sex. Unashamed to air the most lurid details of taboo activities in the otherwise stilted courtroom environment, the State marches those who deviate from its prim standards before grim priests of Justice, to have a portion of their lives ritually excised. This punitive custom has proceeded unabated since the dark-robed death-dealers presided over Salem, distributing their scarlet letters.

To be sure, the class of protected sexual activities has expanded greatly in the past century, even as the class of pharmacological activities allowed has narrowed. Homosexuals, once the target of vigorous raids and legal persecution, have fought, and to a great degree been liberated from, most forms of legal sanction against their lifestyle choices, proving shame is not natural.

This is not to say that all strata of society accept homosexuals, or that the bitter ideological war over full inclusion has been won. The struggles over gay marriage and adoption demonstrate a continuing resistance to sexual minorities. Religious extremists are unafraid to air bigoted opinions, and "right-wing" politicians, who often enough are later unmasked as closet cases themselves, still bank considerable political currency by backing discriminatory legislation.

For the most part, however, the State has abandoned the systematic oppression of homosexuality as such. This is true generally in the Western world, but decidedly untrue in many Muslim countries, where lengthy prison sentences and even the death penalty persist.

Nevertheless, in the United States, expressing an alternative sexual orientation is now a legally enshrined right. Job and housing discrimination based on sexuality or gender identity are forbidden, actionable civil offenses. A person may be proudly gay, and millions are, without fear of criminal reprisal.

This, of course, was not always so. Civil liberties for sexual minorities are a relatively recent development, and the change has transpired over a single generation. Until 1961, when Illinois abolished its statute, every single one of the fifty States had on the books a criminal prohibition of homosexual acts. In fact, it was not until 2003 that sodomy laws were categorically struck down by the Supreme Court, in the landmark decision *Lawrence v. Texas*.

The struggle for LGBT rights parallels the movement for neurochemical liberty, and the success of gay liberation is instructive for those of us striving toward drug policy reform. In many ways, the marginalization of substance users resembles the oppression of homosexuals. In each case, a bigoted majority employs the mechanisms of police and courts to harass a behavioral minority for reasons which are largely specious.

The difference, of course, is that the LGBT movement has made significant headway. It is no longer legally or culturally permissible to mistreat people simply because they pursue sex and relationships with their own gender. Credit must be given to the tireless activists who refused to accept the dominator definition of inferiority, and fought to end the war on their choices.

The transition toward cultural acceptance of minorities, on the whole, was the great political miracle of the twentieth century. The forces of intolerance have been beaten back on many battlefronts, losing the props which promote majority privilege and oppression of the underrepresented.

As we have seen with other historically oppressed groups, homosexuals bear a disproportionate brunt of controlled substance enforcement. Gay inmates, generally non-violent drug or property offenders, are targets of physical and sexual abuse. Two-thirds of homosexual prisoners report sexual assault while incarcerated.

Another class which suffers disproportionately from prohibition is the sex worker. The drug-habituated prostitute gets it in both ends, so to speak, coming and going as it were, a criminal in livelihood, as well as in seeking relief from the emotional toll of work.

Individuals of both genders take to this sort of freelancing, in order to support overpriced habits, but naturally females find their skills more marketable in a largely heterosexual society. As a result, women, many of them busted for drugs, selling sex to acquire them, or both, comprise the fastest-growing segment of the prison population.

Prostitution has a reputation of being the world's oldest profession, which could imply many things, such as the ancient habit of offering a bridal price, or perhaps the earlier custom of hunters flinging a freshly killed carcass at female feet, as inducement to mate.

The saying brings to mind the Old Testament, perhaps some insinuation that Eve extracted payment from Adam, after getting them kicked out of the Garden. Or perhaps it alludes to an issue more contemporary for the authors of Deuteronomy: the temple prostitutes of competing polytheistic cults.

The Whore of Babylon, as she is contemptuously cast, was a major threat to the founders of what has become Judeo-Christianity. The message of tightly restrained sexuality was prone to be undermined by the lusty worship of the neighboring heathens, so the cops of the day scornfully added such practices to the lengthy list of human diversions claimed to irritate Almighty God.

Today, perhaps the lowest rung on the social ladder is reserved for the professional sex provider, who is hardly considered to have an occupation, let alone a profession. The modern symbol of prostitution is the decrepit crack whore, peddling her diminishing body to those sinful enough to buy it.

The ills of prostitution—and they are significant—are once again due to the legal sanctions against the trade, rather than any inherent corruption of the act itself. Of greatest legitimate concern is the welfare of sex workers themselves, who occupy a dangerous place in an underground market where *they* are the valuable contraband.

Physical threats from pimps, violent customers, and the police, are a constant in the life of the street-level sex worker. Exposure to disease and pregnancy are serious risks, as are the physical demands of the lifestyle. All of these would be ameliorated by a sensible policy which allowed licensed prostitution.

Whatever one might think of the morality of such work, it is undeniably in high demand, and seems impervious to even draconian enforcement. Yet public funds continue to finance the hopeless and hypocritical campaign to churn sex workers through the courts and prison system.

Paying for sex with food, or valuable items which stand for food, is part of animal nature, and noticeably practiced by many species of higher mammal and bird. This transaction is symbolic of the dietary support which is essential to the more successful reproduction endeavors involving cooperation during gestation and rearing of the young.

Examples of such behavior persist in the realm of traditional sexual mores of the domesticated primate, quite without social stigma. The dinner date, the engagement ring, even the barside drink purchase, all constitute different ways in which sexual access is obtained by means of a bribe.

Such institutions are condoned, romanticized by the dominant culture. Yet when it comes to a cash exchange between strangers, this is somehow taboo. The only form of prostitution which is criminalized is the one which does not hide behind pretext, expensive gifts, or artful milking of partners whose most appealing assets are their assets.

Meanwhile, the secret police mount entrapment operations, in which dozens of sex workers or aspiring clients are netted by undercover imposturing. The trend is toward targeting the latter, as it makes more sense to extort the party on the paying end of the date, but city and county jails are nightly filled with professional providers of intimate services, who have come to consider arrest just another part of the exploitation.

The popular conception is that such incarceration is strictly overnight, but the accumulation of multiple convictions can make the consequences quite severe, life-changing, and even life-ending.

Marcia Powell was serving a twenty-seven month prison sentence at Perryville Prison in Arizona for prostitution. Her life tragically ended when she aroused the lethal apathy of her guards, who allowed her to bake in the desert heat while she was illegally confined, without water, in an outdoor cage.

Powell, who was placed in the unshaded fenced cell while awaiting transfer for a psychiatric evaluation, was left unattended in the sun for four hours. Despite being on anti-psychotic medications, which increased her sensitivity to sunlight, witnesses say that her pleas for water, and to use the restroom, were willfully ignored by correctional employees. She died of heat exposure and dehydration, after soiling herself.

The autopsy revealed first-and-second degree burns, and her body was covered by blisters. Medical examiners reported a body temperature of 108°. Although sixteen members of the staff were given disciplinary sanctions, including some firings and suspensions, not *one* was charged by the local prosecution in connection with Powell's death.

This demonstrates the sense of priorities for the county attorney's office, which had not been shy about bureaucratically maneuvering Ms. Powell into the prison system, first for drug violations, and then the prostitution charge which ultimately killed her.

But when it came time to employ the law against agents of the State, who had clearly committed criminal neglect, the prosecutors were suddenly afraid of court. Disregarding a three-thousand page report, detailing the complicity of guards in the senseless death of this physically frail woman, and the Department of Corrections' own recommendation that charges be brought against seven of their officers, the CA's office issued a terse statement indicating that there was insufficient evidence to bring a criminal complaint against of any of the personnel responsible for letting Marcia Powell die.

The Powell case illustrates the fundamental fallacy of the punitive penal system in the United States. We are told that the purpose of this process is to reduce crime and improve the quality of life for all. We are led to believe that these institutions exist to keep us safe from the incorrigibly dangerous.

Instead, we see that the prisons are being used to warehouse society's undesirables, often in concentration camp conditions. The authorities didn't care about the death of a mentally ill, drug-addicted prostitute, apart from wanting the embarrassing incident to go away.

So it rings false when we are told that laws which provide stiff penalties for victimless offenses are for the protection of the people who commit them. As much of a mess as Powell's life had evidently been, putting her in prison had nothing to do with rehabilitation.

One of the complaints we often hear is that the activity of prostitution—by which is meant streetwalking—reduces the quality of life in the areas where it is prevalent. Of course, people could simply ignore these interactions which are none of their business, but that does not seem to be in the busybody American nature.

What people really mean when they complain about prostitution is not that they or their property are threatened, but their sensibilities. While business owners might have a legitimate gripe that sex traffic in front of their property could affect the stream of their customers, one can hardly point to any physical danger to uninvolved parties.

A revolution in personal liberties related to both sex and medicine occurred when the Court abolished the prohibition against abortion, with the historic decision in *Roe v. Wade*. The ruling represents an extraordinarily broad interpretation of the Constitution, and establishes the principle of dominion over one's body, as well as the right to transact medical services, without the interference of the State. If such a mentality were to apply to a case of controlled substances, the last shot will have been fired in the war on pharmacological choice.

We fully support a woman's right to an abortion, and believe it to be an absolute. Nevertheless, *Roe v. Wade* is based on some unusual reasoning for the Court. To extend the logic of due process and privacy to expectant mothers seeking to terminate that status, while denying it to marijuana smokers, is inexplicably odd. Why is the surgical excision of a fetus a protected right, but not the prescription of a therapeutically useful, enjoyable plant or chemical?

Abortion was illegal for many of the same reasons behind substance prohibition: a reactionary prejudice against perceived immorality, largely baseless concerns about the harm to society, and a social reliance on the replicable nuclear family unit. Proponents successfully argued that the damage from illegal procedures, the deadly "back-alley abortions," far outweighed any interest society had in suppressing this activity. Terminating an unwanted pregnancy was medicalized, the choice returning to patient and doctor.

This liberty has prevented millions of unplanned children from entering the world, and would be laudable merely for the curbing effect on population growth. The option of abortion as a legal alternative has allowed that fewer babies are born who are not at least tacitly desired. The question is often framed in terms of morality, but is it really more moral to force women to see these inappropriate pregnancies to term? Is it moral to condemn unprepared parents to burden the world with undesired children, rather than whatever it is they might have wanted to do with their lives?

Like LGBT rights, reproductive freedom is under constant assault from what is known as the "conservative religious Right." Despite typically supporting the death penalty, and hawkish postures in foreign relations, such activists style themselves as "pro-life." Such is the stance, even when it includes bombing clinics, or shooting physicians for providing legally sanctioned access to pregnancy termination services.

Three of the last five Presidents—the Republicans—officially opposed the right to an abortion. Reversing *Roe v. Wade* is basic to the platform of "conservatives" who are quite liberal with support for government intrusion into our personal lives.

One set of laws which have thankfully been abolished this past century are the miscegenation laws, which forbade the sexual mingling of different ethnicities. A side effect of institutional racism, both criminal law and vigilante lynch gangs enforced violent separation of gene pools for most of the nation's history.

The proscription against interracial marriage predates the formation of the Union. A strange Maryland law, passed in 1662, prescribed that any free woman, regardless of race, who deigned to marry a slave, would by virtue of this union be downgraded to slavery herself, and that this status would bind all of her descendants into oppression. Virginia passed, in 1691, the first act specifically forbidding marriage between individuals of European extraction, and those originating in Africa.

Of course, such laws were only applied to the voluntary association of mutually respected equals; the profligate sexual subjugation of slaves was widely ignored, for example, as it was regarded as part of a master's privilege.

The hateful laws against mating with someone of differing skin tone are, again, not at all ancient history, but were a reality for most of the century recently completed. Thirty States maintained statutes forbidding marriage between individuals of different ethnicity until 1948. Sixteen States were still clinging to such antiquities when they were struck down by the Supremes, in the 1967 hit *Loving v. Virginia*.

Sex offender status is one of the harshest criminal penalties one could be burdened with, apart from incarceration itself. Every individual on that mandatory list becomes a pariah, judged by strangers for acts they have no opportunity to explain.

Public urination, as in leaning behind the dumpster to loose an urgent stream, can haunt one for life. Hit with charges of indecent exposure, the hapless alley pisser is lumped in with the schoolyard van-snatcher.

Worse still, even the most wholesome of all human activity, the nursing of an infant, has fallen under the misguided application of laws punishing sexual improprieties. Jacqueline Mercado, a Peruvian immigrant, was indicted for felony child pornography in Richardson, Texas, due to a photograph showing her breast-feeding her yearling son. Before wiser heads prevailed to dismiss the charges, she faced loss of custody, prison, and a lifetime on the list of society's most hated criminals.

Opportunities for housing, employment and family life are sharply diminished for those on the list, whom most folks will assume are guilty of some horrible perversion. Failure to comply with registration requirements is an offense itself, which can remand one to prison.

An extension of this concept is the current crusade against photographic images of the underaged. Again, this is an uncomfortable issue, charged with many emotions. But the prosecution of these images has reached such a height of insanity that we would like to bring some perspective to this sensitive topic.

First off, the involuntary exploitation of anyone, regardless of age, for pornographic purposes is a violation of rights in itself, and the production of such material may include nonconsensual involvement. The viewing of such images does not, in itself, constitute an intention to commit the depicted act. After all, most Americans see hours of televised gun battles each week, but only a small minority go on to commit shooting sprees.

The absurdity really begins to come clear around the fringes of this technology-spurred hysteria: the prosecution of minors for possession or transmission of nude images of themselves. The phenomenon—labeled "juvenile self-exploitation"—can cause a teenager to be branded as a sex offender for something which studies show may be common for up to one in five individuals in that age range.

Such protectionism related to adolescent sexuality is indicative of the low regard which adults in authority have for the choices of the underaged, and is utterly out of joint with the reality of human development. No other species prolongs weaning nearly two decades, as modern Western culture promotes. Normally, the attainment of reproductive capacity signifies adulthood, and animal parents cease having an interest in controlling the behavior of their adult offspring.

Biologically, the individuals involved are adults, and teenagers have historically been treated as such in nearly all cultures. This, fundamentally, is the issue we take with the criminalization of adolescent sexual behavior, and with laws in general which discriminate based on age. Such laws create an artificial incapacity, which, we would argue, renders the entire population more immature.

There is nothing about being a particular age which embodies good judgment and rational decision making. Some exceedingly intelligent children make impressively nuanced choices, and some adults seem never to grow up. Maturity is not wholly a function of calendar years.

The drive to control, through prosecution, the unauthorized pursuit of happiness, be it chemical or sexual, is deeply embedded in the very concept of law. In general, as society grows, the welcome trend is to liberalize the more obnoxious and intrusive controls on victimless behavior.

It is our sincere hope to see this evolution reach the point where every personal choice is a protected right, that every crime have a discernible victim with a legitimate grievance, and that every energy be expended to seek an alternative to incarceration.

We believe that confining any human being to a cell is a tragedy, and if it must be done at all, it should only be to those who have committed a violent act.

Even these should be guaranteed humane treatment while guests of the correctional system, being treated with the dignity due a citizen, with every effort made to work on a humanistic level for genuine reform. Until the violent are shown some degree of respect, they will continue to practice violence.

Greater strides have been made in just the past century. If so much progress could be made toward a truly egalitarian society in the span of a human life, how free could we all be, if we work for abolition of all laws which sit in judgment over perfectly common personal choices?

The progenitors of prohibition were as concerned about sex as drugs. Much of the angst which drove the legislation of consumptive morality was concerned with loose women lounging in the saloons and consorting with men in marijuana or opium dens. The hype which criminalized cocaine dwelt on the idea that it drove black men to seek white women, while the smokescreen behind which cannabis was banned depended heavily on the idea that stoned women would accommodate them.

As Harry Anslinger, always good for quote, put it, "This marijuana causes white women to seek sexual relations with Negroes, entertainers and any others." Here he achieves the rare trifecta of bigotry: racial, sexual, and pharmacological.

Today, such sentiments are better veiled, but worries about promiscuous behavior still underly popular support for stricter social enforcement. There are both rational and irrational reasons to be concerned about young people having sex. Parents, in particular, have to confront these issues.

Of all these fears, the idea that one's teen offspring would conceive or germinate a pregnancy, is the most reasonable. The antidote for this is safe sex education, and access to contraception.

Less reasonable, although perhaps more common, is the emotional reaction many parents develop, regarding the power and control they have exercised over this being for their entire lives. In the last few years before they surrender this authority entirely, such parents tend to become tyrannical and invasive, obsessed with the conduct of this suddenly sovereign entity.

This preoccupation with the keepers of the culture translates into policy, heedless of any collateral damage. Politicians do very well among straight-laced family voters of either party, by proposing legislation that helps keep their kids in line and locked down.

Sex may be the fundamental political issue. When social conservatives stump in the name of their venerable values, it seems that authorities have indeed forbidden most forms of sexual conduct throughout the majority of human history. The power of sex, to unify, to defy, to procreate, belongs to each individual, and patriarchs have always tried to hold it for their own.

Courtrooms are curiously dirty places, where lurid details of the most extreme sexual acts are daily brought to public light. Names, faces and intimate depictions splash across the press at the mere allegation of some forbidden act.

The prudery and voyeurism of the judiciary may seem to be in conflict, but it is not. The Puritan is obsessed with sex every bit as much as the sinners they so passionately flog. Expressing a reaction formation so powerful it dominates the globe, patriarchs derive as much perverse pleasure in the denial of sex, as others feel from the attainment of it.

We see the roots of this dynamic in nature, where males compete for sex, using physical force to cock-block their rivals. In human society, this biological urge, not only to achieve mating success, but to deprive others of it, has shaped the psychology of a culture in which what happens in the bedroom is everybody's business.

As the sexual revolution of the 1960s loosened these strictures, the preoccupation with the pleasure indulged by others shifted focus, to repressing the private use of herbs and drugs. Unsuccessful at containing the sodomites and fornicators, the evangelical fury against impudent sinners turned toward what seemed to be precipitating all this wantonness: those hippies and their dope. This obsession would grow rapidly to cover the globe.

ARTICLE XII:
To The Shores of Medellín

"There are no boundaries in this struggle to the death. We cannot be indifferent to what happens anywhere in the world, for a victory by any country over imperialism is our victory; just as any country's defeat is a defeat for all of us."—Che Guevara

Up to this point, we have focused almost exclusively on the domestic pharma-war within the United States. There are several reasons for this; primarily to avoid the complexities of analyzing international law, and the various policies of foreign nations in the context of this book. It is somewhat meaningless to assert that the actions of foreign governments are inconsistent with the US Constitution.

Be that as it may, nearly every country on earth has adopted a detailed criminal code punishing substance-related offenses, and very few are lenient. Some countries, like the Netherlands and Portugal, have varying degrees of tolerance in both legislation and enforcement policy. Others, like Iran, Singapore and Malaysia, have stricter penalties than the United States, and even practice execution for possession offenses.

Purely in terms of penalties, such countries are much harsher on cognitive dissidents and unauthorized distributors, but these nations tend to generally be less free in a variety of other ways, as they are often under theocratic or militaristic regimes. Yet still the United States, with its purportedly civilian, nonreligious representative rule, manages to outdo every one of these countries in rates of incarceration per capita.

The utility of these laws as an instrument of oppression make them tempting for any authoritarian hierarchy, which is probably a fair description of virtually all governments on Earth. The ubiquity of these laws mean that one can't simply relocate to escape them. This reality is partly, but not entirely, the doing of drug warriors in the English-speaking world.

There seem to be few places where the rulers have not seen fit to impose this kind of regulation. The inclination, to an American activist, may be to blame our government for the violent interdiction activities in the world. This is only partly the case.

In truth, most ruling bodies which employ this form of repression on their citizens very likely would continue with it, even without the leadership of the US. The same dynamics which entrench social engineering through brute force in the United States occur to some degree in all hierarchical structures. Like territorial war, it is a side effect of the power-distribution pyramid, and the steeper the slope, the broader the bottom must be.

No other country, however, has pursued military aggression as a tactic to the degree that US agencies, particularly the DEA, have. With tendrils in every production region of the world, the international eradication campaigns have the character of scorched-earth brutality visited on some of the poorest farmers in the world.

The paraquat spraying program began in 1975, as a policy designed to wipe out the marijuana and poppy fields of Mexico. The herbicide is nonselective and highly toxic; not only does it decimate the target crops intended, but makes other farming in affected regions impossible. It is harmful to wildlife, contaminates the food chain, and poses hazards to indigenous populations.

Inhalation of the sprayed product can cause nasal hemorrhage, chest pains, severe nausea, and lung issues such as fibrosis, asthma attacks, and lesions. High doses have been shown to cause irreversible kidney damage, convulsions, and death. Nevertheless, the Mexican government consented to, and eventually began participating in, this poisoning of their people for the sake of social control in the North.

At the same time that these crops were being suppressed for allegedly being dangerous, the spraying project brought actual hazards into the lives of casual smokers. Obliterating the farms outside the national borders was underhanded, but the eradication program had another effect: tainted marijuana being imported.

Here we see where the true priorities of prohibitionists lie. All this concern about the health effects of marijuana, ostensibly the pretext for the hostile policies toward it, did not dissuade them from unleashing toxic chemicals onto the users of the widely consumed plant.

By 1978, the herbicide had become a real epidemic. Tests from the NIDA showed thirteen out of sixty-three busted pot samples, just over twenty percent, contained paraquat, in concentrations as high as 2264 parts per million, with an average level of 452 ppm—*about nine thousand times* the level considered acceptable for products sold domestically.

The considerable imperial might of the United States has successfully pressured production-nation governments into line with these operations, and the pursestrings of foreign aid have been tied to cooperation with eradication programs.

In 1983, the poison was brought home, introduced by the DEA into the National Forests of northern Georgia, despite a restraining order from Judge Charles Moye against the spraying, amidst a nation-wide panic about adulterated cannabis supplies.

The herbicide-bombing of Latin America is one noticeable war crime committed under the cover of anti-drug vigilance. Dousing the Columbian countryside with chemicals and blight, the consequences of this bio-chemical warfare extend far beyond the *cocaleros* who are the ostensible target.

Eradication is literally counterproductive; that is, it obliterates resources, labor, and potential earnings. In fact, prohibition as a whole is a negative economic activity, producing negative value, measuring success in tons seized, lives smashed, and markets denied.

These supposed victories mean that land has been rendered unusable, and that a desired commodity is all the more sought after.

This is the very antithesis of capitalism. The systematic destruction of value, the expenditure of tariffs toward the frustration of industry, the draconian level of regulation, are all inherently hostile to economic development and growth. Put more simply, these policies help make and keep people poor by rendering the market anything but free.

Nowhere is this effect more palpable than Colombia, where the number one cash crop is afflicted by the wholly man-made blight of airborne herbicides. Coca is a part of the indigenous culture in the northwestern region of South America, where it has been used for thousands of years as a mild natural stimulant.

Today, it is both the weapon and target in a civil war which has raged over four decades. Both the leftist FARC and right-wing paramilitary fund their conflict through production and trade of cocaine. To a significant degree the fate of the coca plant, along with its farmers, is what this war is all about.

A rich, fertile tropical land, Colombia is naturally inclined to agriculture, and would normally prosper from these advantages. Their other major cash crop, coffee, once set the standard in the world, but global cultivation has glutted the supply, and the beans are caught in the grinder, as it were. Only gigantic plantations with generally lamentable labor conditions are able to prosper in that market.

For the freelance farmer, these are the variables that go into the choice of what crop to plant. Historically, there also have been many large coca fields controlled by the FARC, the paramilitary, or the cartels, but the slightly inflated value of coca products makes small plots, for family subsistence, viable as well.

Farmers complain that they'd be happy to grow anything, but nothing else they grow can be sold at a price greater than the cost. Small-scale coca planting is not a way to get rich; coca paste, which is the product not only of a season of farming, but an expensive extraction process as well, sells for under one thousand USD per kilo. Processed and shipped to the United States, it becomes worth fifteen times that much.

The usual procedure for obtaining the active ingredient from whole leaf requires large amounts of diesel fuel and other chemicals. The processing cost, in which the farmer must invest up front, can be two-thirds of the raw product's sale price. A harvest might bring only a few hundred dollars profit.

Still, this pittance is a reliable way to support a family, so, despite the risks, tiny plots continue to be the mainstay of cocaine production. These fields tend to coexist with the food crops, on which these poor people depend in a more direct fashion. When the planes drop herbicides on this land, the farmers and their families are apt to starve, as well as plunge into protracted poverty.

Since these fields are so small, they make a difficult target for eradicators, who must be precision bombers to land their deadly cargo on the coca. Often enough, they miss entirely, instead devastating some cassava or plantains that a poor *campesino* family was hoping would sustain them.

The majority of these operations are carried out by the Colombian authorities, at the insistent behest of the US government, and with generous funding from the taxpayers in the North. The violent war on *cocaleros* is the central political issue at the heart of civil conflict; the rebels want, among other concessions for the poor, that the Colombian government sever this Faustian relationship with the United States over cocaine.

Each side engages in brutal repression within the territories they control, and it is by and large the poor who are caught in the crossfire. Death squads and cartel violence blot the countryside, producing a fatalistic culture seeped in blood.

One might point to all of this and say that it is the cocaine causing all this misery, but in reality that is like saying that slaves are the cause of slavery. The *status* of cocaine, and the unnatural market conditions which inflate the value of it, are what drives this internal struggle.

The pattern in Colombia is more or less replicated in every nation where illicit crop production is a considerable, even dominant force in the economy. These countries, such as Mexico and Afghanistan, are notable in that their standard of living is dramatically lower than the United States or most of Europe, as well as in the degree to which they are ruled by collaborators with US policy.

Whereas the horizons of cultivators are limited, and these coveted substances should be a bonanza enriching the general welfare, the fruits of these labors are destroyed, becoming a symbol of strife and poverty.

Under the 1961 UN Single Convention on Narcotics, every member nation is obligated to engage in prohibition. This remarkable conspiracy to deprive the world of cognitive liberty stands as perhaps the most formidable barrier to reform of all. Even if the SCOTUS were to reverse itself, and strike down all controlled substance legislation in the United States, the Single Convention would still rule the world.

The original treaty uses a scheduling system similar to the one later adopted under the Nixon administration. Any substance which is "similar" to morphine, cocaine, or cannabis is automatically placed on the most restrictive category.

One consequence of this is the burden it places on producing countries, where agriculture depends heavily on poppies, marijuana, or coca, to restrict the prospects of their own people. This is not a trivial matter in poor economies where the alternative is starvation.

What is tragic is that the criterion for entering a plant or chemical on this list seems to be bound up in the punitive effect on these "third-world" nations. This is practically a subsidy for commodities, produced in wealthier countries, which would otherwise occupy an inferior share of the market.

For example, both alcohol and tobacco benefit in their competition with marijuana, in that the latter is dependent on an informal distribution system and is subject to a high margin of loss. On an equal footing, consumers who are currently resorting to beer or cigarettes, because of their legal advantage, might choose to forego both in favor of cannabis, at a tremendous net benefit for their health.

How much wealthier these countries would be, if their productive capacity was not being assaulted by the US and UN-sponsored rain of poison from the sky!

There is a long history of the Federal government appointing itself arbiter of agriculture during the twentieth century, not merely in relation to psychotropic crops, but in regulating the supply and price of food harvests as well.

When a government promotes farming, this is a positive and beneficial function which improves the general welfare. Abundance is logically the goal of any regulatory hand in the fundamental production of goods. Yet, as Joseph Heller famously satirized in *Catch-22*, the instinct of authorities is often to discourage production, using obscure and absurd subsidy schemes where farmers are paid to let their lands lie fallow and grow nothing at all.

In exporting this madness to the so-called "third world," the elite countries are practicing the most unfair of all trade: the active sabotage of a struggling nation's most valuable export. That the leaders of these countries comply with prohibition policies is a horrible betrayal of their most disadvantaged populations, but they are not the primary target of our criticism here.

This lamentable state of affairs, in which the US foments internal strife through bribing and threatening governments to act against their people, is the global war stemming from the combative domestic campaign to control psychotropics. This war, like many catastrophic conflicts of the twentieth century, has a multinational character and pits different classes of each country against each other.

Furthermore, like prohibition at home, these policies are completely ineffective in stemming the overall manufacture of the feared substances. On the contrary, eradication simply shifts the sites deeper and deeper into the forests, where even more environmental devastation will attend the poison planes which follow them.

The plants and their tenders are not the only victims of the vast, yet hopeless, campaigns in furtherance of this dubious goal. It takes many human beings to evade the patrols, checkpoints, and borders between these tropical farmlands, and the northern cities where their yield will be consumed.

These individuals are at great risk due to the large cash and valuable cargo in their hands, and often do unspeakable things to protect their interests. They are also due a grisly death, if they mishandle their freight or allow it to be seized. The retribution from a large loss may even be visited on uninvolved family members.

If we accept for the moment that this trade is harmful—and illegality does confer many undesirable features on any commerce—the end result of US interdiction policies is that the export focus has broadened to the rest of the world, especially Europe. Even nearby countries like Brazil are absorbing a rapidly climbing share of the cocaine market, proving that it will take more than blocking one border to wipe out the industry.

The boundaries of the United States were traditionally porous, as the premise of this land has always been that newcomers had every right to emigrate here, even at the expense of those already established.

As the poem proclaims at the foot of Lady Liberty, who still graces the gates of Ellis Island, it would be counter to the basic character of America to turn economic and political refugees away. After all, there She is, a gift from the much-maligned French, depicted on a million postcards, inviting the world to export and expatriate its wretched huddled masses to this uniquely shaped and situated nation of immigrants, in order to breathe free.

Considering the current policy on illegal immigration, however, the inscription ought to be redacted to read: "give me your rich tourists, your foreign business moguls bearing campaign contributions, your defectors with valuable intel, everyone else gets deported."

Border enforcement was largely a formality during much of US history; when the first immigration legislation was passed in 1891, the most restrictive barrier was a head tax of fifty cents. Today, limits are set on resident visas based on country of origin, which means that Latin American applicants, especially from Mexico, are put on a waiting list years long. Meanwhile, more vigorous drug enforcement along the borders makes illegal entry quite hazardous.

The suppression of undocumented immigrants is one of those "hot-button" issues where folks tend to react emotionally and irrationally. In fact, hatred of Mexican immigrants is the most socially acceptable form of ethnic intolerance in the United States.

Proponents of strict immigration enforcement will deny that they are advocating racism, claiming that their objection is merely with the *criminality* of such people being present without paperwork. Groups like the recently disbanded Minutemen vent their resentment, under the pretext that undocumented workers are an economic burden, but the truth is that most are extremely hardworking, and contribute more than their fair share in underpaid labor.

The dispute over illegal immigration is again a bit outside the scope of our primary focus on cognitive liberty. Yet it is intertwined so much with the international struggles over substances, and is cause of so many Constitutional crises, that we feel compelled to briefly comment.

First of all, it is our contention that borders, as a barrier to travel, are at the core a foul and unnecessary accoutrement to an open society. Liberties enshrined in the Bill of Rights are routinely compromised as an introduction to the "Land of the Free." Blocking passage on the basis of birthplace is as arbitrary a form of discrimination as exists, and it is unconscionable that all who wish to enter for dire reasons are not in some way accommodated.

That the border acts as a marginally effective filter, for both humans and commodities which are banned, tends to combine the never-ending effort to smuggle them. Circumventing the controls is most conveniently arranged by placing contraband on the backs of border jumpers, who if all go well will get paid for their efforts once reaching the safety of a city. If not, then it is the hapless immigrants, rather than the cartel members, who will serve a trafficking sentence, before being unceremoniously shipped back across the invisible line.

Insofar as the violence related to getting people and product over that artificial hurdle is directly tied to the degree of border enforcement, those who advocate tightening the net are guaranteeing more bloodshed. As increasingly ruthless cartels fight to control critical supply lines, much of Mexico is consumed in large-scale turf wars, which cannot help but spill over to the US. This relevant reality has become a common rallying cry for legalization, as the evils of smuggling can only be abated by obviating the need for transporting contraband.

While American politicians are ranting about the drugs seeping through the border from Mexico, the southbound product is far more deadly. Seventy percent of the guns seized in Mexico are of US origin. The drug enforcement entities of the US have infiltrated Mexico and dictate internal policies there, although no reciprocal extension of Mexico's very strict gun control policy meddles in US affairs to stem the flow of lethal contraband weapons exported from the North.

Creating a sound policy, which actually reduces harm to the public, calls for more than just a ban-hammer; it requires nuance of understanding, an appreciation for the economics of contraband and collective human nature.

The old adage is manifest and more apt than our rulers seem to credit: laws are made to be broken. Keeping foreigners and a fraction of cartel shipments on the other side of the fence may become marginally successful, but it will never seriously reduce the supply of either undocumented workers, or controlled substances.

Meanwhile, there are plenty of people in the world with nothing to lose willing to risk even the most draconian penalties. East Berlin was sealed by perhaps the most fortified barrier in the world. The Iron Curtain was intended not only to prevent unauthorized travel *into* the Communist East, but to contain the many unsatisfied customers who desperately wanted *out*.

The Berlin Wall was a symbol of the worst sort of repression, and the whole world cheered when it was finally torn down. Nevertheless, thousands of people risked life and limb simply to be on the other side of the most heavily guarded border on Earth.

There is something inherently offensive about deeming a human being illegal, simply because they are away from the land of their birth, on the wrong side of an invisible line carving up the Earth we all share. While it promotes the general welfare to have some procedure new immigrants must follow, the tightening enforcement on immigration is a detriment, to both the foreign-born, and this society which has always depended on them for cheap and obliging labor.

Some of the most outrageous examples of law replacing decency can be seen in the deportation of certain undocumented residents, who were brought to the United States as children, grew up speaking English, and were discovered to be non-citizens in the course of pursuing the American Dream.

Such people have no ties in the country to which they are being shipped away, often no knowledge of the language spoken there, and are effectively being exiled from the only land they have ever known.

One step toward addressing this monstrous inequity is the DREAM Act, which provides paths to permanent residence to such individuals, provided they meet strict educational requirements or military service. While we would submit that this reform, which at time of this writing is negotiating the Senate, does not go nearly far enough, we applaud the rationality, and compassion, behind this principle.

In a perfect world, there would be no borders. We firmly believe that the world belongs equally to all of us, and that barring passage on the basis of nationality is flagrant unacceptable discrimination. To legally enjoin the employment of poor economic refugees is a despicable abridgment of the basic human right to earn a living.

Immigration law is theoretically the sole domain of the Federal government, but in the past few years there has been a push to enforce it locally, particularly in the border State of Arizona. Spouting rhetoric which is protectionist, and often outright racist, the supporters of strict border enforcement style themselves "Nativists," despite being only a few generations removed from ancestors who were themselves among the huddled masses.

Spearheading this movement in Arizona are powerful politicians, such as Senate President Russell Pearce and Sheriff Joe Arpaio of Maricopa County. Catering to a vocal and reactionary movement, which often includes open neo-Nazi posturing, the State Legislature in the hot summer of 2010 passed the controversial measure known as SB1070, marking a shift toward policies reminiscent of 1930s Germany.

If you want an idea of what the Nazification of the United States would look like, take a hard look at Maricopa County. We say this at the risk of violating Godwin's law, which automatically discredits any comparison with the Third Reich. Nothing, the popular wisdom goes, can compare with the Holocaust, and it is considered at the very least indelicate to suggest otherwise.

Nevertheless, the parallels between the Nativist fiefdom in Maricopa County, and the rise of National Socialism in Germany are potent. In each case, an alien class is targeted as the cause of economic troubles, and strict, militarized forces are emplaced in order to purge society of this scapegoat.

The Nativist movement is not merely *like* Nazism; it is, at least in part, unquestionably Nazi. Many of the core supporters are out-front, proud White Supremacists, clad in SS uniforms emblazoned with Swastikas. Pearce and Arpaio have both been filmed fraternizing with members of the National Socialist Movement, which turns out in small, but conspicuous, numbers to burn or stomp on Mexican flags and harass the giant civil rights marches against SB1070.

Known as the "papers, please" law, the controversial and unconstitutional act mandates systematic racial profiling. Requiring local police departments to enforce Federal immigration legislation, SB1070 turns the entire State of Arizona into a border checkpoint. Under the highly protested legislation, anyone could have identification demanded from them, based on a reasonable suspicion of foreignness. Civil penalties are provided to punish any police department in the State failing to sufficiently enforce this offensive exercise in racial profiling.

Naturally, this presents a problem for the State's many legal residents and citizens of Latino descent, who are expected at all times to prove their permission to be on Uncle Sam's turf, even though many Hispanic-Americans have greater longevity in the area than the Caucasian-Americans raising pitchforks at them.

In addition to running one of the most disgracefully corrupt county jail systems in the United States, Joe Arpaio puts most of his time and taxpayer money toward harassing the area's many undocumented residents and petty nonviolent offenders.

He has made a name for himself as the "Toughest Sheriff in America," an assessment we have no quibble with. What is he tough on, though? Violent crime? Thefts? No, Joe's minions put their paramilitary might towards raiding restaurants and carwashes, to arrest people for the dangerous crime of working hard for a meager living.

Joe's real claim to fame, though, is his gulags. Erected not in some secluded frozen forest, but in downtown Phoenix, the sprawling jail complex under his personal control is a testament to the callousness of which the police State is capable.

Unwilling to accept that overcrowding of jails should lead to any leniency, or one single early release, Joe enhanced the carrying capacity of his human warehouse by opening concentration camps, using surplus Korean war barracks tents, in the hottest desert environment in the country.

Tent City, the pride and joy of a man who measures success by the misery he's created, sits in the sun under blistering temperatures in excess of

120° Fahrenheit during spring and summer. Joe won't brook any complaining about this; after all, the barracks are no worse than what soldiers in Iraq put up with. Of course, none of the guests of Maricopa County Jail signed up for this treatment, although Joe seems to think they did. His blanket response to critics: "If you don't like it, don't go to jail."

Thanks to this inexpensive innovation, there is always room for more jaywalkers and dishwashers, as well as, of course, drug possessors. In Arizona, simple possession of marijuana or paraphernalia is charged as a felony, so the cells and tents are crowded with marijuana smokers who can't make bail. Over ten thousand detainees attempt to survive in Joe's jails at any given time, the size of a small college. His expressed philosophy is deliberate inhumanity, saying, "I want to make this place so unpleasant that they won't even think about doing something that could bring them back."

Although seventy percent of the inhabitants of the jail have not yet faced trial, and are not convicted, the evident mentality behind the administration is that anyone who has found themselves under arrest is subhuman, unworthy of medical care, simple information, or the least bit of compassion.

The food service is an absolute scandal. Inmates are fed the worst quality of surplus food, including green bologna and the disgusting concoction used for punishment known as "Nutraloaf." Much of the food is moldy and unfit for human consumption, but starving inmates will still fight over the meager portions. Arpaio's captives are also fed with meat salvaged from sick emus who died on his relatives' farm.

Joe boasts of feeding the jail inmates on pocket change, spending approximately forty cents per day on two meals, while spending over three times as much to feed police dogs.

In 2008, the Sheriff began a policy of charging for these "meals," at triple the cost, deducting payment from the commissary funds of the few who have money on the books. A court order from Judge Neil Wake requires pre-trial detainees to be fed according to Fed standards, a judgment Arpaio vigorously appealed, and has so far ignored.

Arpaio's lawyers spend a lot of time in courts, at a price of about three hundred dollars per hour, and a veritable fortune of taxpayer dollars has been spent defending the many lawsuits against his department. By 2007, forty-one million dollars had been drained from county coffers in order to settle or pay judgments against the MCSO for wrongful death and civil rights violations, as well as attorneys fees and staggering liability insurance premiums. Over two thousand Federal lawsuits were pending in US district court, along with hundreds more in the county system.

Just between 2004 and 2007, over twenty-seven hundred lawsuits were filed against the Sheriff's office, *fifty times* the number in New York,

Chicago, Los Angeles, and Houston *combined*. Arpaio has been the target of numerous Federal probes and grand jury investigations for racial profiling, political intimidation, and prisoner abuses, but no one seems to be able to make charges stick. The largest settlements have come from the deaths in the inhumane, diseased rat-traps, which hold mostly pre-trial detainees and misdemeanor convicts. Medical neglect and conspicuous battery on the part of Joe's guards are sometimes beyond the ability of inmates to physically bear, and a number have unhappily ended their lives in custody of the MCSO.

Joe Arpaio exercises nearly dictatorial control over the government of the county, and is unafraid to dispatch his deputies on a mission of political shakedown. His abuse of power is legendary and seems to know no limits. During his infamous feud with the Board of Supervisors over funding, a number of county employees and elected officials ran afoul of investigations and arrests, facing baseless criminal charges as retribution for daring to tamper with Joe's cash flow. Not even high-level judges are immune from intimidation by the High Sheriff. When a Superior Court judge ruled that it was unconstitutional for the MCSO to restrict visits by defense attorneys, his henchmen responded by demanding all e-mail correspondence from her office.

A public buffoon, Arpaio is given to startling gaffes, such as the time he revealed that being compared to the Ku Klux Klan is, in his eyes, a compliment. Confronted with the unkind accusation on the Lou Dobbs show, the flaccid fool stated, "It's an honor, right? At least we're doing something!" Later, after someone told him how bad that sounded, he backpedalled, but one must wonder at the mind of such a man.

The Sheriff is a Media fixture, a darling of talk shows who has put in hundreds of hours of airtime to promote his fascist approach to law enforcement. A natural blowhard, Arpaio can be counted on to leave no dead air hanging. Feisty and unapologetic, he touts without a trace of self-consciousness the virtues of making people miserable, and the ugly science he has mastered toward this end.

He shamelessly takes every opportunity to highlight the cruelty of his jails, including a book he "co-authored," but has admitted, in a videotaped disposition, that he has not fully read, containing racist statements he hastily disavowed. His abuses need no exposure; Arpaio is quite willing to detail and defend his medieval practices in any Media venue that will have him. He earnestly believes that civil rights are a concoction of lawyers and that he has no responsibility to recognize them.

His "lock-em-up and throw away the key" schtick plays well with the aging voter pool in sunny Arizona, but what shocks the conscience of freedom-loving folk is the wantonness with which he broadcasts his contempt for basic liberties, and the lives under his brutal care.

The Sheriff got his start working for the DEA, where he was known as "Nickel-Bag Joe," for his success at making petty pot busts. Operating in Mexico without Constitutional limitation, Arpaio developed a taste for totalitarianism that he is all too thrilled to import across the border. Such is the future of America, under the encroaching dominance of prohibitionist control-freaks.

The phony link between terrorism and drug traffic is one of the popular new memes in the disinformation programming of the new millennium. Following the destruction of the World Trade Center, the forces of repression have repeatedly gained authority by falsely associating the two.

The abridgment of civil liberties known as the USA PATRIOT Act, rushed through Congress under the pretext of guarding against terrorism, confers unprecedented surveillance powers on government agents. The legislation adds controls on finance, personal travel, and political action which can be as readily used to prosecute controlled substance offenses or domestic activism as to combat any violent conspiracy.

One such provision is the use of so-called "sneak and peak" searches, officially called "delayed-notice" warrants. Whereas agents executing a warrant normally would be required to present it as their authorization to enter, sneak and peek searches could be conducted without the target's knowledge, until well after the fact.

Although this practice had been gradually declared Constitutional by the privacy-hating SCOTUS, the Patriot Act codified the procedure for utilizing this uniquely odious form of intrusion. In fiscal 2009, according to the annual report from the US Court Administration, out of a total of nearly nineteen hundred applications for such exceptional warrants or extensions of them, close to fifteen hundred, or seventy-seven percent, were in support of drug investigations. Only *fourteen* pertained to terrorism. A cynic might suggest that these abrogations of liberty are the real purpose of this Trojan Horse law, to strip away civil rights under the guise of responding to the threat of foreign extremists.

In fact, a number of individuals have postulated that the Twin Towers attack itself was a "false flag" operation, in which rogue elements of the government itself conspired to engineer the hijacking, or even fabricate it, precisely so as to enable the passage of such measures. This is not the place to explore such theories, other than to note how consistent this behavior would be with the past performance of the CIA, especially considering how the late Osama bin Laden, like the many "Goldsteins" who have been transformed into objects of patriotic hate, was once on the Company payroll, and had deep ties to the Bush ruling family.

Some have even presented convincing arguments that Al Qaeda does not exist at all, that the organization itself is an imaginative fabrication foisted on the world as a CIA provocation. Some have observed that the term in Arabic, meaning "the Base," is also a common term for a toilet, and is hardly a name designed to rally support.

We note that over *eleven hundred* architects and engineers have joined an organization, specifically to convey their professional estimation that the WTC buildings were brought down by thermite demolition, rather than jet fuel fire. You don't need to be an engineer to figure this out; just watch how quickly and evenly the gigantic structures collapsed, with sequenced bursts of explosion rippling down the structures as they neatly fell.

Suffice it to say that we don't believe the official version of events on that fateful day. Nor do we believe that the threat of Islamic terrorism has ever been significant enough, even if real, to justify the surrender of domestic civil rights, or the world-churning military invasions in Iraq and Afghanistan.

The War on Terror, like that on drugs, is an instrument of continuous accumulation of State power, predicated on a fantastic amplification of a purported emergency. Unlike possessors of drugs, however, terrorists, insofar as they exist at all, are not plentiful low-hanging fruit on which the prison-industrial complex can feast. It turns out that domestic terrorism is exceedingly rare, considering the provocative excesses of US foreign policy. The handful of terror-related incidents since 9-11 have, for the most part, featured the bumbling efforts of inept and disturbed individuals, rather than any organized conspiracy to destroy the institutions important to national security.

As part of the new war, the Feds began disbursements to local jurisdictions in order to equip their police with instruments of destruction. As Norm Stamper, former Seattle Chief of Police and member of LEAP, Law Enforcement Against Prohibition, put it, "There's nothing 'para' about it. It's just plain military."

Under the guise of equipping local first responders to contain outbreaks of terroristic violence, Federal grants, directly from the Pentagon, were made available to outfit even small towns with the paraphernalia of combat: bulletproof vests, armored personnel carriers, and M-16 rifles. The armed occupation of America has been forwarded, not by the marching of platoons into city squares, but in the quiet transfer of hardware and mandate to civilian police.

SWAT teams, which operate as quick-strike combat units, are the chief beneficiary of this largesse. Since the early 1980s, when the Reagan

Administration made the war on drugs literal, deployment of strike forces inside the US has increased thirteen-fold, from three thousand annually, to forty thousand in 2006. Such units are at the ready in ninety percent of the nearly seven hundred cities surveyed.

Naturally, the weapons provided in order to squash terrorist cells couldn't be allowed to languish. These expensive exercises in overkill are a sledgehammer in search of a nail, which lands squarely on homes which may or may not harbor illicit stashes of party favors.

Pentagon-provided assault units find constant employment in the service of search warrants for drugs. The ridiculous levels of force, and huge numbers of personnel accompanying the typical no-knock raid, signify the overcapacity of law enforcement and disproportionate application of military might.

The hostilities in Iraq and Afghanistan have brought thousands of combat-trained veterans to the job market, with skills related primarily to population suppression. Many of these have been happily absorbed by the imprisonment industry. The skill set of military incursion applies neatly to the demands of drug enforcement. On the streets and in the jails, former soldiers apply the same tactics and gear to US citizens, as they have in foreign invasions.

The use of military force on noncombatant civilians is disturbing, and possibly illegal under the Geneva Convention, whether outside the borders or inside them. Bringing this deadly might to bear on citizens of the United States is an outrage to the Constitution as well. How can the residents of a supposedly free country reconcile the idea of liberty with doors being kicked in on an often erroneous quest for controlled substances?

Since 9-11, there has been an obnoxious tendency in the Media to equate drug use with support of terrorism. Some terrorists, depending how the term is defined, capitalize on the concentrated value of contraband, as do some governments. The difference between terrorist and ruler is principally a matter of perspective and power. Most people and organizations thus designated view themselves as freedom fighters. The word "terrorist" is prejudicial, and while it certainly is a demerit against imported drugs that the handlers are often military gun-toters, who belong to combat units of varying legitimacy, it wouldn't be possible without prohibition.

Perhaps the message would be more effective, if they pointed out that the crack you're smoking may have come to you courtesy of Uncle Sam.

That might be enough to make many quit.

ARTICLE XIII:
Cocaine Importation Amalgamated

"Paranoia is simply having all the facts"—William S. Burroughs

There is an even darker, more hypocritical side to the US activities in Latin America. While the DEA is busy conducting military exercises and chemical warfare in combat against agriculture, another alphabet-soup agency is implicated in repeated large-scale trafficking of the very drugs so many public resources are invested in suppressing.

The first popular awareness of this double-dealing emerged in 1987, with the exposure of the Iran-Contra scandal. As the story leaked out, it appeared that top-level military officials had engineered a sordid, and highly illegal, plot to trade arms for hostages held in Iran, and to facilitate the transport of cocaine. The goal of this subterfuge was to finance the Administration's unauthorized aid to the right-wing revolutionary army in Nicaragua.

The second part of the plan is what concerns us here. The arms supply flights to the *Contras* were illegal in themselves, but considerable public ado accompanied the shocking revelation that these planes were returning stuffed with kilos of cocaine, en route to the inner cities of America.

These missions began to come to light when such a supply plane was shot down by Nicaraguan forces as an invading aircraft. The lone survivor, Eugene Hasenfus, was captured, along with some damaging information related to US operations at Ilopango airbase in nearby El Salvador. The *Sandinista* government tried Hasenfus as a CIA spy, sentencing him to twenty-five years in prison, although he was quickly recovered from captivity by US authorities and returned to the United States.

The *Sandinistas*, led by Daniel Ortega, rose to power in the same season as the Reagan-Bush cabal that would hold power in the US over the next twelve years. Installed after guerilla-war victory over the right-wing Somoza dictatorship in 1979, Ortega's Marxist government was a particular thorn in the Administration's side, because it extended the Soviet sphere of influence to the narrow bottleneck separating the Northern and Southern American continents.

Determined to control this strategically important piece of turf, the CIA immediately began organizing and funding counterrevolutionary insurgency. Because the whole of their political agenda was to remove the socialists from power, the pro-US militias became known as the *Contras*, from a Spanish word meaning "opposition."

Public support for this kind of meddling in the internal affairs of small countries was historically low in the United States, and beginning in 1982, a series of riders on the Defense appropriation bill, called the Boland Amendments, prohibited the diversion of official military budget funding for aid to the *Contras*.

Undeterred, the covert operatives at some point found a brilliant end-run around this restriction. The CIA would broker the Agency's ability to circumvent interdiction measures, on behalf of the fledgling capitalist rebels. This would allow for secret cash to be generated at will by the *Contras* and their abettors. This operation was known colloquially as the "Enterprise," and was personally implemented by National Security Advisor Lt. Colonel Oliver North.

Congressional hearings were held, and it quickly emerged that the plot went right to the top; strong evidence pointed to then Vice-President Bush, who had at one time been Director of the Agency, and who had been given command over the entire intelligence infrastructure by Presidential decree in 1981.

Suspicions also surrounded the Teflon President, against whom nothing could stick, the very same Ronald Reagan who made "Just Say No" the national policy, and who was convinced of the utter destructiveness of drugs. When asked about these shenanigans under oath, the Commander-in-Chief evaded both responsibility and perjury charges, choosing to profess amnesia. While several White House military aids were scapegoated, to appease the public cry for accountability, their convictions were rapidly reversed, and criminal or impeachment proceedings against the President were never initiated.

Chip Tatum, a pilot whose code name was "Pegasus," worked as a CIA mule during the early 1980s. According to his account, Tatum's mission, directed by Lt. Colonel Oliver North, was to transport coolers marked as medical supplies to Little Rock Airport, and deliver them to a certain Dr. Dan Lasater.

In the course of making one of many such deliveries, Tatum opened his cargo, discovering kilos of cocaine and money, stored in what he had assumed was a delivery of transplantable organs. When he asked North, his immediate superior, about this discovery, Tatum was told that the mislabeled stash was "evidence," and it was being transported for the purpose of indicting the *Sandinista* government in World Court.

Under orders, he had no choice but to deliver the contraband to Lasater and his entourage of law enforcement officers, including Raymond "Buddy" Young, who at the time was acting as security officer for the Governor of Arkansas. One William Jefferson Clinton also was present to receive the coolers.

Lasater, who had made his fortune as founder of the Ponderosa steak franchise, had moved on to bond dealing, and was a major political contributor to the free-wheeling First Couple of Arkansas. He was also an enthusiastic participant in the upper-class cocaine culture that swept the fast-paced high-financed world of paper trading during the 1980s, a trend which also snared Clinton's brother, Roger.

This extravagant penchant led to Lasater's unfortunate bust by Federal authorities in 1986. For most defendants, that would simply be the end of the matter, their lives smashed, but not every defendant is dealing for the government. He served six months for Federal cocaine distribution charges.

Clinton, who as President would waste no time employing his pardoning authority on behalf of Lasater, was allegedly present at this delivery, and ultimately took possession of the coolers. According to Tatum, these shipments were a regular event, and he places both future presidents— Clinton and Bush—at the scene of a cocaine production camp site.

Tatum, who has released detailed documents supporting his account of these missions, was subjected to government harassment and railroading criminal charges in retaliation to his public airing of these misdeeds.

A veteran of clandestine operations, Tatum had accumulated what he called "insurance," including photographic and video evidence that he felt the government would not want to see released. Part of this cache was a set of flight plans, which he had filed following each of these suspicious missions, detailing the passengers on board, and including, on the backside of each document, notes relating to the illegal cargo he identified on board.

The breaking point for Tatum came, by his account, when he was assigned to "neutralize" billionaire and independent Presidential candidate Ross Perot, who was challenging the incumbent, Bush, for the fiscal conservative vote in the upcoming election. Tatum explained that he had followed several orders to neutralize foreign foes, and that neutralization is a term which denotes not merely physical, but also character, assassination, extortion, or threats. The mission is to nullify enemies by whatever means are necessary. Using this tactic on an American politician, to undermine the democratic process, violated Chip's sense of patriotism, so he ceased to serve what by his measure was a rogue government.

History notes that Perot did indeed drop out of the race for a time, in reaction to some undefined harassment targeting his daughter, although he eventually returned to play a colorful, if insignificant, role in the eventual election of Bill Clinton. He demonstrated the principle that charts and graphs may be effective boardroom props, but turn voters into snoozers.

Evidently someone was found to do the dirty work Tatum had refused. Although he had committed multiple nefarious acts during his career in covert operations, Tatum balked at smearing a prominent US citizen for purely political reasons, and instead sent an incriminating tape to Bush, as incentive to keep the election tamper-resistant. He tendered his resignation directly to DCI William Colby, who would later turn up dead, under hazy circumstances, perishing in 1996 due to a suspicious boating accident.

By 1994, Tatum had gone completely off the reservation, and began feeling pressure to hand over incriminating evidence he had compiled against, among other people, the sitting President Clinton.

When he refused to surrender his documents, he was jailed on a charge of treason. In response, Tatum released some of the paper trail tying the current President of the Commander-in-Chief and others, to large-scale drug trafficking. He published his papers, and sent copies to the individuals implicated within.

Both Chip, and his wife, Nancy, were brought up on charges which kept morphing, ranging from the original charge of treason for him, to an eventual indictment and conviction for wire fraud charges. To spare Nancy, he later said, Tatum pled to these charges, which amounted to illegally transferring approximately seventy thousand dollars of his own money across State lines.

After serving his time, Chip was again brought up on criminal charges, this time along with Nancy, despite the deal he had made to leave her innocent name out of the harassment. This double-cross was all Tatum needed to make the decision to unleash the next round of insurance.

The two published the *Tatum Chronicles*, and extensively briefed the public on the nature of Chip's work for the Company. The allegations contained in Tatum's memoirs paint a picture of systemic corruption rivaling and surpassing the famous graft of Latin American governments which are notoriously infiltrated by *narcotraficantes* posing as prohibitionists.

Tatum has become *unperson*; all that remains is his humbly self-published book along with many fantastic hours of interview with radio personality and former FBI agent Ted Gunderson. Despite the documentation he supplied to substantiate Tatum's insider whistle-blowing, the mainstream Media ignored his assertions, allowing them to fade into obscurity.

Tatum disappeared in 1998, shortly after completing an extensive interview with Gunderson, and unconfirmed reports indicate that his tortured body was found on the shores of Panama in 2007. If true, the body showed signs of torture, and was missing part of the face. Perhaps his insurance had finally been neutralized.

Quiet, mysterious mortality seems to befall the tellers of these tales, and it is with no small trepidation that we share them here with you, albeit second-or-third hand. All of this shocking information is available in a number of books, as well as on the internet, and for reasons we will go into shortly, we have every reason to believe in its veracity.

Another figure who was hounded to death for revealing these secrets was Gary Webb, a Pulitzer prize-winning reporter for the San Jose *Mercury News*. His reports on the cocaine connection with the *Contras* in Nicaragua merely accused the CIA of knowing about and turning a blind eye to this dealing, rather than actively engaging in it.

Nevertheless, the revelations in his series, called *Dark Alliance*, were too controversial for his bosses, who eventually killed the piece. Webb was exiled to the newspaper's version of Siberia, a distant inconsequential post a hundred fifty miles from his home, and essentially forced from a career in journalism.

He was found dead in 2004, from two gunshots to the head, in an apparent suicide. No explanation was offered for the anomaly of a suicide firing off two successive rounds into one's own skull, but Webb *had* been depressed, according to his wife. The coroner ruled these consecutive shots to be self-inflicted.

The *Dark Alliance* report focuses on the cocaine pipeline leading from Nicaragua to Los Angeles, where tons of Columbian marching powder landed in the hands of "Freeway" Ricky Ross, an enterprising distributor who allegedly pioneered the innovation of crack. He was getting a sweetheart connection from a *Contra* representative named Danilo Blandón, who had previously led the FDN, the largest faction of the revolutionary movement in Nicaragua.

The infusion of pre-based cocaine fueled the violent expansion of the Bloods and Crips gangs, who fought vicious turf wars over the right to vend the product. A similar pattern quickly emerged in every US city, and bloody feuds between the gangs only ramped up the volume on the loud calls for crack-downs.

The money, in turn, went back to Central America in the form of guns, where US policy worked to destabilize the local regime. The CIA was partially successful in attempts to subvert the elected *Sandinista* government, which peacefully passed power to the opposition party in 1990, but regained it through elections in 2006.

The recurring theme of Company-sponsored cocaine importation came to sudden public light, at a town hall held at Locke High School, in south Los Angeles. In response to the damning allegations contained in Webb's *Dark Alliance* stories and elsewhere, Director John Deutch of the CIA came to reassure the angry community that, no, the Company had *not* been dumping crack on their neighborhoods.

Mike Ruppert, a veteran of law enforcement, took the microphone to say, dramatically, "I will tell you, Director Deutch, as a former Los Angeles police narcotics detective, that the Agency has dealt drugs in this country for a *long* time." He identified, by codename, three such operations: *Amadeus*, *Pegasus* and *Watchtower*, indicating that he had in his hands some heavily redacted paperwork related to the latter.

He also said that he had been personally recruited by Company men, to look after their interests in the drug trade, as far back as the 1970s. After trying to get this information about CIA criminal connivance out for eighteen years, he finally aired this scandal in a public forum, directly to the DCI's face.

Deutch, denying the allegations, condescendingly suggested that *if* Ruppert had evidence of such trafficking by the CIA, he could bring it to either the Los Angeles Police Department, the Office of the Inspector General, or, he could write his Congressman.

The crowd, which had stood up to cheer Ruppert's courageous declaration, loudly grumbled at this unsatisfactory buck-passing response. Deutch did *not*, as he might if in earnest, demand that the damning documents be immediately forwarded to his office for close examination.

We must not be too hard on Deutch, though; he may have actually been in the dark. Otherwise, why would he have even personally travelled, to a high school of all places, to discuss these sensitive matters? Not by any means a Company man, the Director had been in office for a little more than a year, having come from the State department after a career in the sciences. He was not necessarily street smart, and this naiveté may have been his most attractive credential in qualifying him for the job of Spook-in-Chief.

One almost believes in the eggheaded sincerity of Director Deutch, when he states on the record that *if* there has been any wrongdoing within the CIA, he would see to it that the perpetrators be "brought to Justice." Considering what the average American is aware of in terms of Company misdeeds, we might wonder what exactly Deutch thought the Agency he was ostensibly running was really all about.

At any rate, he was replaced, exactly one month later, as Director of Central Intelligence, perhaps having learned something at Locke High School that made him unfit for the job.

Celerino Castillo was the DEA representative in El Salvador during the Enterprise period. A dedicated drug warrior, Castillo became concerned when he realized that two particular hangers at Ilopango airfield were being used for cocaine trafficking by suspects well known to him, through his investigations, as major players.

He also discovered that the Company was actively providing passports to these individuals, many of whom had extensive files with the DEA. It should come as no surprise that these hangers were jointly owned and operated by the CIA and the NSA, Oliver North's outfit.

Then, in 1986, what started as a drug raid on a residence in San Salvador turned up something very odd indeed: a large cache of weapons and munitions of US origin, as well as equipment belonging to the US embassy. All departments of the delegation to El Salvador disavowed any ties with the suspect, a supposed civilian named Wally Grasheim.

As Tatum had done, Castillo followed procedure, notifying his superiors about his discoveries. Instead of being rewarded for uncovering such massive, blatant corruption, he was warned to keep quiet, and ordered *not* to close his investigations on the subject, lest the files become accessible through the Freedom of Information Act.

Castillo's story is an instructive case study illustrating what happens when a "good cop," that is, one with integrity, attempts to apply the law to the government imposing it. Like many narcotics officers, Cele got into the game believing he was working for a just cause. When he found out that his bosses were more crooked than the cartels he had signed on to fight, he was pushed into an early retirement, at the tender age of forty-three.

After spending much of the next two decades publishing his book, and conducting interviews relating his perspective on drug war corruption, the patient long arm of the law finally reached out for Castillo.

He was brought up in 2008, on charges of weapons dealing, for trading in firearms at gun shows. In 2009, Castillo was ordered to begin a 37-month sentence in prison, despite his contention that his prosecution was selective, and in retribution for his speaking out about the criminals in high places.

We don't always celebrate when a narc meets such a fate. Cele is a victim of the war on truth.

Terry Reed was yet another former operative with a tale to tell about trafficking cocaine under the color of authority. The players are familiar; like Tatum, he had personal associations with Oliver North, Vice-President Bush, and the Governor of Arkansas, in this period during the 1980s when cocaine traffic, and the "war" against it, simultaneously spiked.

Reed's story corroborates Tatum's, and is curiously parallel. Hired as a flight instructor for *Contra* pilots, at an airbase outside of tiny Mena, Arkansas, Reed was intimately familiar with the inner workings of the domestic side of covert operations relating to Nicaragua. His job was to drill the pilots at an unserviced airstrip in a place called Nella, twelve miles from town.

One of Reed's projects was the oversight of weapons manufacture, for use in Central America. Because arms manufactured in traditional facilities are trackable, through serial numbers and associated paperwork, they were unsuitable for illegal military aid. Under the direction of the CIA, he set up a machine shop to craft untraceable weapons which would seemingly appear from nowhere.

Mena, a remote rural town of some five thousand locals, was certainly an odd place for any kind of large-scale undertaking. Lacking interstate highway access, and off the beaten path, the quiet community in the Ozarks would not seem to have the infrastructure, skilled labor pool, or technology to support such a facility.

It was, however, an ideal location to launch clandestine operations away from prying eyes. Mena became the hub for a complex set of activities in support of *Contra* operations, and rapidly developed into the staging ground for the exchange of arms, cocaine, and the money fueling them.

One contact Reed made in Mena was Barry Seal, a colorful character from Baton Rouge, Louisiana, who was described to Reed as a CIA contractor, working to resupply the *Contras*. At the young age of sixteen, he had joined the Civil Air Patrol, along with another famous Louisiana native: Lee Harvey Oswald.

The two were linked in another way; Seal's CIA recruiter was David Ferrie, which is a name familiar to those who are versed in JFK assassination lore. Both Seal and Oswald were recruited by this strange figure. Seal's involvement with the CIA goes back at least as far as Operation 40, which was a shadowy task force created to combat Castro's communist regime in Cuba in the early 1960s.

By 1980, Seal had found his calling in the import/export trade, hauling large cocaine shipments by plane, on behalf of the cartels in Latin America. This was excellent business for him, until he ran afoul of authorities in Florida, being indicted for bringing Quaaludes into the country. He struck a deal with the government, and in 1984 went to work for the Feds.

At the same time that Oliver North was arranging for massive shipments of cocaine to finance the *Contra* rebellion, he was choreographing a disinformation campaign designed to implicate the *Sandinistas* in the same thing. Barry Seal was part of this frame job; at this point he was something of a triple agent, working for the cartels in Columbia, the Company and

NSA in its coke-for-weapons scheme, and the DEA as an informant.

Seal boasted to Reed that he had, "names, dates, places...even got some tape recordings. Fuck, I even got surveillance videos catchin' the Bush boys red-handed." Like Tatum, he considered this information to be his insurance, in case the tables turned.

Unfortunately, when the time came for Seal, it was allegedly the Ochoa cartel who took his life, execution-style, outside the Salvation Army where he was court-ordered to live and eventually to die, reportedly with Vice-President Bush's *personal* telephone number in the trunk of his car.

By his account, Reed, who had worked in the clandestine operation for two years, discovered the cocaine connection when, in his words, he came "face-to-face with a C-130 full of cocaine...stored in ammunition boxes on a flight which was returning."

Realizing the position he had been put in, Reed did the proper thing: he informed his superior officers of his find. Unfortunately, he put the request for a full-scale investigation to Oliver North, who was not amused. Reed was labeled a security risk, and brought up on bogus charges, which seems to be the favored method of silencing insiders who show signs of not playing ball.

Another of Reed's projects working for North was the management of a loss brokering scheme, a sort of shell game in which different front companies partake in insurance and tax fraud. When he started becoming a threat to the Enterprise, these misdeeds on behalf of the Company became the basis for prosecuting him.

Although he and his wife were acquitted of all charges, the Reeds' quest for justice in the civil courts met an agonizing brick wall. In their lawsuit against Tommy Baker, as well as Buddy Young, who had since been rewarded for years of service with a post at Clinton's FEMA, the judge ruled that the plaintiffs were precluded from presenting their case, insofar as it might incriminate powerful people. The show-stopping order forbade:

"Any reference to President or Governor Bill Clinton and/or Hillary Clinton and the Mena or Nella Airports. Any references to Barry Seale [sic] and any alleged drug smuggling operation or other references to the Mena and Nella Airports, or to a business relationship of Barry Seale [sic] and Dan Lasater..."

With that, the quest to uncover the cocaine conspiracy from Arkansas to Central America in open court was effectively quashed.

One might wonder at this array of bombshell allegations, pointing fingers to corruption at the very top. Surely, given the Media frenzy which follows every financial or sexual scandal related to a President or candidate aspiring to the office, there would be more press on these damning charges of international cocaine and arms conspiracy.

To doubters, we point to the perfect seamlessness linking the detailed reports from Tatum, Reed, and Castillo. Although they were each posted at different points along the supply route, there is startling precision in the way their accounts piece the puzzle together. Dozens of hours given to reviewing this material revealed not a single inconsistency between these players, who name the same figures in the conspiracy, and are indisputably in a position to know. Don't take our word for it. The video is readily available to anyone capable of utilizing a search engine. Look up these names and see for yourself.

The Company has always had a hand in the business of narcotics traffic. Perhaps it is natural for a covert organization to gravitate toward this kind of commerce. The lure of unofficial funds is too great a temptation for above-the-law cabals with an imperative to travel the world in search of power. Secret intelligence outfits are a repository of dirty dealing, as their purpose is to maintain control at any cost.

Across the Ocean, in southeast Asia, a more classic drug dominated the landscape: heroin. The hostilities in Vietnam, which spread to surrounding countries like Laos and Cambodia, provided prime opportunities to bring heroin home. Not only were enterprising soldiers freelancing in this smuggling as they were shuttled back and forth, but the CIA was doing it, too, using the front company Air America to ship heroin under the guise of commercial flight.

According to a report which was entered into the Congressional record by Rep. John Conyers of Michigan, the involvement is as old as the agency itself, beginning in the very first year of operation. Having inherited a relationship with the Sicilian Mafia from its predecessors, the OSS and ONI, the CIA supported the ultra-capitalist mob, as a valuable ally against Communism.

Over the years, this friendliness between Central Intelligence and organized crime has blurred the line between the two, and in reality there is little difference. Each exploits government regulations to profit off desirable goods, whose scarcity is the result of prohibition. Each exercises brutal discipline on its own members, especially those who spill their secrets. Each employ assassins, extortionists and fixers to achieve nefarious ends and prevent or punish security breaches.

The CIA's fascination with drugs goes beyond merely selling them at inflated prices. During its formative years, the Company was very intrigued by the pharmacological potential for mind-control. The newly discovered psychedelic compounds, especially LSD, were of particular interest.

From the late 1940s on, experiments on what promised to be a new class of powerful psychological weapons were conducted under the auspices of Central Intelligence. The MK-ULTRA project was the most well-known of these, as it was exposed during Congressional hearings in 1975, and again in 1977.

Senator Ted Kennedy, in his opening remarks before the Select Committee on Intelligence, asserted, "The Deputy Director of the CIA revealed that over thirty universities and institutions were involved in an 'extensive testing and experimentation' program which included covert drug tests on unwitting citizens at all social levels, high and low, native Americans and foreign."

As in the volatile street-level market which resulted from these clandestine activities, shifting loyalties, betrayal and scapegoating have been a constant feature among the players in the governmental drug trade.

Exemplifying this is the case of Manuel Noriega, who as military commander of Panama had been a valuable ally of US interests, during the 1980s. In an ad criticizing his opponent, George Bush I, the campaign for candidate Michael Dukakis made mention of this close relationship, showing a grainy black and white photo of the two men meeting, and noting that cocaine traffic had spiked three hundred percent under Bush's supposed stewardship of the war on drugs.

When Bush took office, however, he turned on his former pal Noriega, in a backstabbing move characteristic of the style both he, and his Presidential son, have embodied. Using psychological warfare and rock music, the tiny country was invaded by a strike team, whose mission was to overthrow Noriega, and remit him to the US court system to face charges of drug trafficking, money laundering, and racketeering.

The international community, as represented by the UN General Assembly, was outraged, passing a resolution condemning the incursion by a margin of 75-20, despite a veto from close allies of the United States on the UN Security Council. At his trial, Noriega attempted to defend himself by putting his crimes in context: he had conducted these activities under the auspices of the CIA, which had paid handsomely for these services.

The judge refused to allow the presentation of such evidence, although the State was willing to stipulate to the payment of $320,000 passing from the CIA to the General, during the period these crimes were alleged to occur. Noriega countered that the amount was closer to $10 million, and that he ought to have been permitted to detail the work that this hefty paycheck had compensated.

Given the clandestine nature of "The Company," the full extent of CIA drug trafficking may never come to light. It is unlikely that the documented conspiracies, which were largely revealed through mishap and whistleblowers, truly represent the entirety of what appears to be an ongoing exploitation of the restricted drug market to raise funds for secret wars.

When we consider the enormity of the scam, any semblance of moral justification for drug interdiction dissolves. What we have is not so much a concerned nanny-State ignorantly attempting to implement controls for the sake of public health. Rather, one part of government acts to impose price controls through prohibition, while another secretly pockets the enormous profits generated by artificial scarcity. While one hand is pushing drugs, the other is spanking the buyers and competition into a cell.

Any illusions that these forays into drug-running are a thing of the past, an isolated incident among a few high-level zealots, were further eroded in 2007, when an alleged CIA torture jet crashed in Mexico, and was found to be hauling four tons of cocaine.

The plane, which had previously been utilized on rendition missions to Guantanamo Bay, had been registered to something called Donna Blue Aircraft, which gave every appearance of being some sort of front company. First of all, the address to which the company was registered, in the Florida incorporation papers, turned out to be vacant, other than an incongruous six-pack of plain white unmarked cruisers lined up in the parking lot.

Then there is the corporate acronym, *DBA*, which alternatively stands for "*Doing Business As.*" While it is the stock-in-trade of the CIA to make proving clandestine links very difficult, all of this makes some people wonder: why would the government rent an airplane from a shady nonexistent company, which also, coincidentally, hires out air transport for massive cocaine shipments?

All of this—and we have barely scratched the surface of this secretive subject—points to a motive in controlled substance policy which has nothing to do with public safety, or even diversion of funds to the prison-industrial complex. At the highest level, the least accountable faction of government has repeatedly exploited prohibition to fund State-sponsored terrorism.

ARTICLE XIV:
At the End of the Tunnel

"There is absolutely no greater high than challenging the power structure as a nobody, giving it your all, and winning." —Abbie Hoffman

As we complete this journey, we'd like to thank you for being a part of this book. You are the reason we have set aside these months to explore these issues, and why we have so devotedly filled these pages. We expect that some of this material was quite familiar to you, perhaps poignantly so. It is our hope, though, that we have added to the perspective of even the most seasoned veterans of this long war.

We have dwelled at length on the problems, but at this point the question must be, "What do we *do* about all this? How can change be brought about? Let's stop bitching and plan the Revolution!"

The short answer is that we continue do what our kind have always done: organize, transmit pertinent information, equip ourselves with arguments which penetrate the veil of lies cloaking the police State. We do as reform advocates have done for forty years: we celebrate every half loaf, catch our breath from each step forward, just in time to mourn two backward steps, and we pray, perhaps for another forty years, that we will live to see the day when sanity will reign.

We must not underestimate the scope of what stands against us. The artifice of prohibition is so deeply entrenched in the mechanisms of the State, it is so vital to the vampiric agencies feeding off the endless stream of victims, that we may never be free.

It is all well and good to prate about enhanced tax revenue potential from legalization, or depriving the cartels of blood money. These are valid angles, but peripheral. Activists have been reduced to begging for our freedom on the premise that our liberty will profit our captors. We hear that reform measures will save budget appropriations for police, courts and prisons, but we don't hear nearly enough about saving *people* from these things.

Such meek arguments are fine for the squares, in fact it may be just what this money-minded culture needs to hear. Let there be no confusion in our own ranks, though: what we are working to save is not the finances of government, but the flesh and blood of human beings. The primary issue is not the economics of drugs. The issue is what happens to those who are arrested for them.

Nonetheless, there are reasons to hope. The truth about cannabis is out, and getting results, with a growing trend of States enacting medicalization measures. Members of Congress, like Dr. Ron Paul, Barney Frank, and Jared Polis, are speaking out in uncompromising terms about ending this pointless and destructive campaign against a useful, harmless plant, and the humans who love Her.

We have just heard the news that these representatives are sponsoring the first ever bill to decriminalize marijuana at the Federal level; we are pessimistic, yet wish the sponsors well in their quixotic battle with their intolerant colleagues. Tilting at windmills may do no good, but the effort is truly inspiring. Every upheaval of the status quo has followed persistent failures to dislodge entrenched interests, until finally they topple under the pressure of dedicated activists.

Most pointedly, police themselves, along with judges and prosecutors, are beginning to stand up against the system which has used them to do its dirty work. Perhaps this insanity has, finally, nearly run its course.

We want to change the world, but what do we want to change it to? This is the meditation on which this examination shall conclude. What model of control would constitute a victory? At what point would reform be considered successful?

Many people use the words, "legalization" or "decriminalization" to characterize the position that no one ought be arrested for their ingestion habits. We submit that there is an older, more resonant term which applies to this struggle: *abolition*.

Abolition of prohibition is what we demand, an absolute, unequivocal striking down of all legislation which applies a penalty to the victimless possession of substances. Nothing less would honor the principal of individual sovereignty over our own minds and bodies.

This seems like an impossible goal from where we sit, given the intractable economic and social forces at play, the many people and institutions which are so heavily invested in these controls. Yet we are heartened by the historical evolution away from even more regressive systems, which were even more deeply entrenched. Overall, there has been a movement away from the persecution of one group after another, and we are confident that one day this liberation will encompass the free exercise of biochemical choice.

Let us wax idealistic for a moment, and consider what a sane drug policy would look like, how it would address the real issues of psychotropic substances, and how pharmacognitive liberty could be safely restored.

First and foremost, this policy would distinguish between chemically synthesized drugs, and natural bounty from the Earth. There is no reason to have any criminal penalties whatsoever regarding the cultivation, possession, or use of any vegetable. This would include not only cannabis, but also coca leaves, poppy pods, and psilocybin mushrooms, as well as the African entheogen khat. These plants have valid and venerable use in human society over thousands of years, are no more toxic in their natural form than other herbs, and could be safely tolerated without controls, beyond regulations ensuring quality and perhaps warning labeling.

To be sure, the constituents of some of these plants are somewhat habit-forming, as is anything which is pleasant and useful. From the standpoint of harm reduction, however, it seems that making the balanced raw form of an herbal entheogen available would dramatically reduce demand for the distilled version. This is a pattern we saw with the ban on alcohol, when high-potency and dangerously contaminated product displaced more benign forms like beer and wine. Given a choice, many people prefer the low-impact version, and much of the harm of drug addiction derives from restricting this choice. In any given year while alcohol was illegal, ethanol-related fatalities occurred at a higher rate than prior to the enactment of the Eighteenth Amendment, or following adoption of the Twenty-First. To this day, we see among underaged drinkers a disturbing trend of binge consumption due to the glamor of forbidden fruit and the need to capitalize on each opportunity to indulge.

Of course, there would be questions about distribution. In a perfect world, we'd prefer to see cannabis and the others take up their place in the bulk herbs section of the health food store, beside kindred psychoactive herbs like kava, gingko, or nutmeg. Failing that, there are the regulated distribution channels currently applied to tobacco or alcohol, or the coffeehouse model used in the Netherlands.

For synthetic drugs, it seems there are a number of reasonable concerns. One is the possibility of overdose, which might follow from too-ready access. This can be ameliorated by simply abolishing Schedule I, and removing the legal fiction that anyone would take or prescribe a drug which has no medical value. Let physicians decide what prescriptions to dispense, be it heroin for addiction, MDMA for couples counseling and depression, or LSD to aid in psychoanalysis.

We feel confident that health care professionals would be willing and able to provide such services, with fewer bad reactions than occur in the unregulated illicit market. Doctors, rather than police, would have control of pharmacology, and be responsible for minimizing the damage associated with drugs.

There are several avenues by which such change might be effected within the legal system, none of them terribly promising at present. Each branch of government, in fact, has the power at the Federal and even State level to immediately call a cease-fire.

A President could abolish the DEA, and issue executive orders halting the Federal prosecution of controlled substance cases, as well as categorically pardoning all prisoners of the drug war. We have seen disappointing results in this regard; Presidents Clinton and Obama, for example, were both widely expected to loosen interdiction efforts, but instead betrayed their constituents and ramped up enforcement.

The SCOTUS could also declare aspects of the war to be unconstitutional, on the grounds we have mentioned in previous chapters. Here, too, the prospects are dismal. Barring some kind of lethal contagion suddenly and simultaneously wiping out the current occupants of the bench, we can expect decisions from the Supreme Court to follow the same convoluted path of reasoning which has virtually stripped Constitutional protections from the system.

Nevertheless, we have seen such powerful reversals in the past, most notably in ending racial discrimination, and legitimizing medical termination of pregnancy. If the Court in a single decision can declare a universal right to abortion, against a backdrop of decades-long criminalization, the same could happen in some future version of SCOTUS with *this* set of rights.

Congress could veer hard to the social left, and repeal the legislation at the heart of this war. This would require a social revolt on the issue, but there are certainly members of both Houses who would support such a move. Additionally, either the Congress, or three-quarters of the States could adopt a progressive Amendment, settling once and for all that the limits of government preclude interference with sovereignty of self.

We propose, for what it's worth:

Congress shall make no law imposing criminal penalties for private acts which in no direct way infringe on the rights of others, nor shall any State; neither shall any law presume to supersede the individual's sovereignty over one's own body; and for every criminal charge there shall be a discernible victim, who has suffered definitive loss, injury or death, on whose behalf and at whose discretion prosecution will ensue.

Theoretically, such an Amendment could be passed by public referendum in thirty-eight States, thereby becoming the law of the land. Non-compliant courts, as well as willful legislators pushing the envelope to tests the bounds of such a radical decision, would be a perpetual problem, as is the case currently with the shifting sands of abortion politics. Still, it would be a start down the road toward a meaningfully restrained government. Perhaps you can devise an even better set of guarantees.

On the State level, the ballot initiative is a powerful tool for democratic local change, as we have seen in the push for medical marijuana, but a concerted grassroots effort could force national reform as well. We don't have to wait for the politicians to get on board with abolition to make it happen, though of course ending prohibition by any avenue promises great struggle.

We demand the immediate release of all prisoners of war. Every single person who is locked up on drug charges ought to be released without delay, with an apology and a rectification of their criminal record. All those held on probation, or in drug courts or diversion programs, should also have their burden lifted, and walk as free people once again.

Reparations will be a long time coming, but we demand them anyway. Each of us knows how much time and money has been taken from us by this systematic injustice. Sadly, many who suffered the most are no longer with us. But millions more are owed tens or hundreds of thousands of dollars, for legal bills, the theft of property, and years cut from our lives. Justice will not be done until every penny is repaid.

There may be some who doubt our equation between behavioral repression related to controlled substances, and the ethnic or sexual oppression which it replaced and perpetuated. We hope at this point these doubters are not among our readers, or else we have done our job quite poorly indeed.

Whenever the State singles out a class for persecution, whether the basis is racial or social minority, the principles of equality and liberty are betrayed. The stage is set for even more refined witch hunts. How long before the hunters come after other liberties? How long before the war machine calls upon local police to mute critics of State-sponsored terror at home and abroad? How many people will be searched in their vehicles and homes for displaying their political preference?

Don't look now, but all of these have taken place, in one form or another, for quite some time, and certainly with notable regularity since the dawning of the new Millennium. If it doesn't offend the sense of liberty that police search without serious restrictions for evidence of controlled substances, how do you feel about a search predicated on political premises?

This has already been happening to some degree, not only to legalization activists, but environmental organizers, anti-war protesters, even supporters of challenging candidates who threaten the powers-that-be. Despite all the doom and gloom, there remain powerful reasons to hope for a new day on the horizon. More and more airtime is being devoted to these ideas, and some fairly distinguished voices have started publicly backing them.

Consider the Global Commission on Drug Policy Report, issued in June of 2011, literally days before we are writing these words. The panel reached many of the same conclusions, regarding the misguided policy of international war on the pharmacological underclass, which we have presented here.

Chaired by Fernando Henrique Cardoso, former President of Brazil, and composed of such establishment luminaries as former US Secretary of State George Shultz, and Federal Reserve Chairman Paul Volker, as well as an impressive consortium of international leaders, including George Papandreou, Prime Minister of Greece; Ruth Dreifuss, former President of Switzerland; César Gaviria, former President of Colombia; Ernesto Zedillo, former President of Mexico; and Kofi Annan, the former Secretary General of the United Nations, the pedigree of this body is impeccable.

This is not a fringe group. These are individuals who have presided as heads of State, over nations most affected by these policies. The findings of the Commission are utterly in accord with the argument we have been advancing, and depends on much of the same reasoning we have been considering.

The report begins without mincing words: "The global war on drugs has failed, with devastating consequences for individuals and societies around the world."

Calling for an end to the "criminalization, marginalization and stigmatization of people who use drugs but who do no harm to others," and imploring leaders to "break the taboo on debate and reform," we are startled and gratified to see this report echoing the same sentiments we have labored to express in this book, over the past several months of its composition.

We expect to hear such radical proclamations from those, like us, who are directly affected members of the cognitive underclass. That world leaders would put their names to these declarations shows that conscientious administrators of these policies are interested in jettisoning them as well.

It is significant that the panel is composed mostly of *retired* leaders, rather than those at the mercy of political forces. Free to speak their minds, we see that even from the top of the pyramid, the very premise of prohibition seems obviously corrupt. Such candor is rarely an option for sitting officials.

Sounding more like a revolutionary manifesto than the work product of prominent statesmen, with comments like, "The time for action is now," and "we don't see the US evolving in a way that is compatible with our long-term interests," this remarkable analysis shines some light at the tunnel's end.

Adhering to tradition, drug czar Gil Kerlikowske called the commission's conclusions "misguided." With typical disdain for common sense, the Lord of Prohibition disavows the compelling argument set forth in the report, agreeing only that the phrase "war on drugs" ought to be abandoned, while leaving the reality intact.

Apparently even the staunch prohibitionists are starting to catch on to how bad their rhetoric sounds. Yet we cannot be satisfied by a clothing of the same human rights violations in benign-sounding words. We need no Ministries of Pleasure to torture us.

Still, the official response from the drug warriors shows that they have no intention of easily surrendering the reins, so long as America can be made to chomp at the bit.

"Drug addiction is a disease that can be successfully prevented and treated," ONDCP spokesman Rafael Lemaitre tersely declared. "Making drugs more available — as this report suggests — will make it harder to keep our communities healthy and safe."

Healthy, by denying medicine to sick people and consigning them to infested cells? Safe, by kicking in doors and invading communities with military squadrons? The lies keep coming from the pharmafascist regime, but even world leaders are beginning to see through it.

Another, much more locally-based, assemblage of executives denouncing prohibition is the US Conference of Mayors. Composed of municipal leaders from across the nation, this powerful voice has gone unheeded by the legislatures for years. As the putative superior to the heads of local law enforcement, under whose auspices most busts occur, these politicians are uniquely positioned to comprehend the devastation the war has brought to their cities.

At the 2011 annual convention, the USCM adopted a proposal backing the National Criminal Justice Commission Act of 2011, sponsored in Congress by Senator Jim Webb of Virginia and South Carolina Senator Lindsey Graham.

A proposal to create a committee to study reform, the bill likely is going nowhere (one prediction in which we sincerely hope to be mistaken), and amounts to little, even if passed. Nevertheless, to see support for the principle of curbing prohibition is heartening. We hope that this book will be obsolete in a few years. It will stand as part of the documentation of a very dark episode in the shadows of history.

Still another ray of hope shines from the magnificent organization LEAP.

Law Enforcement Against Prohibition is this war's equivalent to Vietnam Veterans Against the War. The moral authority of this group is unmatched and unimpeachable. Having implemented these policies throughout their careers, these individuals have banded together in protest against them, with no axe to grind other than a commitment to fairness and human dignity.

The very existence of LEAP exposes a vulnerability that may ultimately bring down the dominance of the prison-industrial complex. As the organization grows, it brings the powerful message that all parties are harmed in this counterproductive endeavor.

Throughout this book, a reader may have gotten the impression that we do not like the police very much. True as this is, with one serious exception it is nothing personal. We'd just prefer there were fewer of them, and that they be reassigned to useful labor. We understand that most officers entered this line of work because they believed they would be contributing to the safety of the community. Many are a decent sort; we have run across that kind, too.

To the extent that this sort of genuine service is part of their routine, we salute them. Emergency response is important. Dangerous situations do require a firm hand at times. People are rescued by the police. Violent criminals do need to be stopped, lest we all be unsafe.

Part of our objection is the way law enforcement, which is otherwise a positive and necessary function of government, has been perverted by prohibition into an occupying army with unchecked power. By forcing cops to be bad guys, their more critical functions are necessarily neglected.

If you are employed, or have been, peripherally or directly, in the persecution of people for their choice of substances, we encourage you to contact this organization in order to become part of the solution. LEAP into a world where peaceful citizens need not fear public servants.

We were lucky. Since we became victims of this war, we have had to tell ourselves that, and it is true. There are so many ways in which we count our blessings, and reflect on our good fortune through adversity. It could so easily have been worse.

In these last few pages, you may as well know how this book came about. It does not have a happy beginning, but it is our hope that we will see a happy ending, to the ongoing tale of how the government ruins lives.

You may recall that we earlier discussed Maricopa County, its horrible jails, and its insane Sheriff. We have more than a researcher's familiarity with this particular piece of geographical Hell. We don't live there, but traveling through on the interstate highway, our lives suddenly came full stop, and we quickly learned from experience, in a very personal way, how truly vulnerable ordinary citizens are, before the evil of the police.

As dusk hit, a few days past New Year's, our lives would change forever, when we were lit up with a traffic stop, allegedly for inoperative break lights. Traveling in the short bus we'd lived in for five years, this was the first time we would be pulled over in it. Our registration and insurance were in order, and we were about twenty hours into the trip from San Francisco. When our progress was so rudely interrupted, we were only about ninety minutes away from our destination, which was a friends' house in Tucson.

Reality turned rapidly upside down, as we were ordered from our mobile home, and more squad cars appeared. They told us that they wanted to search the bus. We told them we didn't want them to. They said they didn't need a warrant. We were taken into custody, handcuffed, placed in separate cars, and watched in horror as several uniformed and plainclothes police swarmed all over our home with rubber gloves and cameras.

We were lucky. We keep having to tell ourselves that.

Within an hour, we had transformed, from free-living hippies, to inmates in the most heartless place we have ever seen, or hoped to. Although we are used to doing everything together, and had been arrested for literally the same thing, the two of us were separated, each plunged into the his-and-hers hellholes Sheriff Joe is so proud of.

Throughout this book, we have used the plural first person to refer to the author-publishing team behind this book. This is to signify what a collaborative effort it has been. We have done it together, each in our domain. I have done the writing, which she edits, while she designs the cover as I ask the impossible. Every phase of this book was conceived in unison. That is just how we roll. Now, for the first time, it is necessary to distinguish between us, for we were no longer in contact at all, which was the very worst part of the experience.

She was arrested on her menstrual cycle, and was not wearing a whole lot in the way of clothing. Like all the women, she was stripped-searched, a procedure that I, strangely, was not subjected to. Because she'd been arrested in a flimsy wrap-around, and deemed a biohazard due to her period, she was issued a set of black-and-white prison stripes and shower sandals. No sanitary napkin or tampon was provided. The arresting officer had verbally abused her for bleeding all over the back of the cop car, as if sitting there were *her* idea, calling her beautiful womanhood "more disgusting than dog shit."

One of the cells reeked of bleach, which the guards informed everyone was due to a recent staphylococcus outbreak. The ladies took turns standing by the single air vent so at least one at a time could breathe. No one wanted to sit on the benches or floor, for fear of infection. Somehow it did not seem the guards were terribly concerned about anyone's health.

Among her holding cell-mates was an African-American lady in her eighties, who said her booking charge was jaywalking. Instead of helping a little old lady cross the street like good boy scouts, the officers had arrested her and brought her to jail. She was horrified, and never stopped praying to Jesus to free her from these trials. The officers had told her that since this happened in the street it was considered a traffic incident. They would likely suspend her license, probably for the remainder of her life.

Another woman had been brought in for assault. Her story was even more insane: a victim of domestic abuse, the woman had called 911 on her husband, but the wise officers had arrested her instead, because in defending herself she had wounded him. She feared losing her nursing license over this incompetence. Her newborn infant was left in the custody of her abuser.

A teenage girl with a broken hand was arrested for harboring her boyfriend, who was wanted on a warrant. Although she had warned the officer that she needed her splint, being seriously injured, she had been taken in custody without it, handcuffed like everyone else, despite her injury and nonviolent offense. The incarcerated nurse, examining the hand, said that it needed prompt medical attention, but calls to the guards went unheeded. The nurse resorted to wrapping the wounded hand in precious toilet paper.

The first night in the holding cell was utterly surreal. No one would tell me anything. I was brought into a little room, where a portly woman behind thick plexiglass began interrogating me. Not about the alleged controlled substance violation for which I'd been booked; about my life in general. This was none of her business, and anyway, her questions didn't make sense. I told her I understood I had a right to remain silent. She dismissed me and threw my paperwork away, warning of ominous consequences.

We were packed, twenty to thirty in a cell, awaiting the judge. Most everyone seemed to be in for a DUI or possession case. Every so often, for reasons that easily could have been explained to us but never were, we were collectively shackled to each other, to be marched in literal lockstep to our new and interesting holding cell.

Each holding cell has a toilet, which you try not to need, because it is not fun for anyone when a turd plops publicly into the water. I began to understand how dangerous any word or look could be, how easy it would be to earn someone's enmity. They had two dozen of us crammed in a literal bathroom. Imagine if the sewage backed up!

I passed the time getting scared. I knew we didn't have much stash in the bus, by West Coast standards, but there were three felony possession charges on the papers. The bus! *Everything* we had was in the bus. Everyone said for sure they were going to take it, and keep it, for a roadside possession bust. Marijuana, evidently, was a Class Six felony, as was paraphernalia.

The third charge, possession of dangerous drugs, was listed as a Class Two felony, which properly scared the shit out of me, once I realized that it was a descending scale: the lower the number, the more serious it was. Murder was Class One. Were they trying to hit us with a transporting charge, because we were from out of State?

We wouldn't find out for months what the Class Two was really all about, but when we went before the bail judge in the morning, he shook his head, and told us he didn't find probable cause for that particular charge. Admonishing me for my uncooperativeness with the social worker, he ordered us each held on $100 bond.

Between the two of us, we'd had ninety-six dollars on our persons at the time of the arrest. No problem. There was a couple hundred in the bank, and her debit card was in her property.

No dice, said the Judge. We don't *take* debit.

Don't take debit? How could they not take debit? Here they are, hustling desperate people through the jail, pricing their freedom, and not letting them use their savings to buy it! Only cash. But if you are arrested with too *much* cash, they take it away, and charge you as a drug dealer.

She got on her knees and begged every non-prisoner in the courtroom for spare change, but none of the court employees could spare four dollars for our freedom. Doubtless such an act of kindness and mercy would place their jobs in jeopardy.

Having come together for the bail hearing, we were again separated. A hundred dollars. For a rotten hundred dollars they wouldn't take from our bank card, we were relocated to different jails, for who knew how long.

Shackled again by hand and foot, we were shuffled aboard transport busses, and moved to Estrella and Durango jails respectively. Durango was bunked four to a cell, and I was placed there in the middle of the night, assigned to the top bunk. I had no idea where to go to the bathroom, and was afraid to ask.

In the morning, I was wakened to a crude tap on my foot. A fairly well-groomed middle-aged man in stripes wanted my attention, and wouldn't go away.

"Hey," he demanded. "Who you run with? Woods?"

Oh, shit. I knew where he was going with this, and I wanted no part of it. I shook my head and shrugged incomprehension. "Wood? What do you mean?"

"You a Peckerwood?" he insisted. For those who don't know, this is the common term for the White Pride gang which controls Caucasians in the jail. I'd been hearing rumbling about it, but didn't expect to be recruited straight away.

"Look, man, I'm just in here for some weed…I'm a hippie. Not much of a team player. Just doing my time."

He grinned cruelly. "An independent, eh? Good luck with that in here. No independents here." He left the cell and went over to speak with some overly buff white men, pointing in my direction and laughing. For the first time, I realized that the mute petty brutality of the guards might be the least of my problems.

It was a few minutes before I understood who the man was, and why he was there to see me, the fresh fish. The jail was racially segregated, not by the guards, who left us more or less alone in the locked pods, but by the gangs. This guy represented the white gang.

My very nature revolted against this. I had no more enmity for any black or Hispanic inmate than these ridiculous White Supremacists, in fact quite a bit less, but rejecting the Woods left me without any guide or protection at all. The answer to where and when I could use the bathroom safely, was part of the benefits of joining with the skinheads chanting "White Pride! White Pride!" and banging on the dayroom tables, with no reaction at all from the guards.

When the "meals" were delivered, I immediately gave mine to the first black inmate I saw, as refusing the miserable sack might bring punishment from the angry looking guard dispensing them. I was not eating any of the food, apart from the sugary fruit juice, as most of it was unsuitable for my strict vegan diet. I was not very hungry anyway, dreaded having to use the bathroom, and felt that passing up these meager rations was hardly a sacrifice.

Back in my cell, the Hispanic gentleman bunking on the other rack was visited by his racial leader, a representative of the *Paisa*, the gang of Mexican nationals. Being reasonably conversant in Spanish, I picked up most of the rundown I had missed, by refusing to ally with the Woods.

Noticing my attention, the *Paisa* head, quite kindly, repeated his last explanation in English for my benefit. I told him that I spoke Spanish from my time in Mexico, and we had what was my first conversation *en español hace mucho tiempo*. He told me that I could join the *Paisa*, which sounded like a good solution for me, since I could not morally bring myself to cooperate with racists. My ethnicity was obviously not being held against me; apparently my halting use of their language and status as an accused *marijuanero* made me one of them.

He held out his fist in the familiar street greeting of Mexico, inviting me to bump my fist and seal my commitment. "But," he warned. "Once you make this choice, you can't go back." That warning gave me pause, for at that point I had no idea when, or even if, I would be getting out of Joe's Dungeon. Seeing this as my best opportunity for survival and community, I tapped knuckles with him, and considered how the Peckerwoods would respond to this. Hopefully they would back off.

Making bail, we both learned, is more complicated than we had imagined. Neither of us remembered any telephone numbers which could help us out of this mess, including those of our friends, who'd have been happy to rush to our aid, had they only known; they were all stored on our confiscated cell phone contact list. Who dials a number anymore?

Each holding cell had a list of bail bonds companies, across the room from the phones, but I quickly discovered two things about these numbers. Painstakingly scrawling the names and numbers on the back of my arrest papers, I went back and forth about twenty times. Most of them didn't answer, and those who did, wouldn't take a collect call from jail. For some reason, despite each arrestee's Constitutional right to make a telephone call, the outbound phone lines cost the accepting party five dollars.

When one finally did pick up the line, I discovered something else about these bail bonds companies—they weren't interested in my measly hundred-dollar bond. Since they'd only be making ten bucks on the deal, it wasn't worth their time. It wasn't even worth taking the call. My bond was too *low* to get out of jail!

She had more success than I did. Having no pencil, she had to scrawl the numbers on the cell wall in soap. She persuaded the bail bondsman that he would get the entire hundred dollars, if he would just get her out, and he agreed, warning her that if she reneged on the deal, he'd void the bond, resulting in an immediate warrant for her arrest.

Right at noon, the time he had promised to pay the bond, she was called, not for release, but to be transferred to long-term holding at Estrella. No amount of reasoning with the guards could delay them; as far as they were concerned, if it wasn't in their computer yet, it wasn't happening. She was shackled up and shipped out, despite her bail already being paid.

Estrella was a dormitory-style jail, filled with prostitutes and drug offenders. Again she was strip-searched, in plain view of the other inmates. Many of the women were actively experiencing the pangs of womanhood, being either on their periods or pregnant, but no accommodation was made for these conditions.

There had been a policy in Maricopa County Jail dictating that birthing mothers be shackled during labor, until public outrage and women's groups demanded this practice be curtailed. Of course, having just carried the infant to term, inmate mothers often never get to see their babies again.

She was not released until 4:00 AM, sixteen hours after bail was posted, when the dark downtown central Phoenix is an unwelcoming place for a woman alone in scant dress. Part of the delay was a regulation prohibiting release prior to that time, due to a lawsuit following several late-night rapes near the jail.

Word came that I was being transferred out; grumbling, jealous voices informed me that meant bail had been made. She'd come through, somehow! I grabbed my bedding, folded it per instructions, and quickly left the cell, singing a happy tune.

Even though I was being brought out for release, I had to wait until enough other transfers had been assembled to make a chain gang. We were shackled at the ankle again, and had to walk the few hundred feet to the transport bay. Having always marched to the beat of an eccentric drummer, this march was particularly tough, and I painfully stumbled on my way to freedom. Upon reaching the bay, I was shuffled between another round of holding cells, where we could watch the busses come in and wonder in vain which was ours.

Not all the transfers were headed for release. Actually, I was one of just a few headed outside. Some were going to prison, or court, or to Tent City. One of these, a genial heavyset African-American gentleman, told me that he was being remanded to the Tents, as punishment for complaining about the shackles. A diabetic, the chains irritated his ankles, which are swollen and vulnerable as a consequence of the disease. For daring to ask that his disability to be accommodated, he would serve his six months in a place where shackling was a regular daily part of the routine.

As quick as they were to throw us in jail, it took an awfully long time to pry us out. I remained in the merry-go-round of holding cells late into the evening, not being released until nearly twelve hours after learning that bond had been posted.

Court was anticlimactic; we were told that our case had been "scratched," a curiously untechnical term meaning "dismissed without prejudice." In other words, the prosecutors were unable to mount the case at this time, and we were free to go, pending re-filing of the criminal complaint. We breathed a sigh of relief and prepared to leave the State, after making sure that not one shred of illegal anything was in our ride.

Over the next six months, we engaged in constant legal research, trying to gauge the outcome of all this. The outlook was not good. Apparently this was standard procedure, to drop the charges, so a stronger case could be presented after lab evidence became available. We put our money together, and retained a NORML attorney, in hopes that we could settle the matter.

We believed we had a good case for a motion to suppress, based on illegal search, but our attorney disagreed. To our great shock, we learned that the summary search was perfectly legal in the eyes of the court, since the officer claimed to have smelled marijuana in our vehicle. That gave them the right to scour the inside for any traces of it.

It took till June for our case to appear on the computerized docket we were monitoring. We learned what the Class Two felony was all about; on the first page of the police report, the lying sack of dung had put down that "several *ounces*" of psilocin mushrooms had been found in our vehicle. The lab report showed a bag containing 2.2 *grams* of dust, barely a single dose.

The cop had tried to railroad us with a trafficking charge by doctoring his report, claiming to have found at least twenty-five times as much weight as was turned in to the lab, but this did not, our attorney advised, present an opportunity to impugn his credibility vis-á-vis probable cause to search. The court was likely to view this as a simple error, rather than malicious fabrication. Since the bail judge had tossed out that count, and it had not returned on the criminal complaint, no harm had been done to us, and this sign that the arresting officer was at best incompetent, and at worst a perjurer, did not provide a defense.

In the end, the lawyer was unable to do much of anything, except line up the standard crappy deal for us, and fix a bench warrant issued due to his negligence. At an expense of $1500 in biodiesel, which we could hardly afford at this point, we sadly drove down in the hottest part of summer to the 100° desert in our twenty-three year old bus.

At this point, before setting a foot in court, the ordeal had cost us over $4000, not counting all the work we'd missed. We had become professional defendants, fully employed in the grueling task of pouring over relevant case-law online in a fruitless quest for some loophole, and trying to raise our attorney on the telephone.

Half of that sum had been paid to our lawyer, but it generally took about a week to get ahold of him, and it had quickly become clear that nothing would get done, unless we spelled out each step. As we learned, nothing got done anyway.

What's the difference between a hooker and a lawyer? The hooker actually gets you off when you pay two grand.

We already knew that the prosecutors weren't offering any better deal; negotiations to reduce the felonies to misdemeanors had failed. The insistence on felony charges was why we had to physically appear. They were willing to let us plead to a felony paraphernalia charge, with eighteen months probation, or else for one year enter a diversion program, called TASC, presumably because it is a lot of work.

It was like being asked to choose between malaria and Lyme disease; either option condemned us to live under legal disability. In the end, we had to go with the softer option, to avoid that felony conviction, and to be done with it six months sooner. We resigned ourselves to loosing another year of our lives, and sat down with the TASC salesman.

First, we were forced to fill out form confessions, short-circuiting any possible defense, in the event that we were booted from the program and had to once again face these charges. We knew from our research that these decidedly coerced statements had already been deemed voluntary in appellate court. When we objected to the self-incriminating language he firmly dictated, we were informed that this part was not optional. We reluctantly signed, lest we become felons for life.

He was friendly enough; he told us that he wanted us all to succeed in the program, because that's how they get paid. "You know," he said, "it's all just a *game*." Yeah. Lots and lots of fun.

Then he laid it out for us: how *much* they expected to get paid. Before we signed up, we'd been led to believe the program would cost about $2200 apiece. Outrageous as that seemed, considering what we'd already spent, our attorney had prepared us for this.

What he hadn't prepared us for were the add-ons. We would have to pay each time for urinalysis, which would begin at ten times a month and gradually reduce. Then we'd have to pay for treatment, twenty-four hours of it, another seven hundred dollars each.

Not only that, but because we'd been arrested for a substance not normally tested for, we would also have to pay a monthly fee for specialized tests to detect psychedelics. So we'd be paying more for our UAs than someone who had been arrested for meth, coke, or even heroin.

To top it off, because we were going to do this out of State, we'd have to locate a facility to collect the urine, and pay an extra $3 for each "kit" to mail it back to them so they could scrutinize our bodily composition in a lab. We were just happy to get the hell out of Arizona.

All in all, the numbers crunched out to over $11,000 for the two of us. Jaws dropped. "Um, that's, like, more than we make in a *year*," we told him. Eventually we'd be able to save some of that cost, by showing our part-time income, but we'll still have forked over about eight grand to these vipers, before we are finally, blessedly through with their extortion.

Our immediate and overwhelming impulse was to sink into a depression.

The balance of our free time was given over to these inane meetings, where we typically held our peace, and collected the signatures we needed. The urine testing was every three days, which in practice meant two or three times a week. The collection facility, which was really just this tiny hippie rehab specializing in meeting court requirements, had to institute this whole extra procedure just for us.

The whole thing was humiliating and degrading, and we settled into a routine which consisted of little more than working to pay the TASC-holes, and running around satisfying their demands. Our lives had been reduced to serving this heartless entity which existed solely to exploit people like us. Neither of us felt that we had any kind of drug problem, knowing that we were actually fairly mild in our habits compared with others we knew. Neither of us drank, for example, or used what we thought of as hard drugs.

We were comfortable with our relationship with natural entheogens, and felt that they had no real evidence otherwise. Mushrooms, however they may have gotten there, do not signify a pattern of abuse, and their presence actually indicates *not* using them. If they had been used, they'd be gone. Our lawyer hadn't liked that logic, either.

Eventually though, as we survived their ridiculous program, we began to have some time of our own again. We still had to submit UAs, but much less frequently, and having completed the hours of mandatory droning as fast as we could, we once again could choose what we did with the days off which we now valued at a premium.

The winter had been cold and cruel, but as spring was born, we felt that this monstrous waste of time and money must somehow be redeemed. We could not accept that nearly two years of our lives would be swallowed by this incident, without some good emerging from it.

Thus this project, which we have endeavored to make a worthwhile and educational use of your time as well as ours. This volume encapsulates the grim reality we had been only peripherally aware of, before the system showed us its power and depravity.

We reiterate that we were lucky. Had the situation been only slightly different, this traffic stop could have easily separated us in prisons for years. We learned that we had stumbled afoul of some of the harshest laws in the country.

There was one bright light in the law: not the product of legislators, but directly of the people, a public referendum in Arizona called Proposition 200. Passed by ballot initiative in 1996, the law eliminated jail or prison terms for first-or-second-time controlled substance offenders, freeing thousands.

It had also legalized medical marijuana and other Schedule I substances, but that particular provision had been crushed by the legislature. A more recent successful ballot initiative, in response to self-righteous politicians undermining the express will of the People, now forbids the legislature from overturning any future referendum acts.

Under Prop 200, we really ought not to have been charged with felonies at all, since the Arizona Constitution specifies that a felony is defined as a crime punishable by more than one year in prison. Since incarceration was never an option in our case, even had we been convicted by jury, the violations charged to us could and should have been filed as misdemeanors.

Had activists and voters not come together for this measure, it is possible that the outcome would have been quite different. Unable to jail us for the trivial amounts listed in the police report, the prosecutors settled for making us miserable in free society, and for that we are truly grateful. We owe no thanks to the State, but to the voters who made this critical reform happen.

With that thought, we shall leave you to ponder what contribution you can make to help change this travesty of justice doing business in your town and across the country. If you are already engaged in organizing on behalf of the glacial reform effort which is creeping across the nation, we thank you for your service and hope it will be enhanced in some way by this time we have spent together.

If you are not, we implore you to consider putting just a little time into supporting a ballot initiative in your area, or wherever the struggle ensues. One humble but effective contribution is to make voter calls encouraging people to vote for their State's ballot. Sign up with groups like the Drug Policy Alliance, NORML, Marijuana Policy Project, or Students for a Sensible Drug Policy, to receive action alerts by e-mail and stay abreast of prohibition issues.

About a month into TASC, we volunteered to make phone calls on behalf of Arizona Yes on Proposition 203, in support of a new medical marijuana referendum item appearing in the November election. After fielding an annoying call from my TASC case manager, a vile woman who was on the prohibitionist committee to oppose 203, we put our time to some rare good use after several weeks of "mis-treatment" sessions.

Dialing from the public library conference room, we used Skype to remind voters about election day, and to clarify the meaning of their vote. Some were confused, thinking a "no" vote would be in *favor* of medical marijuana. We were glad to straighten this out and save two votes...the one they correctly cast in favor, and the mistake they would have made voting for the other side.

We were originally disappointed to hear of the defeat of 203, which at first was reported to have lost, but after the provisional ballots were counted, ended up winning by a slim margin of about four thousand votes. Desperate messages went out from the legalization groups to their membership, repeatedly reminding these voters, who were generally poor, young, or Mexican, to validate their votes.

These provisional ballots, issued in cases of questioned identity, residence or citizenship, were brought in overwhelmingly favoring the proposition in the days following the election, reversing the tally. In our darkness, we finally had reason to celebrate; some people, the neediest, would be spared what we had been through in that awful place.

We entertain no illusions that our few hundred calls made the critical difference, but combined with the other efforts from volunteers, we did help change the law in Arizona by a bare majority. We proved that we didn't have to be hostage to a rogue government serving the interests of ignorant bigots. Until they make them illegal, voter referendum is the last true bastion of democracy, and we ought cherish this tool. Someday, we may use it to overturn or at least dial down this repressive police regime.

So much more remains to be done. At times, we stare down the abyss of prohibition, and wonder if things will ever change, or if millions more like us will have some part of their lives stolen for no good reason at all.

The revolution of the mind happens one at a time, and we have faith that every tyranny must eventually submit to the concerted resistance of the people. More Americans than ever perceive the downsides of prohibition, the costs of incarceration, the increased cartel and gang violence, the neglect of other more vital law enforcement functions.

Aside from these important arguments, we feel that what is often missing from the debate is a focus on the Constitutional rights at stake, and plight of the human beings who must suffer without them. Until the public conscience awakes to these evils, the economic arguments will tend to fall short. It is too easy to vote money for war. So-called fiscal conservatives rarely take issue with appropriations meant for crushing enemies of the State, either at home or abroad.

We must garner more minds to this cause, smash the myths supporting prohibition, and count each victory in terms of lives spared from persecution by courts and police. Every reduction of penalties is a worthwhile achievement, until so little of prohibition remains that they are forced to dismantle jails, decommission narcotics task forces, and end the occupation of our streets by this malicious multi-agency gang.

This is the dream we strive for. Together, some day we will wake up in a truly free country. Let us work toward that day.

Appendix
Selected Source Citations:

ARTICLE I
Cotts, Cynthia "The Pot Plot" *Village Voice* 9 June 1993
Bradbury, Michael "Report on the Death of Donald Scott" Office of the Ventura County District Attorney 30 March 1993
Hadley, Scott, "Officer Criticized Over 1992 Drug Raid Still Wants Vindication" *LA Times*, 3 December 1997
Cook, Rhonda, "Documents Reveal: Cops Planted Pot on 92-Year Old Woman They Killed in Botched Drug Raid" *Atlanta Journal-Constitution* 30 April 2007
"Police: Accused Officer Has 'Credibility Issues'" Fox 10, Phoenix, 14 October 2010
Balko, Radley "Jose Guerena Killed: Arizona Cops Shoot Former Marine in Botched Raid" *Huffington Post* 25 May 2011
"A Look Inside the World of Tucson Police SWAT" Waddell, Jennifer KGUN-9, Tucson 16 May 2011
"Raw Video: Sheriff's Office Interview on Fatal Drug Raid" Interview by Joel Waldman KGUN-9, Tucson 13 May 2011

ARTICLE II
"Crime in the United States 2009," FBI Uniform Crime Report: US Dept. of Justice, September 2010, Table 29
"Prison's deadliest inmate, hepatitis C, escaping." *Associated Press* 14 March 2007.
Balko, Radley "Tennessee Cops Posed as a Defense Attorney To Get Suspect To Incriminate Himself" *Reason Magazine* 8 March 2011
The Stanford Prison Experiment. Dir. &. Prod. Kim Duke Dr. Philip Zimbardo, BBC, 2002.

ARTICLE III
CDC's National Center for Health Statistics Data Brief No. 42, September 2010
Hoffman, Abbie *Soon to Be a Major Motion Picture* Perigee 1980
De Vine, Lester "The Link Between Opioid Addiction And Endorphin Deficiency"
Haasen C, Verthein U, Degkwitz P, Berger J, Krausz M, Naber D. "Heroin-assisted treatment for opioid dependence: randomised controlled trial" *British Journal Psychiatry* July 2007
Duke, John "A Quantitative Analysis of Adverse Events and 'Overwarning' in Drug Labeling," *Archives of Internal Medicine* 23 May 2011

ARTICLE IV
The Constitution of The United States
Supreme Court of the United States *Carroll v. US* 267 US 132 (1925)
SCOTUS *Arizona v. Gant* 556 US 542 (2009)
SCOTUS *New York v. Belton* 453 US 454 (1981)
SCOTUS *US v. Ross* 456 US 798 (1982)
SCOTUS *Atwater v. Lago Vista* 532 US 318 (2001)
SCOTUS *Kentucky v. King* 563 US 09-1272 (2011)
SCOTUS *Illinois v. Caballes* 543 US 405 (2005)
Davis, Aaron "Police Raid Berwyn Heights Mayor's Home, Kill His 2 Dogs" *Washington Post* 31 July 2008
Cormier, Anthony "Warrant to Search All Persons Questioned" Sarasota Herald-Tribune 14 February 2011
Bureau of Justice Statistics on Crime and Law Enforcement 2005
Hawkes, Andrew "Highway Drug Interdiction - Secrets of Successful Highway Drug Interdiction" Webpage, http://www.highwaydruginterdiction.com/ last accessed 1 July 2011

ARTICLE V
Orwell, George *1984* Signet Classics 1949
James, Nathan, "Federal Prison Industries" Congressional Research Services Report, 13 July 2007
American Violet Dir. Tim Disney Prod. Uncommon Productions Perf. Nicole Beharie, Will Patton & Alfre Woodard DVD 2008
Regina Kelly: Drug War Victim Interview with Radley Balko 20 October 2007
Hearne, Texas: Scenes from the Drug War Off Center Media 2005
United States District Court, Western District of Kentucky, *Hammonds v. Corrections Corporation of America* Civil Action #3:11-cv-8-H
Yeoman, Barry "Steel Town Lockdown" *Mother Jones* May 2000
Mattera, Philip; Mafruza Kahn & Stephen Nathan "Corrections Corporation of America: A Critical Look At Its First Twenty Years" Report for Grassroots Leadership, the Corporate Research Project of Good Jobs First & Prison Privatisation Report International May 2003
Boone, Rebecca "ACLU Suing Corrections Corp. of America" *Associated Press* 11 March 2010

Victor, Marc "Pro Tem Recusal Minute Entry" 24 May 2003
Victor, Marc "My Contribution to Science" 31 August 2010

ARTICLE VI:
SAMHSA, Office of Applied Studies, National Survey on Drug Use and Health, 2009
Siegel, Lauren "Pregnancy Police Fight the War on Drugs" (From Crack in America: Demon Drugs and Social Justice, P 249-259, 1997, Craig Reinarman and Harry G Levine, eds.)
Isikoff, Michael "Drug Buy Set Up For Bush Speech" *Washington Post* 22 September 1989
Chavkin, Wendy "Drug Addiction and Pregnancy: A Policy Crossroads" *Public Health and the Law* April 1990
Chasnoff, Ira et.al "Cocaine Use in Pregnancy" *New England Journal of Medicine*, 12 September 1985 Ira J. Chasnoff, M.D., William J. Burns, Ph.D., Sidney H. Schnoll, M.D., Ph.D., and Kayreen A. Burns, Ph.D.

ARTICLE VII
Reinarman, et al. "The Limited Relevance of Drug Policy: Cannabis in Amsterdam and San Francisco" *American Journal Of Public Health* May 2004
Robinson, Rowan *The Great Book of Hemp* Park Street Press 1996
SCOTUS *Wickard v. Filburn* 317 US 111 (1942)
"DEA Release Admits Marc Emery Extradition Politically Motivated" *Cannabis Culture Magazine* 4 March 2006

ARTICLE VIII:
Gonnerman, Jennifer, "Truth or D.A.R.E." *Village Voice,* 7 April 1999
Ostrow, Ronald J., "Casual Users Should Be Shot," *L.A. Times,* 6 September 1990
Office of the City Auditor, "Opportunities for Youth II: Drug Abuse and Resistance Education" Austin, TX August 1994 (Report No. S9305D)
Egan, Dan, "Iowa Cop, Arrested Driving Around With Porno and Stolen Methamphetamine, LSD and Cocaine" *Des Moines Register*, 17 May, 1996
Brown, Abbey, "DARE Officer Charged in Drug Case At School," *Town Talk (LA)* 25 April 2008
US Court of Appeals DC Circuit *Paige V. United States of America*, Case 1:06-cv-00644-EGS 2006
Bovard, James, "Destroying Families for the Glory of the Drug War" *Freedom Daily*, March 1997
Forbes, Daniel "Reading, writing and propaganda" *Salon.com* 8 August 2001
Brady, Pete "TV takes Prohibitionist Payola" *Cannabis Culture Magazine* 17 June 2000
Shire Pharmaceuticals "Operating Review: Central Nervous System"
Cartoon All Stars to the Rescue TV1990

ARTICLE IX
Martin, Brian "The Beating of Rodney King: The Dynamics of Backfire" *Critical Criminology*, Volume 13, Number 3, 2005, pp. 307-326.
McMillian, Thomas, "Top Cop: You're Arrested for Videotaping Us" *New Haven Independent* 11 November 2010
Long, Colleen; Hays Tom, "Cop who made tapes accuses NYPD of false arrest" *Associated Press* 9 October 2010
"Viral Video Officer Suspended" *Valley News Live* Fargo/Grand Forks KVLY 17 May 2011
"Confronting Corruption" Robert Wanek Productions 7 May 2011
"These Streets are Watching: Behind the Scenes of the Arrest of Jacob Crawford" Prod. Jacob Crawford & Josh Wolf 2003
"Eyewitness To Miami Beach Shooting Alleges Misconduct" Rep. Brian Todd CNN News 7 June 2011
Cushing, Raymond "Pot Shrinks Tumors; Government Knew in '74" *Alternet* 31 May, 2000

ARTICLE X
"Ecstasy Rising: History of MDMA" Rep. Brian Jennings *Primetime Special Edition* ABC News 1 April 2004
Shulgin, Alexander& Ann *Phenethylamines I Have Known and Loved; Tryptamines I Have Known and Loved: The Coninuation* Transform Press 1991/1997
"The 'X' Files" Rep. Jane Pauley, Stone Philips, John Larson *Dateline NBC* Special 2001
"The Hansen Files: Bath Salts" Rep. Chris Hansen *Dateline NBC* May 2011

ARTICLE XI
Lemons, Stephen "Arizona's Shameless About the Cage Death of Marcia Powell" *Phoenix New Times* 1 October 2009
SCOTUS *Loving v. Virginia* 388 US 1 (1967)
SCOTUS *Lawrence v. Texas* 539 US 558 (2003)
SCOTUS *Roe v. Wade* 539 US 558 (1973)

ARTICLE XII

Trux, John and Torrey, Lee, "Poison Pot Probe" *New Scientist* 27 April 1978 p.242

"Drug crops hit by weedkiller and spy-planes" *New Scientist* 25 August 1983 p.531

Heller, Joseph *Catch 22* Simon & Schuster 1961

Dickerson, John "Inhumanity Has a Price" *Phoenix New Times* 20 December 2007

Kraska, Peter "Militarization and Policing—It's Relevance to 21st Century Police" *Oxford Journal of Policing* 1 January 2007

Duff, James "Report of the Director of the Administrative Office in Applications for Delayed-Notice Search Warrants and Exceptions" Administrative Office of the United States Courts 2 July 2009

ARTICLE XIII

Tatum, Chip *The Tatum Chronicles* D.G. Chip and Nancy J. Tatum 1996

Webb, Gary *Dark Alliance: The CIA, the Contras, and the Crack Cocaine Explosion* Seven Stories 1999

Reed, Terry, *Compromised: Clinton, Bush, and the CIA* Shapolsky Publishers Inc. New York 1994

Castillo, Celerino, *Powderburns* Mosaic Press

"Police State II: The Takeover " Writ. & Prod. Alex Jones 2000

Report of the Director of the Administrative Office of the United States Courts on Applications for Delayed-Notice Search Warrants and Extensions, 2009

United States Court of Appeals, Eleventh Circuit. *US v. Noriega* Nos. 92-4687, 96-4471.

"Plane Crash in Mexico Involved Colombian Cocaine" *Associated Press* 27 September 2007

ARTICLE XIV

"Marijuana Bill In Congress: Barney Frank, Ron Paul Legislation Would End Federal Ban On Pot" *Huffington Post* 22 June 2011

"War On Drugs" *Global Commission on Drug Policy Report* June 2011

Lederer, Edith "Panel: Drug War Failed, Regulate Marijuana" *Associated Press* 2 June 2011

United States Conference of Mayors "Nation's Mayors Urge Passage of Webb's Landmark Criminal Justice Bill" Press Release 22 June 2011

www.ingramcontent.com/pod-product-compliance
Lightning Source LLC
Chambersburg PA
CBHW020201200326
41521CB00005BA/213